MUSIC IN
GERMAN ROMANTIC
LITERATURE

Music in German Romantic Literature

A COLLECTION OF ESSAYS, REVIEWS AND STORIES

*Translated & annotated with
a critical introduction by*

Linda Siegel

ELRA PUBLICATIONS · NOVATO, CA · 1983

To Joel & Laura

ACKNOWLEDGEMENTS

I wish to express my appreciation to my friend, Heidi Ivanoff-Johnson, instructor of German, San Francisco State University, for her many useful suggestions regarding the translations in this book. I wish also to thank I. J. S. for his encouragement and help with the preparation of this manuscript.

Manufactured in the United States of America
Designed by Kathleen Walkup, Matrix Press
Typesetting by Abracadabra
Production by Marilyn Perry

Contents

Ludwig Börne

Achim von Arnim

Heinrich von Kleist

Preface

REFERENCES TO MUSIC appear in German Romantic literature more frequently than in the literature of other periods. The reason for this is that music during the age of German Romanticism was a national cult. This unusual devotion to music is but the logical culmination of the position that music occupied in German life for centuries. As far back as the Renaissance the ruling German class provided not only staunch patrons of music, but talented performers and composers as well. In the Romantic era instruction in the rudiments of music theory and lessons on one instrument or another were considered a necessary part of the education of both the middle and upper classes in Germany. It is a typical German Romantic belief that music is superior to all other arts.

As with almost all other young Germans then, the individual destined to become a Romantic literary figure was in his early years steeped in music theory and performance. If music is part of an author's daily life, if his childhood memories are filled with associations with performers, composers and music teachers, and the tones of Sunday family concerts still echo in his ears, opinions regarding the art of music, whether they be good or bad, cannot help but be formed and find expression in subsequent literary pursuits. Such was the case with the German Romantic authors. And, parenthetically, such was also the case with the great early twentieth century German author, Thomas Mann.

It is both unique and highly significant that the majority of German Romantic authors are both musicians and poets. This dual talent runs throughout German Romanticism: Wagner, Schumann, Weber and Liszt, each of whom left behind several volumes of literary works, are part of a tradition started many years before by Jean Paul and other German Romantic writers born in the decade 1765-1775. As far as the relative importance of music and literature to any of the German Romantics is concerned, it is only a matter of emphasis and timing. One finds, for example, that Theodor Körner was writing songs at a much earlier age than Robert Schumann, whose major creative efforts as a youngster centered around literary pursuits.

I do not think it is an exaggeration to describe the age of German Romanticism as an age of musical-literary art. Indeed, to my mind, it is this inseparable bond between literature and music which is one of the most interesting and distinguishing characteristics of this period. Moreover, the German Romantics themselves conceived of art as properly an amalgamation of all of the various art forms—music, literature and painting—in one synesthetic experience.

This bond between literature and music provides a sense of unity to German Romanticism which is a cultural movement otherwise sometimes difficult to define, characterized as it is by a number of conflicting and constantly changing elements. In the literary sphere this complexity has led to the description of various schools of German Romantics whose members are tied together by geographical, philosophical or chronological considerations. It is not the intention of this book to disregard such important distinctions. Yet I feel that this unique synthesis of literature and music is significant enough to break down the barriers of time, place and idea and unites, for example, the satirical realist, Ludwig Börne, whose literary activity centered in Frankfurt, with Achim von Arnim, one of the leaders of the Heidelberg school. Whether one is dealing with the works of Ludwig Tieck, a leading figure in the development of the first Romantic school at Jean, or Theodor Körner, whose patriotic outpourings link him to the Heidelberg group, this love and knowledge of music is always conspicuous.

If one accepts the investigation of the role of music in German Romantic literature as legitimate and worthy, certain interesting aspects of the historical and stylistic evolution of German Romantic music begin to emerge. One striking finding, for example, is that German Romantic music may very well have begun to develop much earlier than is customarily thought. Most scholars are inclined to begin its history with Franz Schubert, Carl Maria von Weber or Carl Loewe, composers born approximately in the last decade of the nineteenth century. It would appear, however, that an earlier phase of German Romantic music existed which parallels the early stages of German Romantic literature. To this period belong such composers as Joseph Weigl (1766-1846), Johann Friedrich Reichardt (1752-1815), Johann Hummel (1778-1837) and many other lesser known musicians whose names fill the pages of this book. This earlier phase of German Romantic music also rightfully includes the group of poet-musicians appearing in this volume. What I am trying to say here is that German Romantic literature is one of the prime musicological sources for the study of German Romantic music. The literary efforts of the German Romantic authors played a most important role in shaping the musical aesthetics of the German Romantic composers.

The list of German Romantic poet-musicians is exceptionally long and it is not easy to categorically say which ones had the greatest impact on the form of German Romantic music. However, to date, Wackenroder, E. T. A. Hoffmann and Jean Paul Richter have occupied center stage in the study of the interrelationship between German Romantic literature and music, with Novalis, Brentano and Heine often sharing the limelight.

The choice of material for this volume has been guided by this consideration. The authors comprising this collection, although equally important participants in this literary-musical *Gesellschaft,* are less well-known for their use of music in literature, and their influence on the development of German Romantic music has not been given as much attention. The exception to this is the figure of Robert Schumann, who was selected to represent the musician-writer of this period. Additionally, although the works of Hoffmann, Jean Paul and others have frequently been rendered into English, the authors included herein provided opportunities to choose works which have not been previously translated, literary examples which add one more dimension to the study of music in German Romantic literature. I have also tried in this volume to include a diversity of literary forms: musical criticism, stories, essays, letters and poems which illustrate the different ways music was used in German Romantic literature.

The primary purpose of this collection, then, is to provide the reader with a group of selections which are not only new in English translation, but also representative of the important interaction between German Romantic literature and German Romantic music. With this objective in mind I have included a comprehensive introduction and several notations which provide the background necessary to understand the references to music which appear in the writings in this collection. The introduction also attempts to bring the authors who appear in this work into the circle of the more well-known poet-musicians by making frequent comparisons between the musical aesthetics of both groups.

From a purely literary point of view the reader will find that these selections, in themselves, constitute highly enjoyable reading. Whether one is a musician or not the description of young Tieck (*Musical Sorrows and Joys*) struggling with his violin and his nonchalant music teacher is as entertaining as Shaw's commentary on Wagner's *Ring*.

LINDA SIEGEL
Belmont, California
August, 1978

PART I
Introduction

1

The Poet-Musician

WHEN EICHENDORFF DISCUSSES the works of Goethe, comparing *Werther* with the oversentimental but highly popular novel, *Siegwart* by Martin Miller, [1] he does so with the aid of musical imagery, expressing his ideas and constructing his sentences in a manner not usually associated with literary criticism. Eichendorff compares Goethe's mode of thinking, his creative process, to a well-tuned harp and the three characteristics of Goethe's writings, feeling, fantasy and intellect to the three main chords of the harp. The shallowness of *Siegwart* with its one-sided emphasis on superficial emotionalism, however, is vividly portrayed by Eichendorff's comparison of the novella to a harp with only one string, i.e., feeling. Ludwig Börne in like manner uses musical imagery to suggest how great minds affect our daily life: "Great minds," he wrote, "are the soloists in the concert of the world and their cadenzas interrupt the monotonous beat of the music of life."[2]

The musical imagery of Eichendorff and Börne is not meant to be a clever mannerism or a playful manipulation of speech. What we have here are examples of that distinctively original mode of expression, that musical-literary language which is at the very heart of German Romantic literature. Indeed it is the credo of this school that one's most heartfelt thoughts cannot be expressed by human speech alone: "Only music," to quote that oft-stated remark of Wackenroder, "is capable of expressing the feelings of

3

mankind."[3] Earlier Jean Paul painted this philosophy with a vibrant palette. Victor, the hero of Richter's *Hesperus* (1795), finds music to be an outlet for his emotions:

> Leaning his head upon his hand, he let his tears flow without thinking or seeing, till he could cry no more. Then he went to the clavier and sang to its accompaniment the most passionate parts of his letter; what strongly moved him always compelled him to singing, especially the emotion of longing.[4]

Of all the countless passages in German Romantic literature in which the unburdening of the soul through music is described, especially revealing are those lines from the third act (scene 2) of Körner's drama, *Hedwig* (1811), in which the heroine, torn by love and duty, reaches for her harp and sings:

> In vain I search for words to express the powerful feelings in my heart. Each happiness we experience in life cannot find expression in words, only in song, only in music can I express myself . . . only in song can I express my tears.[5]

At the climax of almost every scene, be it in a novel or a drama, at the moments of the most intense emotion, how often we find that the heroines and heros of German Romantic literature do not speak. Instead, they rush to the clavier or seize a lute or guitar, they must play, they must sing as Edward does in Körner's fragment, *Eduard und Veronica, oder die Reise in's Riesengebirge* (*Edward and Veronica or The Journey Into the Riesengebirge,* 1809):

> Then in order to quickly subdue the violent storm which raged in his breast he seized the harmonious sounding flute and the sea of entwining tones adroitly resounded until it transformed itself into the soft sorrow of a most holy love. The fleeting song, the strong melody, soared upward and the song of the enraptured youth kindled the world spirit and the power of his longing sank into the waves of the harmonious tones.[6]

This passage vividly brings to mind the scene from *Tristan und Isolde* which may be the most sublime musical expression of the German Romantic belief in the inadequacy of human speech to

4

express human emotion. In Wagner's opera, at the climax of the first act when the hero and the heroine have just drunk the magic love potion and the love buried deep in the heart of each is freed for all eternity, neither speaks, Isolde glances at Tristan and he at her, their silence is more shattering than a thousand words and as they tremble violently the only sound emerging from the stage is the powerful love music of the orchestra.

What I have said thus far is essentially not new; the musical-literary language of German Romanticism has been given considerable attention by numerous scholars.[7] That music played an extremely important role in the literature of this period is an acknowledged fact. However, the role of German Romantic literature as an influence on German Romantic music, as a force which shaped the very spirit, style and goals of this art, has not been given equal stress. This influence could not have occurred if it were not for the fact that the German Romantic authors possessed an extraordinary knowledge and love of music. Schumann once said that he learned more about counterpoint from Jean Paul than any music teacher[8] and E. T. A. Hoffmann was one of Wagner's favorite instructors in music as we see in this passage from the composer's *Mein Leben:* "I had secretly been taking harmony lessons from G. Müller, his teaching and exercises filled me with the greatest disgust . . . for me music was a spirit. . . . I gathered much more congenial instruction about it from Hoffmann's *Phantasiestücke* than my Leipzig orchestra player."[9] The position of music in the lives and works of the authors in this volume present excellent examples of this characteristic.

It is often stated that Tieck's interest in music was in great part stimulated by his friendship with Wackenroder and his association with the composer and literary dilettante, Johann Friedrich Reichardt.[10] Admittedly Reichardt figures to some extent in the lives of Tieck, Wackenroder, Brentano and especially Arnim. But I rather think that Tieck's association with Wackenroder and his introduction to the musical world of Reichardt only awakened in him memories of his own childhood acquaintance with music.[11]

The most important source regarding Tieck's musical ability is his novella, *Musikalische Leiden und Freuden (Musical Sorrows and Joys)* which according to Köpke is biographical for the most part.[12] The novice in the story is Tieck himself and through him we learn that the poet played the violin for many years, from his early childhood until he left for the University of Halle. Evidence that Tieck did indeed play the violin is also convincingly supported by the descriptions of violin technique which occur in the novella. The references to the use of the mute, proper bowing procedures, problems of intonation, execution of tremolo passages and technical terms relating to parts of the instrument could only have been written by someone who played the violin and played it rather well.

Tieck's father, a rope-maker, had an avid interest in the theater, especially opera. As a youngster Tieck attended the performances of several operas; this fact is brought out by the novice as he looks back upon his childhood. The poet's favorite opera composer was Mozart; Tieck was especially fond of the composer's *Die Entführung aus dem Serail (The Abduction from the Seraglio,* 1782). This opera is mentioned in the novella and again in an important letter Tieck wrote to his family dated January 25, 1825.[13] Köpke mentions that one of the greatest joys of the young poet occurred when at the age of sixteen he accidentally sat next to Mozart in a theater in Berlin.[14]

Tieck revealed his love and knowledge of music in several of his literary works.[15] Among his earliest essays on music are the four contributions Tieck made to Wackenroder's *Phantasien über die Kunst (Fantasies on Art,* 1798-99), "Unmusikalische Toleranz" ("Non-musical Tolerance"), "Die Farben" ("Colors"), "Die Töne" ("Tones") and "Symphonien" ("Symphonies"). I find the latter particularly significant as it foreshadows two of the new orchestral forms of German Romantic music: the tone poem and the concert overture. In "Symphonies" Tieck in describing Reichardt's Overture to *Macbeth* wrote:

> No poet can create such a colorful, intricate and beautifully developed drama as . . . overtures can. . . . I cannot remember ever

6

having experienced such joy as that afforded me during a recent journey. I went to the theater where *Macbeth* was supposed to be performed. [Reichardt] had written an Overture for this magnificent tragedy, this composition enchanted me and caused such rapture in my heart. . . . I cannot describe how marvelously allegorical this impressive tone poem was. . . . After this Overture everything that followed was an anticlimax . . . this Overture was in effect the more poetic representation of the plot. It seems to me furthermore that it is degrading to use the Sinfonia which is called an overture today as an introduction to operas or plays . . . for if these musical compositions are supposed to blend in with that which follows then we are robbing the overture of its significance. . . . Why have music here at all?[16]

Tieck, I would venture to say, personally knew more composers than any other German Romantic writer, E. T. A. Hoffmann excepted: Beethoven, Zelter, Reichardt, Taubert, Meyerbeer, Schubert, Weber, Mendelssohn and the famous violinist, Benda, were only a few of his musical acquaintances.[17] Tieck was also instinctively drawn to the aristocratic German residences where the performance of little known music flourished. In 1802 Tieck began his long and important association with the family of the wealthy aristocratic patron of music, Count Finckenstein.[18] The three daughters of the Count were all talented singers, especially the oldest, Henriette, a great admirer of old Italian vocal music and one of Tieck's closest friends. Tieck paid homage to the Finckenstein family in *Musical Sorrows and Joys:* the Baron and his daughter are none other than the Count and Henriette.

Theodor Körner was born into that kind of refined cultural atmosphere which Tieck enjoyed. One might even say that Körner's father resembles the Baron in Tieck's novella. Christian Gottfried Körner was a well-to-do Counselor of Appeals and as such was on intimate terms with many German noble families; he was Schiller's intimate friend as well as a close associate of the important Leipzig music publisher, Christoph Gottlob Breitkopf (1750-1800) in whose home he met his future wife, Minna Stock, an accomplished musician and daughter of a well-known engraver. Körner's father was a great admirer of music and a member of Zelter's choral group in Berlin, the so-called *Singakademie*. [19] The Counselor's home in Dresden became the scene of many important musical events: Mozart, Paer, Zelter, Hiller were but a few of the many composers who frequented the Körner residence. It was a common occurrence in the Körner household to celebrate an important family occasion with the performance of an opera. On March 11, 1806, for example, Theodor Körner, his aunt, Dora Stock, and his sister, Emma, surprised Minna on her birthday with a performance of Cimarosa's *Il Matrimonio segreto* (*The Secret Marriage,* 1792).

Theodor Körner was the real troubadour of the early German Romantic writers, an aristocratic poet-musician who set his own lyrics to music. [20] One can almost imagine him as a young boy singing to the accompaniment of his guitar as if he were a knight serenading some fair lady. He was not a music critic like Börne, Tieck, Brentano, Heine or Schumann, nor did he philosophize about music like Jean Paul or Wackenroder, he simply knew that music was an important part of his life and something he could not do without.

Körner like Robert Schumann possessed at an early age a marked talent for both music and poetry. Körner played the violin, flute and piano, but was especially adept at the fretted instruments, the mandolin, lute and guitar, and like his father he was known in later life for his fine bass voice. [21] The guitar became his favorite instrument and he played it in a masterful fashion: one of his most prized possessions was a very fine instrument his father gave him on his twenty-third birthday. [22] The poet's correspondence mentions several of his own musical compositions such as a set of bagatelles which he wrote for the daughters of the Prussian Minister of State, Wilhelm von Humboldt. [23] Körner is also said to have composed a set of variations for flute and guitar and a number of songs based on poems of Schiller. [24]

Although poetry was to become the passion of Körner's life it is impossible to separate his literary efforts from his love of music. A large group of his poems, for example, deal with musical subjects

Facsimile of Theodor Körner's song, *Resignation* (poem by Schiller).

and could be grouped into the following categories: sets of verses which express the feelings aroused in him by some particular musical composition he recently heard, new lyrics which Körner provided for many of his favorite melodies and poems which deal with minstrelsy and singing (examples of these are included in this volume).

One of the high points of Körner's short life was his association with the Theater an der Wien and the Burgtheater in Vienna (1811-1813). In this city, which was one of the most important centers for the development of opera in Germany, Körner soon became one of the most sought after librettists of his day.[25] His own dramas, incidentally, were frequently set to music here. I find it especially interesting to note that Körner sang in many of the operas performed in Vienna such as Mozart's *Figaro*.[26] The poet was also one of the basses in the Vienna performance of Handel's *Alexander's Feast*.[27]

9

The musical education of Börne and Schumann shares one important element, a love for the works of Jean Paul. Richter's novels are translations of music into words abounding in passages describing the divine powers of music. Could anyone reading Jean Paul fail to be entranced by the magic of music or not be curious to hear *Don Giovanni*, especially after reading Jean Paul's hair-raising description of Mozart's opera in *Titan*. Robert Schumann and Ludwig Börne were like spiders caught in his web: to the consternation of their families they spent more time reading Jean Paul than attending to their school work. Jean Paul not only drew these two budding musicians into his magical world of musical sounds, but he became their source of inspiration, their model, their consolation. Börne once wrote, "I must read Jean Paul, not so that I can copy him: on the contrary! He represents to me all that a good general does, he gives me courage to express myself boldly as I otherwise would scarcely dare."[28] One of Börne's earliest essays on music, *Über Musik-und Talentbrüder* (*On Music and Brothers of Talent*, 1811) is profoundly influenced by Jean Paul, especially his musical similes and metaphors. Schumann and Börne were the heirs of Jean Paul and it is to him that we must look for part of their early musical education.[29]

Schumann and Börne both studied the piano as children; Börne also played the flute. Schumann's first creative efforts were, however, literary and his early poetry, essays and fragmentary novels bear the stamp of Jean Paul. When Schumann, who was to become a brilliant pianist and one of the greatest composers of the Romantic era, turned to music as his prime means of self-expression, he still continued his literary pursuits, excelling particularly in the field of music criticism.

Börne became a journalist, but one irresistibly drawn to music; his music reviews like those of Schumann form a very large part of his literary output. Articles on the musical life of his time fill the pages of *Die Wage (The Venture)*,[30] *Die Zeitung der freien Stadt Frankfurt (Newspaper of the Free State of Frankfurt)* and *Die Zeitschwingen (The Trends of the Time)*, daily newspapers he edited himself, as well as the many *Briefe aus Paris (Letters from Paris)* which were mainly written for Cotta's *Morgenblatt (Morning News)*.[31] In addition Börne's writings include a group of musical tales such as *Die Karbonari und meine Ohren (The Carbonari and My Ears*, 1818) in which the hero hears about the activities of an Italian political organization (the Carbonari) during a performance of Rossini's *Otello*.

It would appear that Börne as a child was exposed to more music than Schumann. As a boy Schumann spent a great deal of his time browsing through his father's bookshop, helping his father with editorial tasks and organizing various literary clubs. Börne grew up in an atmosphere quite similar to his childhood acquaintance, Meyerbeer. As a son of a wealthy Frankfurt merchant, Börne had several tutors one of whom was the family clavier teacher, Buchweiser. While Schumann passed his holidays engrossed in his books, young Börne sat through one concert after another at the homes of his father's friends, the Mendelssohn and Herz families.[32] As a boy of thirteen he already exhibited a passion for singing and opera; while studying at Heidelberg he attended the theater more than he did class. Schumann, incidentally, was no more conscientious; rather than attend his law classes, he preferred to stay in his apartment writing novels in the style of Jean Paul. Börne died before Robert Schumann had made a name for himself as a composer. Unfortunately, he never knew Schumann nor how much the composer admired him; Börne's name was to appear many times in Schumann's own journal, the *Neue Zeitschrift für Musik (New Journal for Music,* founded by the composer in 1833).

Heinrich von Kleist was another member of this literary-musical *Gesellschaft* who was profoundly devoted to music. Letters, documents and remarks of those who knew Kleist well always mention the musical side of his nature. Karl von Bülow[33] described Kleist as a self-taught musician who composed instinctively and who possessed a remarkable musical memory, being able to sing back everything he heard with flawless intonation.[34] Rühle von Lilienstern[35] confirms Bülow's statement that Kleist played the clarinet and while in the army organized a quartet in which the historian also participated.[36] Some sources maintain that Kleist also played the flute.[37] Tieck in his Foreword to Kleist's *Gesammelte Schriften (Collected Works)* wrote that Kleist "showed at an early age a beautiful talent for music and played various instruments."[38] Friedrich Koch seems to feel that Kleist's interest in music and study of the clarinet developed while he was an officer in the Prussian army (1792-1799).[39] But I rather think that as in the case of Tieck, Kleist's interest in music stems from his childhood; Kleist's letters seem to confirm this:

> Thus from the days of my earliest youth I have related all my general ideas about poetry to musical tones. I believe that in the art of figured bass may be found the most important information about poetry.[40]
>
> I do not know if you were ever fortunate to experience something similar or whether you are able to consider the following possible. But now and then at twilight when I am walking alone facing the blowing breath of the west wind and especially when I then close my eyes, I hear whole concerts complete with all the instruments from the tender flute to the rustling cello. Thus I remember to have heard as a boy of nine when I was walking against the current of the Rhine and against the evening wind, simultaneously surrounded by the waves of the air and the water, a melting Adagio with all the magic of music, with all the melodious turns and the entire accompanying harmony. It was like a performance at Vauxhall;[41] truly I even believed that everything which the sages of Greece wrote about the harmony of the spheres was not any more gentle or beautiful or any more divine than this strange dreaming. But as soon as a thought interferes with these tones immediately everything is gone as if by magic: disappeared! melody, harmony, sound, in short the entire music of the spheres.[42]

This last passage illustrates the very distinctive musical quality of Kleist's sentence structure. Whenever I read Kleist I feel as if I am listening to a melody rather than reading words, and by melody I mean that special type of Romantic melody which spins out endlessly, expanding like one long breath, spiralling upwards as if imbued with some type of magic force, pushing forward as it carries the listener along with it, gathering more and more momentum as it swells until at last this continuous flow of sounds finds its peak of intensity and then quickly dies out like a flame.

Music is also the source from which so many of Eichendorff's writings spring. More profoundly influenced by music than Kleist, music may be called the very soul of Eichendorff. In the past decade three important studies have appeared which well document the way in which Eichendorff's literary efforts originated from his own musical experiences.[43] The story, *Die Zauberei im Herbst (Magic in Autumn)*, included in this collection is an excellent example of Eichendorff's dependency on music. In this and other works Eichendorff's musical background comes to life.

As a child Eichendorff exhibited a most remarkable sensitivity to instrumental color, a talent which grew steadily throughout his life; instruments functioned for him like the colors of an artist's palette. Eichendorff heard, for example, the eerie sound of the wind in the tones of the clarinet and, as did Weber, the mysterious voice of the forest in the hunting horn. The poet was a superb orchestrator in every sense of the word. Notice this passage from *Magic in Autumn:*

> At this point the stranger suddenly jumped up. Outside could be heard a strange song flying past the castle windows. It consisted only of single phrases which now and then sounded at one moment like a human voice and the next like the high tones of a clarinet.[44]

This acute sensitivity to instrumental color was nourished at an early age by his father, the wealthy aristocratic patron of music, Adolf Theodor Rudolf von Eichendorff (1756-1818). The Eichendorff family lived in a magnificent castle at Lübowitz (i.e., Silesia) in whose specially designed concert hall the young poet heard a variety of musical sounds. His father was particularly fond of strolling musicians; clarinettists, drummers, trumpeters and flautists frequently performed for the young Eichendorff. The poet's father even owned a glass harmonica upon which the young boy often played.

Eichendorff's formal musical education began at the age of thirteen when in 1801 he and his brother, Wilhelm, were sent to study at the Gymnasium in Breslau. The young poet noted in his *Taggebuch* (November 8, 1802) that it was here that he had his first piano lesson.[46] Eichendorff also noted in his diary that one year later his father bought a new pianoforte upon which he played.[47] It should be noted here that the oldest of the five Eichendorff children, Wilhelm, was an especially talented pianist and composer and performed the flute and violin with some dexterity.[48] Wilhelm had studied music before he went to Breslau and now the younger brother had a chance to follow in his footsteps.

The activities at the Gymnasium centered a great deal around music. The students at the school participated in several musical performances; works such as Haydn's Oratorios, *Die Schöpfung (The Creation,* 1798) and the recently composed *Die Jahreszeiten (The Seasons,* 1801), were performed while the two Eichendorff brothers were in Breslau. Eichendorff, his brother and classmates also often attended musical performances at the Breslau theater. The poet's great love of Mozart's operas can be traced back to his experiences in Breslau: as a student at the Gymnasium he heard Mozart's *Figaro, The Abduction from The Seraglio, Don Giovanni, Die Zauberflöte (The Magic Flute),* and *La Clemenza di Tito (The Clemency of Titus).*[49] Scenes from these operas were to appear in Eichendorff's later novels.[50] The young poet also heard in the Breslau theater Ferdinand Kauer's popular *Donauweibchen (The Woman of the Danube),* the source of *Magic in Autumn.* Brandenburg records how after the performance Wilhelm sat at the piano and played the Overture, the hunting motive and several other selections from this opera as Eichendorff and his friends sang to his accompaniment.[51]

Eichendorff's subsequent experiences at the Universities of Halle (1805-1806) and Heidelberg (1807-1808) increased his already vast knowledge of music. The young poet and his brother like so many German Romantic writers participated in the musical activities at the estate of Reichardt at Gibichenstein near Halle. Here Wilhelm played the piano and Eichendorff sang. The poet also noted in his *Tagebuch* that in the summer of 1807, before he left for Heidelberg, he began to take up the guitar.

At the University of Heidelberg Eichendorff began his important association with Anton Friedrich Justus Thibaut (1770-1840), professor of law and amateur musician. Schumann, who attended Heidelberg in 1829, was also greatly influenced by Thibaut, so much so that he actually allowed the professor to persuade him to attend some classes. Thibaut organized the well-known student music society (the so-called Heidelberg *Singverein*) for the purpose of performing Renaissance and Baroque vocal music. As members of this group Eichendorff and Schumann were introduced to much of the music of the past.

Arnim's musical background has certain features in common with Eichendorff. Arnim's father, Baron Joachim Erdmann von Arnim, was also a wealthy aristocratic patron of music; in 1776 Frederick the Great (i.e., Frederick II, King of Prussia from 1740-1786) appointed Baron von Arnim as his director of court entertainments. Karl Otto von Arnim, the poet's older brother, similar to Wilhelm Eichendorff, was a talented musician and followed in the footsteps of his father. Like Eichendorff, Arnim also participated in the musical activities at Halle and Heidelberg along with his close friend and future brother-in-law, Clemens Brentano. Arnim's favorite instrument appears to be the guitar;[52] his love of singing is also well-documented in his essay, *Von Volksliedern (On Folksongs)*.

The most important musical influence on Arnim was the composer Reichardt, a close friend of the poet's father. At the age of twenty-four Reichardt was appointed Royal Kapellmeister to Frederick the Great at the same time Arnim's father received his own appointment as director of court entertainments. Reichardt and Baron von Arnim frequently met to discuss musical matters. Throughout his life Arnim was a frequent visitor to the Kapellmeister's residences in Berlin and Gibichenstein. Of the several German Romantic writers who knew Reichardt, Arnim was the closest to the composer.[53] The poet's great admiration of Frederick the

Great's Kapellmeister, moreover, never changed in contrast to Tieck and Brentano whose later writings reveal a decided ambivalence toward the composer.

Arnim's association with Reichardt is mirrored in several of the poet's writings: Reichardt's experiences as a composer, for example, form the basis of the plot of *Angelika und Cosmus* and the heroine of *Gräfin Dolores* (*Countess Dolores,* 1810) is none other than Reichardt's talented daughter, Louise.[54] Arnim also dedicated his essay, *On Folksongs,* to the Kapellmeister and contributed various articles on the German folksong to Reichardt's journal, *Berlinische Musikalischen Zeitung (Berlin Musical Journal).*

Because of their own musical talents and vast knowledge of music and particularly because music meant so much in their lives, the German Romantic writers watched over this art form with the greatest love and concern. Each of the poet-musicians included in this collection took an active part in the musical life of nineteenth century Germany. They felt compelled to allow no one to abuse their precious adopted child, continually drawing their reader's attention to those compositions which they felt debased the divine quality of music. They were the defenders of the champions, Beethoven, Mozart, Haydn and Gluck, as well as lesser-known composers whom they felt had merit, but were overlooked. As will be shown they also brought about a true Renaissance of the music of the past and developed a philosophy of music which directly affected the style of German Romantic composers.

NOTES

1. See Eichendorff selections, pp. 225-248.
2. Ludwig Börne, *Sämtliche Schriften,* 5 vols. (Düsseldorf: Joseph Melzer, 1964), I, 147.
3. Ludwig Tieck, ed., *Phantasien uber die Kunst für Freunde der Kunst* (Hamburg, 1799), p. 195.
4. Jean Paul's *Sämtliche Werke,* 30 vols. in 17 (Berlin: G. A. Reimer, 1860-62), V, 115.

5. Theodor Körner's *Sämtliche Werke*, 2 vols. (Berlin: G. Grote'sche, 1885), II, 34.
6. *Ibid.*, I, 197.
7. See Bibliography.
8. Karl Storck, ed., *The Letters of Robert Schumann*, trans. by H. Bryant (New York: E. P. Dutton, 1907), p. 128.
9. Richard Wagner, *Mein Leben*, authorized translation (New York: Tudor Publishing Co., 1936), p. 38.
10. See, for example, Walter Salmen, *Johann Friedrich Reichardt* (Zürich, 1963), p. 96.
11. Tieck was introduced to Reichardt in 1788 by the Kapellmeister's stepson, Hensler. In 1798 the poet married Amalie Alberti, Reichardt's sister-in-law.
12. Rudolf Köpke, *Ludwig Tieck, Erinnerungen aus dem Leben des Dichters*, 2 vols. (Leipzig: Brockhaus, 1855), I, 55-57.
13. Fife, Matenko and Zeydel, *Letters of Ludwig Tieck* (New York: Modern Language Association of America, 1937), p. 302.
14. Köpke, *op. cit.*, p. 87.
15. For example: *Die Sommernacht* (1789), *Phantasus* (1816), *Alma* (fragment, 1803), Franz Sternbald (1799), articles for Cotta's *Morgenblatt*, etc.
16. Tieck, *op. cit.*, pp. 91-98.
17. Tieck worked closely with Taubert, Meyerbeer and particularly Mendelssohn during the years 1840-42 when the poet was invited by the newly crowned King of Prussia, Frederick Wilhelm IV, to supervise the performance of Greek tragedies and the plays of Shakespeare at the Berlin court. Tieck met Beethoven in Prague in 1813 and Weber and Schubert in 1819. The poet had intended to write a biography of his favorite violinist, Friedrich Wilhelm Heinrich Benda (1745-1814), based on certain writings and letters which Reichardt possessed.
18. Tieck met Count Karl Ludwig Friedrich von Finckenstein (1745-1818) through his friend, Wilhelm von Burgsdorff. Under the guidance of the Count and Henriette, Ziebingen became an important musical center during the early nineteenth century. Kleist also knew the Finckenstein family; in a letter dated August 26, 1813 he described an evening with Henriette and Tieck. Brentano, a frequent visitor to the estate, paid tribute to the Finckenstein family in *Der Sänger*.
19. Carl Friedrich Zelter (1758-1832), composer, conductor, musical theorist and founder of the *Berlin Singakademie* (1792). Zelter was a close friend of Goethe and Mendelssohn and his songs, which play an important part in the early history of the German Lied, were greatly admired by Schubert.
20. Theodor Körner was the godson of the Duchess of Courland.
21. For more information concerning music in the life of young Körner see: Christian Gottfried Körner, *The Life of Carl Theodor Körner*, trans. by G. F. Richardson, 2 vols. (London: Thomas Hurst, 1827), I, 5, and E. Peschel and

E. Wildenow, *Theodor Körner und die Seinen*, 2 vols. (Leipzig: E. A. Seemann, 1898), I, 227. Vol. II (P. 106) contains a painting by F. W. Heine which depicts Körner playing the piano and singing.

22. Körner, *op. cit.*, II, 338 (letter dated September 23, 1812).
23. *Ibid.*, p. 336 (letters dated June 24, and February, 1812).
24. Friedrich Blume, *Die Musik in Geschichte und Gegenwart*, 15 vols. (Kassel: Bärenreiter, 1958), VII, 1396.
25. For a list of Körner's librettos see: Albert Schaefer, *Historisches und Systematisches Verzeichnis sämtlicher Tonwerke zu den Dramen Schillers, Goethes, Shakespeares, Kleists und Körners* (Leipzig: Karl Merseburger, 1886), pp. 131-136. To this list may be added the unfinished libretto, *Faust*, for Spohr. Beethoven also approached Körner for a libretto *(Ulysses Return)*.
26. Körner, *op. cit.*, II, 236 (letter dated January 20, 1813).
27. *Ibid.* See excerpts from Körner's letters, page 254.
28. Karl Gutzkow, *Börne's Leben*, vol. 6 of *Karl Gutzkow's Gesammelte Werke* (Frankfurt: J. Rutten, 1845), p. 149.
29. See this author's "The Piano Cycles of Schumann and the Novels of Jean Paul Richter," *The Piano Quarterly*, Fall, 1969.
30. George Brandes translates this title as *The Balance (Main Currents in Nineteenth Century Literature)*, 6 vols. (London: William Heinemann, VI, 48).
31. Johann Friedrich Baron von Cottendorf (1764-1832), publisher of many well-known journals. Tieck also contributed to his publications.
32. Marcus Herz (1747-1803), physician, philosopher, and friend of Kant and Lessing. His home in Berlin was another important gathering place for artistic and literary personages. After his death his wife, Henriette (1767-1847), an accomplished musician and literary enthusiast, continued to maintain the position of the Herz family. Her influence on young Börne is well documented; the young journalist boarded with the Herz family while studying medicine in Berlin (1802-1804).
33. Karl Edward von Bülow (1803-1853), disciple of Tieck who collaborated with him in 1848 on a second edition of Kleist's works (G. A. Reimer, publisher).
34. Helmut Sembdner, ed., *Heinrich von Kleist's Lebensspuren, Dokumente und Berichte der Zeitgenossen* (Bremen: Carl Schunemann, 1957), p. 8.
35. Rühle von Lilienstern (1781-1831), historian, close friend of Kleist and the painter, Caspar David Friedrich.
36. Sembdner, *op. cit.*
37. Blume, *op. cit.*, VII, 1211.
38. Ludwig Tieck, ed., *Heinrich von Kleist's Gesammelte Schriften*, 3 vols. (Berlin: G. A. Reimer, 1826), I, iv.
39. Friedrich Koch, *Heinrich von Kleist* (Stuttgart: J.B.Metzlersche,1958), p.3. 3.
40. Heinrich von Kleist,*Sämtliche Werke* (Berlin: Tempel-Verlag, 1964), p.1363 (letter written in the summer of 1811).

41. Vauxhall Gardens, a park in Lambeth, England, used for concerts in the eighteenth and nineteenth centuries.

42. Kleist, *op. cit.,* p. 1230 (letter dated September 19, 1800).

43. See Bibliography under Siara, Wendler and Worbs.

44. Joseph Freiherr von Eichendorff, *Werke und Schriften,* 4 vols. (Stuttgart: J. G. Cotta'sche Buchhandlung, 1957), II, 981.

45. Erich Worbs, "Waldhornruf und Lautenklang-Musikinstrumente in der Dichtung Eichendorffs," in *Aurora: Eichendorff Almanach* (Wurzburg: Verlagkulturwerk, vol. 22, 1962), p. 74.

46. Worbs, *op. cit.,* p. 75.

47. *Ibid.*

48. Concerning Eichendorff's brother see: Hans Brandenburg, *Joseph von Eichendorff* (Munich: Oskar Beck, 1922, p. 30) and Paul Stocklein, *Joseph von Eichendorff* (Hamburg: Rowohlt, 1963, 31).

49. Eichendorff heard *La Clemenza di Tito* conducted by the young Carl Maria von Weber in Breslau in 1804.

50. See: Norbert Siara, *Szenische Bauweise des Erzählers Eichendorff nach dem Opernvorbild Glucks und Mozarts,* Doctoral Dissertation (Frankfurt: Goethe Universität, 1973).

51. Brandenburg (n. 48), *op. cit.,* p. 134.

52. Mention of Arnim playing the guitar can be found in John Warrack's *Carl Maria von Weber* (Cambridge University Press, 1976), p. 90.

53. For a full and authoritative discussion of Reichardt's relation to Arnim see: Hedwig Wahl Reinhardt, *Johann Friedrich Reichardt, His Importance to the Romantic Movement in German Literature,* Doctoral Dissertation (New York University, 1947).

54. Reinhardt (n. 53.), *op. cit.,* p. 102.

2

German Romantic Literature and the Caecilian Movement

ACHIM VON ARNIM could have given his hero Halbgott any one of a multitude of popular songs to sing at the crucial place in his tale, *Fürst Ganzgott und Sänger Halbgott (Prince Whole God and the Singer Half God),* when the princess sends him a note hinting that he come to her boudoir. But Halbgott sings neither an aria from an opera, a romance, or a popular song, in fact nothing of a secular nature. Instead Arnim chooses the melody of Pergolesi's *Stabat Mater,* a Catholic church composition, and what an effect this melody has on its audience (Orpheus himself could not have elicited such an ovation): the stuffy chamberlain kisses Halbgott's hand, the nightingales moan, the fountain pushes its stream of water up to the stars in the sky, the glowworms fly intoxicated around the singer's head, a cat cannot restrain himself from joining in and the princess sends a second note requesting that Halbgott keep her company.

But all this is rather mild if we compare it to the effect of Catholic church music on Kleist's group of blasphemous ruffians, who in the novella, *Die heilige Cäcilie (Holy Cecilia),* are about to raze the convent of St. Cecilia to the ground; but just as the riot is about to take place, the choir intones the "Gloria in excelsis Deo" ("Glory to God in the Highest") from the second part of the Ordinary of the

Mass and all at once not a breath stirs, not a particle of dust is disturbed on the floor, the unruly mob stands like statues and their leaders, the four brothers from the Protestant Netherlands, fall to their knees, shaking violently as if struck by lightning and never again regain their senses.

These incidents from Kleist's and Arnim's tales might appear somewhat strange and paradoxical considering that both writers were Protestants and Arnim a staunch one at that. Yet Kleist's and Arnim's glorification of Catholic church music is understandable if placed within the context of the Protestant church music reform movement which began in the eighteenth century and continued to flower in the nineteenth.

This movement was launched in 1762 by the Protestant theologian and philosopher, Johann Georg Hamann (1730-1788), who in his "Klaggedicht in Gestalt eines Sendschreibens über Kirchenmusik" ("A Complaint about Church Music in the Form of an Open Letter"), called attention to what he felt was a decline in the standards of German Protestant church music. At the time Hamann wrote this article Protestant church composers such as Johann Friedrich Doles (1715-1797) and Carl Philipp Emanuel Bach (1714-1788) were freely paraphrasing the words of the Bible, ornamenting and altering the chorale melodies to such an extent that they were hardly recognizable, and employing theatrical and operatic devices in their cantatas, characteristics which can also be seen, although to a lesser extent, in the church music of J. S. Bach.

Hamann's interest in the reform of Protestant church music bore fruit in the works of his pupil, Johann Gottfried Herder (1744-1803), whose philosophy had a profound influence on early German Romantic thought. Herder himself was a gifted musician and it is not surprising that he should give so much attention to the problem of Protestant church music. In his *Briefe, das Studium der Theologie betreffend* (*Letters Concerned with the Study of Theology*, 1786, i.e., Letter no. 46) Herder systematically set forth his ideas concerning Protestant church music. By way of summary I have listed the six most important concepts in his *Letters:*

1. Sacred music is the holiest form of art.
2. Church music of the late eighteenth century has lost its dignity and taken on the characteristics of the "dainty court song" and the ornateness of the operatic aria.
3. Church music should be a humanitarian form of art, "its text is the word of all mankind."
4. The foundations of Protestant church music are the choir and the sacred hymn (the chorale); the choir is the basis of sacred music, not the solo song; the choir and the congregation intone the song of praise, the hymn in which lie the mystical, sacred secrets of the church.
5. The individual, be he the composer, the poet or the performer, should not be allowed to express his individuality.
6. Religious music has no connection to anything theatrical. "Drama and religion are as separate as the eye and the ear."[1]

The influence of Herder's *Letters* on the early German Romantic Protestant writers is especially noticeable. Herder's initial premise, for example, is restated by Tieck when the novice in *Musical Sorrows and Joys* says, "I believe that music's true destiny was to soar to heaven, to proclaim the divine and the belief in God."[2] In Jean Paul's "Elende Extra-Sylbe über die Kirchenmusik" ("Poor Little Extra Syllable on Church Music," *Hesperus*), Herder's third point is supported by Richter's satirical condemnation of the way church music in his time seems to have been written in a style which could only be understood by intellectuals. The choir director in this excerpt who sings bravura arias is also an example of an individual who misuses church music to express his own talent. Ernst Moritz Arndt (1769-1860) also took up Herder's cause in his *Von dem Kirchenliede nebst Geistlichen Liedern (Concerning Church and Spiritual Songs,* 1819).

Herder discussed the reform of Protestant church music in his other writings. Of particular significance are his two essays, "Vom Geiste der Ebräischen Poesie" ("On the Spirit of Hebrew Poetry," 1783) and "Cacilia" (1793). At the end of the earlier article Herder attached a short essay entitled, "Über die Musik" ("On Music"), written by Matthias Claudius in 1771.[3] This article, which glorifies the art of church music, draws examples from Hebrew, Greek and Renaissance sacred music. In discussing the latter, Claudius related the oft-told story of how Palestrina saved the art of sacred contrapuntal music from banishment by the church through his *Pope Marcellus Mass (Missa Papae Marcelli,* 1567):

> Pope Marcellus II wanted even to banish music from the altar, but Palestrina appeased him with a Mass which moves forward in a slow dignified manner, devoid of all wantonness . . . its tones turning toward heaven and touching the heart with every step.[4]

The mention of Palestrina at this time is of the utmost significance as the music of the Renaissance master was to become the paragon of true church music in the Romantic era. In Herder's later article, "Cäcilia," several other old Italian church composers such as Leo, Jomelli, Pergolesi, Durante and Marcello were recommended as models for Protestant church composers to follow along with Palestrina; the entire group Herder described "as the favorites of Saint Cecilia."[5] These Italian church composers were as important to early German Romantic literature and music as the Italian painters, Titian, Correggio and Raphael, were to the Nazarenes.

In his article of 1793 Herder also prophesized that the Catholic Saint of Music would return to earth and temples would be erected to her. The first to erect such an edifice was, perhaps, Johann Friedrich Reichardt, Herder's close friend. In 1783 the composer journeyed to Italy describing the Catholic music he had gone there to hear as "the highest form of all art . . . especially the old simple style."[6] Upon his return to Germany in 1784 Reichardt organized the so-called "Concert Spirituel" for the purpose of performing old Italian church music. These concerts were later heard by Wackenroder and Tieck whose works were the first of a long line of German Romantic literary efforts to glorify the music of Saint Cecilia's favorites.

Wackenroder, although a Lutheran, depicted his literary alter-ego, Joseph Berglinger *(Fantasies on Art),* as an Evangelical Kapellmeister every fiber of whose being was deeply affected by Catholic church music. Palestrina's music casts a spell over him and before he dies Joseph prays to Saint Cecilia for that last spark of divine inspiration which he needs to finish his great masterpiece, a Catholic Mass. In 1802 Tieck, who had journeyed to Italy the year before, paid tribute to Catholic church music in a series of poems entitled, "Die heilige Cäcilia," "Marcello," "Pergolesi," "Stabat Mater," and "Palestrina, Marcello and Pergolesi." These are, incidentally, "the few meagre poems" which the novice mentions he wrote as a young man enchanted by the sound of old Italian church music (see *Musical Sorrows and Joys,* p. 111).

Tieck's series of poems is an excellent example of the way German Romantic authors romanticized Saint Cecilia and her favorites. In Tieck's "Pergolesi," for example, the composer is portrayed as a terribly lonely young man, ill, wandering in a forest, wringing his hands in agony, yearning and longing until at last an angel appears to him. Praying for divine inspiration for which he would gladly sacrifice his life, Pergolesi at last receives the ray of magic light, writes his *Stabat Mater* and dies shortly thereafter. But as Romantic as this poem is Tieck blends fact and fantasy together as he does in *Musical Sorrows and Joys:* the last work of Pergolesi who died at the age of twenty-six is believed to have been the *Stabat Mater* which he wrote in the midst of great suffering.

No less imaginative is Theodor Körner's portrayal of Saint Cecilia. In his poem, "Heilige Cacilia" (c. 1810), Cecilia is depicted as a young, extremely talented harpist who one day hears the wondrous music of the angels. Tormented by the realization that she can never achieve the beauty of these heavenly sounds on earth, she breaks the strings of her instrument. Urged on by a mysterious force the young girl takes her own life so that she may make this stream of magic harmonies her own for eternity.

The most important literary stimulus behind the Romantic cult of Saint Cecilia and Catholic church music is most likely Kleist's novella, *Holy Cecilia.*[7] In this tale the Patron Saint of Music[8] miraculously comes back to earth and seated at the organ conducts the choir saving her convent from ruin. In the novella Saint Cecilia is vividly portrayed as the protectoress of church musicians, the source of divine inspiration and the symbol of the mystical power of music and in particular Catholic church music: her organ playing affects the soul in the way Raphael's portrait of her[9] brings about the death of the painter Francesca Francia in Wackenroder's *Herzensergiessungen eines kunstliebenden Klosterbruders (Confessions from the Heart of an Art-Loving Friar,* 1796-1797).

The profound religious tone of Kleist's novella reflects how deeply the poet was moved by the spirit of Catholic church music. His great admiration for this art form seems to have first evidenced itself during a visit the poet made to the predominantly Catholic city of Dresden in 1801. In a letter by Kleist dated May 2, 1801, is foreshadowed the intense reverence for Catholic church music which is expressed in *Holy Cecilia:*

> I felt so good upon this first entry into a world full of beauty, a world which was completely new to me. . . . But nowhere did I find myself so profoundly moved as in the Catholic church where the greatest most exalted church music combines with the other arts to move the heart with such power. Ah, Wilhelmine,[10] our divine service is nothing. It speaks only to cold intellect, but a Catholic service speaks to all the senses.[11]

By the end of the first decade of the nineteenth century the Protestant conversion to Catholic church music was complete. Herder had not only given the members of the Protestant church music reform movement a platform to follow, but a name as well, i.e., the Caecilian Movement. Stimulated in great part by the literary efforts of Herder and the early German Romantic writers societies sprang up all over Germany dedicated to the performance of the music of Saint Cecilia's favorites; in the late eighteenth century the term, *Caecilien-Bündnisse,* was used for many of these organizations, particularly in Vienna and Passau, in the nineteenth century the term, *Cäcilienverein,* was used in Frankfurt, for example. To this group of choral societies also belong Zelter's *Singakademie,* Thibaut's *Singverein* and Schumann's *Singekränzchen* which the composer organized in Dresden in 1851, and the many private performances of Renaissance and Baroque choral music which took place in the residences of the German aristocracy. Mendelssohn also played his part in the dissemination of old Italian sacred music introducing many little known compositions to his audiences in Düsseldorf, as demonstrated by the comments he made to his sister, Rebecca (letter of October 26, 1833):

> I could not find among all the music here even one . . . single work of the old Italian masters . . . so I got into a carriage and drove to Elberfeld where I hunted out Palestrina's *Improperia* and the *Misereres* of Allegri and Baini . . . and went off to Bonn. There I rummaged through the whole library. . . . I found some splendid things and took away with me six Masses by Palestrina and one of Pergolesi. I found two motets of Lassus in Cologne, one of these . . . we are to sing in church next Friday. [12]

Along with this Renaissance of old Italian church music, the Protestant church music reform movement set the stage for a Catholic musical counterreformation. The situation which occurred is not that different from Luther's reforms of sacred music which elicited some counteraction on the part of the Catholic church. The difference being, however, that in Germany in the Romantic era, both sides were glorifying the same type of music. Many Protestant composers of this period were writing Catholic church music and a great deal of it at that.

I attribute this state of affairs not to the fact that among the Protestant sects there was continual dissension or that the Protestant liturgy was newer and less well-defined than the Catholic, but rather to the musical-aesthetic taste of the time. As Kleist's letter so well demonstrates Catholic church music like Catholic paintings appealed to the senses, to the Romantic love of the mystical, otherwordly and ritualistic, qualities which one does not truly associate with the Protestant service.

The Protestant church music reform movement began to flourish at a time when Catholic church music had reached a low ebb, as evidenced by Rossini, for example, in whose sacred music whole sections from his operas were often used without changing a single note, only the text. Catholic church musicians soon agreed with Herder that the solution to the problem of sacred music was to adopt the style of old Italian church music; it was not long before the views of the Protestant Caecilian Movement began to appear in the writings of Catholic church musicians. Herder's belief in the need for a humanitarian form of church music found expression, for example, in the writings of the Catholic music scholar and admirer of Herder, Karl Proske (1794-1861). Notice, for example, this passage from Proske's works: "True church music does not serve any single human being, but it is an integral part of prayer and the whole Catholic liturgy and cannot be separated from it."[13]

Franz Liszt was a zealous reformer of Catholic church music and in the following quotation from his *Über die Kirchenmusik (On Church Music,* 1834) we sense the influence of the Protestant church music reform movement:

> Church music! We no longer know what this word means anymore. The great revelations of a Palestrina . . . or a Marcello . . . live only in libraries. . . . The church music of our day lacks the spiritual power of the Middle Ages. . . . It does not have the inner strength . . . or vigorous roots or the depth which illuminates heaven and earth with wonderful flaming beams.[14]

Several years after the Catholic Caecilian Movement began to flower Franz Witt (1834-1881), ordained priest, composer and friend of Wagner and Liszt, in his *Zu Zustand der Katholik Kirchenmusik (The Position of Catholic Church Music,* 1865) summarized the goals of the new reform movement. The most important of these are as follows:

1. To unify Catholic church music practices.
2. To revive Renaissance, Baroque and Medieval Catholic church music.
3. To encourage the composition of new works which adhere closely to the old style of Catholic sacred music.
4. To revive, reform and encourage the use of Gregorian chant.[15]

The three most important centers of the Catholic Caecilian Movement in Germany were Regensburg (Ratisbon), Eichstätt and Saint Michael's in Munich. Church musicians associated with these centers made a great effort to discover and collect manuscripts of old Italian church music. Leading the way in this endeavor was the earliest of the three centers, Saint Michael's. Here in 1816, for example, Caspar Ett (1788-1847) directed the choir in a performance of the long forgotten *Miserere* of Gregorio Allegri (1582-1652), one of the Italian church composers mentioned in *Musical Sorrows and Joys*. The reintroduction of this work and Ockeghem's Mass, *Missa cujusvistoni* (directed by Ett in 1827), were landmarks in the history of the Caecilian Movement. It was also at Saint Michael's that the works of Palestrina's great contemporary from the Netherlands, Orlando di Lasso, were revived.

The revival, reform and use of Gregorian chant was in some respects the pivotal point of the whole Catholic Caecilian Movement as the chorale was for Herder the foundation of the Protestant liturgy. In 1807 Caspar Ett established the earliest German Romantic institute for the study of plainsong at Saint Michael's. Of special importance is Ett's publication in 1827 of a new edition of Gregorian chant (the so-called *Cantica Sacra*) based on the old medieval form of plainsong which challenged the authenticity of the Renaissance *Editio Medicean* (1614-1615). It would seem as if Tieck was aware of the controversy over the Renaissance edition of the chants for he makes a point of mentioning in his novella that he was greatly impressed by the way he heard the old canti-firmi while in Italy. this manner of singing plainsong, he noted, was not only totally new to him, but he never heard it again either in Rome or in Germany.

Despite all the efforts of the Protestant and Catholic church music reform movements to provide guidelines for composers to follow, one perplexing problem remained: how to reconcile the goals of the Caecilian Movement with the church music of the beloved German composer, Mozart, for example, in whose sacred music instruments are used and the influence of opera is quite pro-

28

nounced. Was the sacred music of Mozart, Haydn and even Beethoven to be considered profane?

Guided by the theories of Wackenroder, Hoffmann in his *Alte und Neue Kirchenmusik (Old and New Church Music,* 1814) offered a solution which was palatable to many German Romantics: let the true religious devotion of the composer, he argued, be the yardstick by which to judge the worth of a sacred composition, not style. This concept runs like a leitmotiv through German Romantic literature. In Eichendorff's writings (page 225), the poet states that it is only the religious devotion of the old church artists which has kept their work alive; the great beauty and power of the music of the nuns in Kleist's *Holy Cecilia* is intimately connected to their piety and sincere devotion to God.

As far as our Romantic composers were concerned this dilemma presented no problems. Despite their love of rich orchestration, bold harmonies, lyricism and literary stimuli, traits which are, admittedly, contrary to the simple church style Herder envisioned, German Romantic composers still found ways to recapture the spirituality and mysticism of old Catholic church music. They found these means not because they felt it necessary to reconcile the views of the reform movements with their own concept of musical style and form, but because of their own sincere love and reverence for the music which resounded through the halls of the old Catholic churches. Like the early German Romantic writers, it little mattered to them what religion they were, this art form satisfied a definite spiritual need as in the case of Kleist. Schumann, for example, only wrote two liturgical compositions during his entire life, a Catholic Mass and a Catholic Requiem and he did so during that period when the shadow of his fatal illness finally engulfed his entire being, his anxiety finding release in the mystical visions of the Catholic liturgy. Mahler also found spiritual relief in old Catholic church music; the whole emotional and intellectual message of the first movement of his gigantic Eighth Symphony is to be found in the Gregorian chant, *Veni creator Spiritus* (Come Holy Ghost, Creator, Come from Thy bright heavenly throne, come take possession of our souls and make them Thine own), which is not only the central musical theme in this movement, but an expression of Mahler's plea for salvation.

Echoes of the Caecilian Movement are found in many spheres of German Romantic music, the oratorio, the opera, the symphony as well as liturgical music; the following is a brief discussion of some of the more notable examples of this influence. It is not common to find the life of a composer as subject for an oratorio, but knowing this period's fondness for Palestrina, it is not surprising to find that the Protestant composer and theologian, Carl Loewe, wrote an oratorio based on the life of the Renaissance master. Loewe's greatest tribute to the goals of the Caecilian Movement, however, is his oratorio, *Die Apostel von Phillipi* (*The Apostles from Philippi*, 1834), which is scored for an unaccompanied male choir and is characterized by a clarity of declamation and simplicity of rhythm, features associated with the so-called Palestrina style. Several of his other oratorios also use Protestant chorales.

The first half of Wagner's *Das Liebesmahl der Apostel* (*The Banquet of the Apostles*, 1843) which shows the influence of Loewe is written for men's voices alone. *Das Liebesmahl* also forms the preliminary sketch for *Parsifal*[16] (premièred in 1882), one of the Romantic era's most important products of the Caecilian Movement. In his last opera Wagner vividly recaptured the essential sound and spirituality of Palestrina's music. That particular passage in *Parsifal* (Act I) in which the knights partake of the Eucharist while from the gallery under the dome of the Hall of the Grail the sounds of an unaccompanied boys' choir float down like the music of angels is one of the most soul-stirring portrayals of the mystical power of Catholic church music in the nineteenth century. *Parsifal* represents the goals of the Caecilian Movement in yet another manner, one of the most important themes of the opera, that associated with the Eucharist, is a Gregorian chant, *Momento Domini David et omnis mansuetudinis ejus* (Psalm 131, verse 1, Remember O Lord the meekness and patience of David).

The Catholicism of *Parsifal* as well as that of *Tannhäuser* and

Lohengrin is rooted in Wagner's earlier experience in Dresden as is Kleist's *Holy Cecilia.* Wagner came under the spell of Catholic music while a young conductor in that city (1842-1848). The design of the Hall of the Grail in *Parsifal* was undoubtedly influenced by Wagner's visits to the Dresden *Frauenkirche* in which he heard music cascading down from the famous cupola gallery. It was also in this city that the composer wrote *Das Liebesmahl* and met Franz Witt who gave him a copy of Palestrina's *Stabat Mater,* a composition which Wagner studied many times.

The German Romantic composer who was most intimately connected with the Catholic Caecilian Movement was Franz Liszt. Despite his wayward youth, Liszt is the only composer of this school who was a devout Catholic and a member of the clergy. It is for this reason, perhaps, that we find several uses of Gregorian chant in his music rather than in the music of Schubert and Weber who although Catholic lacked his ecclesiastical background. Gregorian chants can be found, for example, in Liszt's *Quasi stella matutina,* the oratorio, *Elisabeth,* part III of *Christus,* etc. Liszt gave considerable thought to the study and proper performance of plainsong and his correspondence with Witt and other Catholic church musicians and editors of sacred music journals reveal that his knowledge of Gregorian chant was considerable.

Palestrina's music is characterized by a style which is basically in agreement with the principles of chant singing. Liszt's small sacred work, *Die heilige Cäcilia* (1874) is one of several of his compositions which evidences a conscious attempt to imitate the characteristics of plainsong. The mezzo-soprano solo line, which is the most important part of the work, is rigidly constructed: its range is narrow, it proceeds with an even unmodified beat devoid of strong and weak accents (there are actually no bar lines in the score, long note values predominate and the text is set in a strict syllabic style). In addition the four-part choir *(ad libitum)* sings much of its material in unison. *Die heilige Cäcilia* also derives its entire thematic material from the medieval antiphon, *Cantibus organis* (see n. 8). The austere medieval style of singing is, however, accompanied by optional orchestral parts highly reminiscent of Wagner.

The veneration of Palestrina further resulted in a large repertoire of Latin texts set for unaccompanied choir by the Catholic composers, Schubert, Spohr and Bruckner. Schubert, in particular, wrote several a cappella sacred works including a large group of Masses. The Protestant, Brahms, also contributed to this repertoire with his setting of three Latin texts, *O bone Jesu, Adoramus te* and *Regina caeli* (op. 37, 1866). Amongst the unpublished church music of Meyerbeer are also twelve Psalms written for unaccompanied double choir.

Hoffmann particularly enjoyed alternating between the old and new styles of church music: his Mass in D Major (1805) and his *Miserere* in B Minor (1809), for example, employ the same large orchestra as Beethoven's Mass in C Major (op. 86, 1807) and the texts are set in a similar dramatic manner. In contrast, Hoffmann's *La Santa Virgine,* a set of six Latin hymns for unaccompanied choir (1808), pays homage to Palestrina.

To the list of Catholic church compositions already mentioned might be added Mendelssohn's three Latin Motets (op. 39) for women's choir and organ which were supposedly inspired by the singing of the nuns of Trinità dé Monte in Rome (letter of December 30, 1830 to Zelter). Mendelssohn possessed a remarkable knowledge of Catholic church music as evidenced by the scholarly accounts of the music heard in Rome during Holy Week included in his letters to Zelter (1830-1831). Passages like the following demonstrate how deeply he was affected by Catholic church music at that time:

> During this silent prayer a deathlike silence prevails in the whole church; presently the *Miserere* commences with a soft chord breathed by the voices. . . . This beginning . . . made the deepest impression on me. For an hour and a half one voice alone has been chanting; after the pause comes an admirably constructed chord (this is wonderful) causing everyone to feel in his heart the power of the music.[17]

As moving as the Eucharist scene in Wagner's *Parsifal,* incidentally, is Mendelssohn's use of a solo boy's voice to announce the coming of the rain in the composer's masterpiece, *Elijah*.

One of the favorite Catholic texts of the Romantic era was the *Stabat Mater* which no doubt influenced Arnim when he chose this medieval poem for his hero, Halbgott, to sing. We notice also that in Tieck's *Musical Sorrows and Joys,* the first time Julie is allowed to perform she sings Palestrina's *Stabat Mater.* The fondness for this text and the *Salve Regina,* which appears in Kleist's novella, reflects a particular aspect of the German Romantic intense interest in Catholicism, i.e., the veneration of the Virgin Mary. Although the idealization of the Virgin stems in part from the Romantic identification with the Gothic, Goethe's image of the redemptive power of woman which is so vividly portrayed in the concluding "Chorus Mysticus" of *Faust II* also contributed to this cult. Arnim's Princess, who at the end of his tale saves both brothers from disgrace, is a Gretchen-like figure and the *Stabat Mater* which is sung to her aptly fits her elevated character.

Following Wackenroder, the earliest German Romantic literary work to glorify the text of the *Stabat Mater* is, perhaps, Tieck's poem which belongs to that series mentioned previously (p. 24). Tieck's *Stabat Mater* captures the central image of the medieval sequence in that it is a most compassionate description of the emotion of the Virgin as she stands nobly beneath the cross watching her Son die. To my mind the musical summation of the German Romantic worship of the Virgin has always been the fourth movement ("Urlicht") of Mahler's Resurrection Symphony.[18] After a movement of the utmost turmoil and torment, of dissonant clashes and violent sounds, "Urlicht" ("Primeval Light") opens with the unforgettable quiet entry of a solo contralto singing the words, "O Roschen rot," which refers to the Virgin Mary.[19] As in Dante's *Divine Comedy* and Goethe's *Faust,* the Virgin is the only mediator between God and man and it is to her that man must pray. Thus Mahler through the words, "O Red Rosebud," appeals to the Virgin for spiritual salvation. In addition might be mentioned that scene in Act IV of Schumann's opera, *Genoveva,* when the heroine is saved from being murdered by a ray of light which miraculously shines down upon her from a cross with the image of the Virgin on it, the statue being hidden in the bushes.

Amidst this veneration of old Catholic church music one wonders how the great Lutheran composer, J. S. Bach, fared. Reichardt's attitude toward Bach well reflects the position which the great composer occupied in the early decades of the Romantic era. From his writings it is evident that Reichardt revered Bach the keyboard composer, not Bach the church musician. Bach was to him the greatest of all organists and works like the *Goldberg Variations, The Well Tempered Clavier* and the organ chorales were greatly admired by him and he arduously studied the unmatched polyphonic writing which is contained in them. But Bach's choral music was another matter. For a composer who idolized the simple songs of Johann Peter Schulz,[20] Bach's highly ornate vocal parts were "unnatural," "unsingable" and contrary to the laws of proper declamation.[21]

Knowing Reichardt's attitude, Tieck's discussion of the music of J. S. Bach in his novella is quite significant. However, in spite of Tieck's forward looking comments Bach's position little changed. We notice, for example, in Schumann's little tale, *Monument für Beethoven (A Monument for Beethoven,* 1836), that the Bach whom Schumann glorifies is an organist who, sitting upon an organ bench, weaves wondrous chorale variations. There is, however, a most significant passage in Schumann's tale that should not be overlooked. I am referring to that place where, after sketching Bach playing the organ, Schumann suddenly says, "There you are Felix Meritis, a man whose heart and mind equal his, playing one of his chorale variations."[22] Felix Meritis is Schumann's name for Mendelssohn, the composer whose great love and understanding of Bach Schumann knew far surpassed that of his contemporaries. It was Mendelssohn who was responsible for the revival of Bach's complete *Saint Matthew Passion;* the performance of this work in the hall of Zelter's *Singakademie* marks the debut of Bach the church composer.

In 1869 Witt's *Cäcilienverein* (Bamberg) was given official recognition by the German Catholic clergy in Innsbruck; with this act the revival of old Italian church music was complete and with it had come a rich harvest of German Romantic literature and music which embodied in a variety of ways the goals and philosophy of the Caecilian Movement. Schumann often used the *Tagebuch* as a literary form. One such journal bears the title, *Aus dem Tagebuch der heiligen Cäcilia (From the Diary of Saint Cecilia)*.

NOTES

1. Johann Gottfried von Herder, *Sämtliche Werke zur Religion und Theologie,* 10 vols. (Vienna: G. Haas'schen, 1819-1820), IV, 67-76.
2. Ludwig Tieck, *Werke,* 12 vols. (Leipzig: Bibliographisches Institut), II, 357.
3. Matthias Claudius (1740-1815), son of a Lutheran pastor, poet, philosopher, amateur musician and close friend of Herder.
4. Matthias Claudius, *Sämtliche Werke* (Berlin: Tempel-Verlag, 1964), p. 47.
5. Herder's *Sämtliche Werke,* 34 vols. (Vienna, 1821), XXXIV, 101.
6. Blume, *op. cit.,* XI, 158.
7. *Holy Cecilia* was dedicated to Cäcilie Müller, a convert to Catholicism like her brother, the philosopher, Adam Müller.
8. Saint Cecilia was first looked upon as the patron Saint of music in the fifteenth century. Her association with music originated from the text of an old medieval antiphon (Laudes) performed on her Feast Day (November 22, Vespers II) which directly refers to her singing to the accompaniment of the organ. The text of the antiphon reads: To the accompaniment of the organ, Saint Cecilia, the Virgin, sang in her heart saying to the Lord alone, O Lord let my heart and body be immaculate that I may not be confounded.
9. In the fifteenth and sixteenth centuries many artists portrayed Saint Cecilia as singing or playing the organ; the most famous representation of her as a musician is Raphael's painting (Pinacoteca, Bologna, c. 1513) which Wackenroder mentioned in his *Confessions*. Mendelssohn as well as Liszt saw this portrait and described it in glowing terms in their writings.
10. Wilhelmine von Zenge, Kleist's former fiancée.
11. Heinrich von Kleist, *op. cit.,* 1292-1293.
12. G. Seldon Goth, ed., *Felix Mendelssohn, Letters* (New York: Pantheon Books, 1954), p. 216.
13. Blume, *op. cit.,* X, 1655.

35

14. L. Ramann, ed., *Gesammelte Schriften von Franz Liszt,* 6 vols. (Leipzig: Breitkopf und Härtel, 1881), I, 48.

15. Anton Walter, Franz Witt, *Gründer und erster Generalpräses des Cäcilienvereins* (Regensberg: Puset, 1889), pp. 59-63.

16. For more information concerning the relation of *Das Liebesmahl* to *Parsifal* see Arnold Schering, *Geschichte des Oratoriums* (Leipzig: Breitkopf und Härtel, 1911), pp. 424-429.

17. G. Seldon Goth, *op. cit.,* p. 139.

18. The text of "Urlicht" is taken from Brentano and Arnim's collection of folksongs, *Des Knaben Wunderhorn.*

19. See Dante's *Divine Comedy,* "Paradise," last canto, the biblical use of the term, Rose of Sharon, and note the German name for the Virgin Mary, Marien Roslein.

20. One of the few biographies of Schulz was written by Reichardt for the *Allgemeiner musikalischen Zeitung* (Leipzig: 1800-1801).

21. Salmen (i.e., p. 17, n. 10), p. 209.

22. Martin Kreisig, ed., *Robert Schumann, Gesammelte Schriften über Musik und Musiker,* 2 vols. (Leipzig: Breitkopf und Härtel), I, 133.

3
Opera, Singing & Song

WHATEVER ELSE can be said about the musical taste of the German Romantics one has to agree that the human voice attained an unprecedented position in the nineteenth century. "Singing is the original speech of the heart, instrumental music is but a translation of this speech," Börne once remarked.[1] Wagner expressed the opinion of many Romantics when he said, "The human voice is an irrepressible fact . . . it is a far more beautiful and noble medium of tone than any orchestral instrument."[2] The German Romantic love of the human voice excluded very few. "Even those who have great difficulty hearing finally learn to enjoy short melodies,"[3] Tieck's novice informs his listeners in *Musical Sorrows and Joys* during his discussion of the songs of Schulz.

I do not mean to imply that the German Romantics were indifferent to instrumental music; Eichendorff, Jean Paul and Hoffman, for example, made many references to instrumental music in their tales. But if we consider the musical writings of this school as a whole it becomes quite evident that only a small percentage of their literary efforts were devoted to instrumental music.[4] Indeed with many members of this circle their love of music goes no further than the vocal sphere. In the realm of German Romantic music we find a similar situation: after the days of Haydn, Mozart and Beethoven the number of symphonies composed sharply de-

clined and of those that were written in the Romantic era several
contain movements in which voices were employed. But in the
field of the solo song, what a wealth, what an abundance of creativ-
ity occurred.

It is quite natural that the German Romantic writers should
have been so enamored of the human voice: the majority of them we
may recall were talented singers who possessed a considerable interest in and knowledge of vocal pedagogy. They also lived in a
world in which singing and discussions of singers and songs was a
favorite occupation. The aristocratic families with whom they associated were particularly proud of the vocal training of their female members; Henriette Finckenstein, for example, was no aver-
age singer. Mörike's description of the talented family of Count
Schurzburg in *Mozart auf der Reise nach Prag* (*Mozart on His Journey
to Prague,* 1856) and especially his account of the beautiful voice of
the Count's niece, Eugenie, singing Susanna's aria from the garden
scene (Act IV, scene 1) of Mozart's *Figaro* while her fiancée, the
Baron, accompanies her at the piano gives us another example of
the typical aristocratic evening of song in which our writers participated.

Tieck's *Musical Sorrows and Joys* is without a doubt the most
learned and longest dissertation on the art of singing to be found in
German Romantic literature, containing as it does several lengthy
discussions of vocal techniques and Italian and German methods of
singing, even the subject of the anatomy of the singer is brought
up. Hoffmann's satirical description of Italian singing in *Die Serapionsbrüder* (*The Serapion Brothers,* 1819), although much shorter
than Tieck's discussion of singing, deserves mention here. We may
also recall that Theodor Körner devoted a number of his poems to
singing; poems such as "Das Reich des Gesanges" ("The Kingdom
of Song," p. 273) are amongst the most moving and beautiful
expressions of the German Romantic love of the human voice.

One of the most astute connoisseurs of singing was Ludwig
Börne who well knew how to single out the good points and the
weaknesses of singers. Kleist demonstrates this same skill in his

review of the opera, *Cendrillon (Cinderella)*, included in this volume; his advice to the aging singer Frederike Bethmann is quite impressive.

The German Romantic idealization of the human voice was also kindled by the study of antiquity which was an essential part of the secondary and university curricula in Germany in the nineteenth century. The magical power of song, the ability of the singer to heal wounds, inspire love, influence the course of nature, affect the outcome of wars, indeed, to rule the world is a theme which runs throughout Greek mythology and German Romantic literature. "How often has it been during war that an inspired song has decided the outcome of battle," wrote Ludwig Börne.[5] The list of solo singers in German Romantic literature who accomplished miraculous deeds well matches that of Greek mythology: Arion, Amphion, Chiron, Orpheus and especially the divine Apollo come back to life in the works of Tieck and his circle. In his poem, "Die Weisung Apoll's" ("The Advice of Apollo"), for example, Körner glorified the singing of Apollo.

In Arnim's tale the singer, Halbgott, who not accidentally wears a coat of arms depicting the head of Apollo, is called a "second Orpheus" by his brother, a title which he quite deserves as it is his singing and only his singing which melts the heart of the Princess (a heart which the Chamberlain compares to the impenetrable ice of the North Pole). Margot's voice in Brentano's fragment, *Die Rose (The Rose,* 1800), also accomplishes miracles. Notice, for example, the passage in which his singing brings peace to King Dringinwalde, who is sorely troubled in mind and spirit:

> As Margot had finished his song they both were silent and then the King spoke: "Oh dear Margot . . . it seems to me as if your song made everything vanish. When I heard you sing it was as if I were bathing myself in the cool sea of the night and now everything is calm again."[6]

Novalis actually incorporated into *Heinrich von Ofterdingen* the myth of the Greek poet-singer, Arion, who, captured at sea, begs

39

to sing one last song before his death thereby charming a dolphin who carries him safely back to shore.

The German Romantics were especially attracted to the myth of the magic songs of the celebrated Sirens of ancient Sicily. German legend usually depicts one Siren, Lorelei, who, singing on a rock in the Rhine, supposedly lured sailors to their death. The story of this water nymph occurs frequently in German Romantic literature (Heine's "Die Lorelei" and Brentano's "Lorelay," for example). The myth of the Sirens also figures prominently in Eichendorff's *Magic in Autumn* and Wagner's *Tannhäuser*. In Eichendorff's tale Raimund cannot escape the magic power of the voice of the beautiful young girl or the singing of her companions; he is lured by the magic of their voices into an enchanted garden where he dissipates his youth in the pursuit of pleasure until in the end he loses all reason.

The singer in the antique world was a person who possessed both the skills of a poet and a musician. Indeed, the name, singer, was commonly used among the ancients for a poet-musician; it is in this context, incidentally, that Börne and Schumann use the term, singer, in their writings. In the Hebrew, Greek and Roman civilizations poetry was not as a rule written except to be sung and very little music was composed which was not used to accompany poetry. The close interaction between song and poetry, however, is nowhere so apparent as in German Romanticism. How much the song meant to Tieck and his contemporaries, how much the poem meant to the German Romantic composers is expressed over and over again in the literary works of this period. "Poets and musicians must be able to reverse their hearts like gloves in an instant," wrote Mörike.[7]

To bring poetry and song together into one art form was one of the goals of German Romanticism and it is to this end that Schumann wrote his youthful essay, "Über die innige Verwandtschaft über Poesie und Tonkunst" ("On the Inner Relationship of Poetry and Music"), included in this collection. It is of particular interest to note the last paragraph of this essay for it vividly brings to mind the Greek concept of the singer. Along with Schumann's article, Hoffmann's essay, "Der Dichter und der Komponist" ("The Poet and the Composer," 1819), also envisioned the ideal composer as one in whom the talents of music and poetry are united.

The veneration of the poet-singer was in many respects also related to German Romantic nationalism. Investigations into Germany's past led scholars back to the Middle Ages and the rediscovery of the German *Minnesänger* who, like the gods and demigods of ancient Greece, united in one being the arts of singing and poetry. Novalis's *Heinrich von Ofterdingen* (1799) appears to have greatly contributed to the glorification of the medieval minnesinger. Novalis described his thirteenth century bard as being endowed with divine favor and inspired by the spirits of heaven who through his voice brought heavenly wisdom to earth.

This striving for a unification of song and poetry which had existed in Greek and medieval cultures led to the German Romantic concept that poetry could not speak for itself; the voice which Tieck's Count Alten informs us "is supposed to be the expression of human feelings,"[8] became the only vehicle which could express the emotions of the Romantic poets, the voice became in the Romantic era as Mörike so well stated, "the poet's second soul."[9]

The song, however, was more than the voice of the poet in German Romanticism, it was the voice of a nation. One of the strongest shaping forces of the German Romantic spirit was the quest for a national identity, an identity that was found to a great extent in the folksong, which was for Herder, "the archives of the people, the treasure of his knowledge, of his religion and theology . . . the source of his ancestry and the history of mankind."[10] Herder occupied an important position in the German Romantic awakening of a national consciousness; his role in the revival of the folksong is as significant as his influence on the development of the Caecilian Movement. Although Herder was a musician in his own right (Reichardt's father was his music teacher), his interest in the folksong was probably more the result of his speculations on the ethical, linguistic and literary evolution of mankind. The philosopher strongly believed in the uniqueness and importance of ethnic groups; the discovery and preservation of the customs, language and characteristics of each race was of great importance to him.

Herder believed that the origins of each group of people were to be found in their folksongs, ballads, proverbs, sayings and sagas, things which took hundreds of years to evolve, which were not the work of any one individual and which had nothing to do with intellect, but which evolved effortlessly and naturally. As he had seen various cultures almost annihilated by more powerful civilizations, he feared that the German race would suffer the same fate, that it would be destroyed by French influence. "That this does not happen to Germany is our main concern," Arnim stated in his essay, "On Folksongs," an essay which although dedicated to Reichardt we recognize as basically a repetition of those views of Herder I have just listed.[11]

The first decades of the nineteenth century witnessed the publication of many collections of German sagas, legends, poems and folksongs such as *Des Knaben Wunderhorn,* Uhland's *Volkslieder* and Karl Simrock's *Die deutschen Volkslieder (German Folksongs).* The term, *Volkslied,* incidentally appears to have both literary and musical connotations: the term can refer to folk poetry as exemplified by Simrock's *German Folksongs* or it can mean a type of song. The German Romantics made a sharp distinction between the genuine folksong and the *Volkslied.* Genuine folksongs as defined by Arnim in his essay are the songs of the folk: miners, soldiers, craftsmen, peasants, they are not sung by skilled singers nor are they written by any composer or poet. In contrast the *Volkslied* refers to popular songs which resemble folksongs but whose words and music are by known persons. Popular songs of this type have a long history in Germany; it would not be entirely incorrect to say that the *Volkslied* already existed in Georg Forster's *Frische Deutsche Leidlein (New Beloved German Songs),* as we read in Arnim's footnote many of the songs in this collection were composed by Forster himself.

The first composer, perhaps, to bring the *Volkslied* to the attention of the learned classes, to elevate this form to a higher artistic level than previously seen was Johann Peter Schulz (1747-1800) whose beloved *Volkslieder* were given special attention in the writings of Tieck and Arnim. Schulz it must be granted was especially conscientious as far as designating that his songs were not genuine folksongs for he called his collection of forty-eight *Volkslieder, Lieder im Volkston (Songs Composed in the Style of the Folksong,* 1782).

Following closely after Schulz is the composer, Reichardt, who although once reported to have said, "It is very difficult to create a song in the true style of the folksong,"[12] was, nevertheless, unusually adept at this task. His success can be seen by the fact that when Johann Nicolas Böhl (1770-1836) published in 1810 twenty-four of the *Wunderhorn* poems with melodies, eight of them were by Reichardt. The composer stands out as one of the most important figures in the collecting and publishing of folk poetry and folk melodies. According to Salmen it was Reichardt who was not only the main stimulus behind *Des Knaben Wunderhorn,* but a contributor as well.[13]

Other composers of the *Volkslied* include such figures as Friedrich Silcher (1789-1860) and Friedrich Kücken (1810-1882). Most of the well-known composers of the Romantic era were also quite skilled at imitating the idiom of the folksong. Perhaps "imitating" is the wrong word to use here; Reichardt and Schulz may have imitated the style of the folksong, but with Schubert, Weber, Brahms and Mahler, for example, the spirit of the folksong was a natural, spontaneous, unconscious part of their musical language and because it flowed so effortlessly from their hearts their songs were the more enduring.

Reichardt, as Tieck mentions in *Musical Sorrows and Joys,* had little respect for Mozart; Mozart's songs were to him "Merely very pleasing operatic cavatinas written in the Italian manner and not in the least German."[14] Tieck does not say that Beethoven's songs are not German, but he does remark that their complex style is not pleasing to him. What Reichardt, Tieck, Arnim and Weber heard in the folksong and particularly in its relative, the *Volkslied,* is important to note, for it is these characteristics that dominate the evolution of the German song in the nineteenth century. Tieck in this regard strikes the key word here, i.e., simplicity: simplicity of accompaniment and rhythm, declamation as natural as German speech, repetition of phrases, vocal lines which arise from the natural impulses of the heart and are devoid of all ornamentation, all embellishments and intellectual contrivances, in a word, divest of all foreign influence.

Weber once wrote, "The creation of a new form of song can only be achieved through the way the composer sets the poetry. With my songs I have always given the greatest concern to reproducing the correct declamation and true meaning of my poet."[15] As the decades passed in the nineteenth century, the *Volkslied* gave way to the development of the German *Lied*, "that more profound style of song," wrote Schumann, "of which earlier composers had no knowledge for it arose out of the new spirit of the poetry reflected in the music."[16]

The German Lied was the most important embodiment of the German Romantic striving to create an art form which was the ultimate fusion of poetry and song as well as the most sublime representation of the human heart. But no matter how intricate its accompaniment became or how rich and striking its harmony, the essential qualities of the folksong as the early German Romantic writers conceived them, as they heard them in the songs of Schulz and in the melodies of the people, still found their way into the Lied as well as into other forms of music at this time. We know how much the folksong meant to Schubert, Weber, Schumann, Brahms, Mahler and Mendelssohn. We even sense its spirit in nineteenth century opera, in the "Spinning Chorus" and the "Spring Song" of Wagner's operas, *Der fliegende Höllander (The Flying Dutchman)* and *Die Walküre,* in Schumann's opera, *Genoveva,* in which the genuine folksong, "Wenn ich ein Vöglein wär" ("If I Were a Little Bird"), occupies such an important position, in the *Schweitzerfamilie (Swiss Family)* of Weigl and especially in Weber's *Der Freischütz* which became such a source of national pride.

The German Romantic interest in folksongs, however, was not

restricted to German sources alone. Although many Romantics such as Friedrich Schlegel were to turn from universalism to nationalism, nevertheless the former still remained an essential part of the German Romantic idiom. We see this universalism in the writings of Börne and in Arnim's essay and in the following remark of Schumann, "Listen carefully to all folksongs, they are a storehouse of the most beautiful melodies and reveal to you a glimpse into the characteristics of various nations."[17] Universalism is also noticeable in the later song collections of Beethoven which include Irish and Welsh melodies, in the music of Brahms and Mendelssohn and particularly in Reichardt's fondness for Spanish folksongs.

Next to the solo song the opera was the favorite musical form of the early German Romantic writers. That opera became the focal point of their attention is in part related to their love of the human voice; it has to be admitted that the highlight of many operatic performances for Ludwig Tieck and his circle was the appearance of a well-known singer, especially a female singer. What rapture the voices of Caroline Seidler, Josephine Schulz, Corona Schröter, Angelica Catalani, Frederike Bethmann and especially the incomparable Anna Milder- Hauptmann and Henriette Sontag caused in their hearts. The beautiful voices of these singers were immortalized for all time in the literary efforts of the German Romantics. No one can ever forget the name of Henriette Sontag after reading Börne's essay about her.

The German Romantics' intense interest in opera is also intimately tied to Germany's dream of a national theater; both the drama and its offspring, the opera, play very large roles in the search for a national identity. There could be no German identity without German drama, drama being the highest form of poetry. "If one feature characterized all dramas, if the poets were all united in their goal," wrote Schiller, "if they selected from national subjects, there would be a national stage and we should become a nation."[18]

To the German Romantics there was little difference between

drama and opera, the fusion which they strove to achieve between poetry and song was also applied to these related forms. For the German Romantics opera and drama both constituted theater, an attitude we recognize as basic to Wagner's art. If we want to find Eichendorff's views on opera, we must look to his writings on drama. What constitutes good or bad drama is the main yardstick by which Tieck and his fellow authors judge opera; this art form was subject to the same type of criticism that the German nationalists imposed upon the drama.

In the latter half of the eighteenth and first years of the nineteenth centuries the most important influence on the drama and opera in Germany was French. The most important figure in the movement to imitate French drama in Germany, perhaps, was Johann Christoph Gottsched (1700-1766) whom Eichendorff mentions in his writings (see p.247). In the field of opera, Gluck (1714-1787), although a German and considered as one of the predecessors of German opera, wrote in a style that was more French than anything else.

The revolt against French influence on the drama began with the Swiss writer, Johann Jakob Bodmer (1698-1783) and the uncle of the Schlegel brothers, Elias Schlegel (1717-1749), whose ideal was the English drama and in particular, Shakespeare. The most important supporter of Shakespeare was the great dramatist, Lessing, and with the appearance of Schiller and Goethe the struggle to end French dominance in German drama was nearly over.

In the field of opera the growing reaction against French influence began to appear in the literary works of Brentano, Tieck, Börne and Eichendorff; Weber's *Der Freischütz* (1821), Hoffman's *Undine* (1813), Beethoven's *Fidelio* (1805) and Weigl's *Schweitzerfamilie* (1809) seem to herald the disappearance of French music in the operatic area, but not until Schumann and Wagner were German composers free of alien symbols. Many composers influenced by the new interest in Shakespeare did turn more and more to the English dramatist for subject matter. But by and large the whole subject of the demise of French influence on German opera in the

46

Romantic era is a complex one. The favorite opera composers of Theodor Körner, an ardent anti-French nationalist, were still French or those who followed French models.

Except for Jean Paul, the early German Romantic writers criticized most strongly the works of Spontini, Paer and Rossini. Jean Paul belonged to a group of French sympathizers along with Hegel and other German intellectuals. Concerning Spontini, for example, Jean Paul writes, "*La Vestale* is a work which usually melts and weakens us by its exquisite beauty . . . . Upon hearing those tones I could depart from life."[19] Hoffman also praised the Italian born composer in his welcome message ("Gruss an Spontini," 1820) to the new music director in Berlin; Hoffman also translated the composer's *Olympia* into German the following year. But Hoffman had erred as far as Spontini was concerned and he knew it as his later writings attest.

Spontini, although an Italian, rightfully belongs in the same way as Gluck to the history of French opera; Spontini's works set the stage for the development of that particular type of French opera known as Grand Opera, a type of entertainment characterized by pageantry, ceremonials, processions, spectacles at all cost, ballets, librettos drawn from heroic or historical subjects and melodies which are for the most part devoid of Italian embellishments, traits we see in the young Wagner's *Rienzi* (1840) and particularly in the works of Meyerbeer. Spontini was Napoleon's favorite composer and there is no doubt that the Emperor's love of lavish display influenced the Spontini "formula."

Spontini's *La Vestale* (*The Vestal*, 1807) and *Ferdinand Cortez* (1809) were the rage in Germany in the early years of the nineteenth century, *Olympia* (1819) coming in a close third. What spectacles these operas contained: *Cortez,* for example, includes an enormous ballet following upon the heels of an even more enormous procession of Mexicans bringing gifts to Cortez (Act II); *La Vestale* had a thunderstorm to beat all thunderstorms with bolts of lightning shooting down upon the stage; but Spontini reached the epitome of the "grand style" in *Olympia* when a huge elephant paraded across the stage in what might well constitute the largest procession in the annals of opera as well as the greatest uproar (the score calls for an extraordinary number of kettledrums and trumpets). To quote Heinrich Heine: "All Berlin sat up in awe. The enthusiast cried, 'Hosanna! Spontini is a musical elephant himself! He is an angel of trumpets!' "[20] When asked what he thought of Spontini, Beethoven remarked, "There is much good in him; he understands theatrical effects and the musical noises of warfare thoroughly."[21]

Börne reviewed *La Vestale* in *Die Wage* (1818). In that biting satirical tone of which he was a master he criticized the confusion, the excessive glitter and the ballet scenes which in his opinion had no place on the stage. But what really got his dander up was the inappropriateness of the music to the drama, a trait which Börne consistently hammered away at in his operatic reviews; it was totally inconceivable to him that Romans should sing Christian church music. This is, incidentally, also one of Brentano's major points of attack; why, he asks in his review of Paer's *Achille* (1801), should Patroklus sing a Polonaise? The popularity of Polish music notwithstanding, Brentano is quite correct in saying that the Polonaise has no place in an opera dealing with a Greek subject. What more can we say about Spontini than to quote the remark of the novice (*Musical Sorrows and Joys*) regarding the composer's operas, "It is difficult to decide . . . just how much the ear can take."[22]

Eichendorff's particular grievance as far as French opera was concerned was the emphasis on the ballet. It is quite possible that the poet had Meyerbeer's *Les Huguenots* (1836) in mind when he wrote that passage condemning the use of ballet in opera. (see p. 246). The dance has been a part of French opera since its earliest inception (Gluck's operas made good use of them). But the ballet as we know it, toe shoes and all, was the product of the Romantic age and one of the highlights of the Grand Opera Style. The ballet, incidentally, usually occurred after the middle of the opera. Wagner in his article, "Bericht über die Aufführung des *Tannhäuser* in Paris" ("An Account of the Performance of *Tannhäuser* in Paris," March,

1861), provides us with the reason for this situation:

> The director of the Grand Opera showed me that a ballet was necessary for a successful performance of *Tannhäuser* . . . . I thought the first act, at the court of Venus, would provide the best occasion for a choreographic scene. . . . The director informed me that it was not merely a question of a ballet, but of a ballet which must be performed in the middle of the evening's entertainment, for it was only at this time that the subscribers . . . appeared in their boxes, as they were in the habit of dining very late.[23]

Ferdinand Paer (1771-1839) was another Italian-born composer who worked in Paris during the Napoleonic era and was a favorite of both the Emperor and German audiences. His *Camilla* (Vienna, 1799), which was an adaptation of an earlier French opera by Dalayrac, enjoyed considerable popularity in Germany. Dent described the plot of *Camilla* as "absurd a story as one would wish."[24] Börne in his review of the opera mentions its "impeccable reputation," but criticizes the unsuitable costume of the heroine. *Camilla,* although it abounds in Italian lyricism, is an excellent example of the popular French hair-raising-at-the-eleventh-hour rescue opera. So for that matter is Beethoven's *Fidelio* (the story of which Paer had set to music one year earlier).

Paer's *Achille (Achilles)* was another German favorite. Brentano's review of this opera (1815) is an excellent piece of musical criticism and deserves mention here. The poet gets to the heart of the matter when he raises the age-old (but never solved) question, what are the roles of music and drama in an opera? "Is an opera a text set to music," he asks, "music set to a text, a text put into music," or a text merely written to provide a composer with a vehicle to display his wares?[25] The answer to this question Brentano feels lies in the type of text the composer selects. If the opera is based upon an excellent drama, an art work of great beauty, then the music must serve it; this type of opera, he maintains, is a true opera, but one which is rare. If the text is a poor one, Brentano continues, then the music must elevate it, must do more than serve it, must make it acceptable theater. Mozart's *Magic Flute,* incidentally, the German

49

Romantics felt accomplished just this task. A third type of opera, Brentano states, is that in which the text is but an empty shell, a thread upon which a composer hangs his music; the text is neither good nor bad, in fact it is almost nonexistent as far as the composer is concerned. Into this category Brentano places Paer's *Achille* in which "the total abuse of the theater has reached its epitome"[26] and Tieck, the works of Rossini.

We come now to the third member of the triumvirate, Rossini, and with the mention of that "divine maestro" (as Tieck's device, the old Italian, speaks of him) the whole problem of Italian opera in Germany emerges. Tieck and his fellow authors considered Italian opera along with French a fierce competitor of German culture. Börne and Tieck, who have the most to say about Rossini in this volume, are agreed on the following points: he has absolutely no concern for the drama or character portrayal, he writes in an all too hasty manner and as such his music is crammed with stereotyped musical phrases, he has no depth, no substance, and what he writes for the voice is more suitable for instruments. In short, neither have one good thing to say about Rossini.

All hopes to end alien influences in German opera were centered upon Weber's *Der Freischütz* which admittedly put Spontini out of business, but did not end the popularity of French or Italian opera in Germany; Rossini merely put on Spontini's shoes. *Der Freischütz* did contain many qualities which are German, a large symphonically conceived overture, leading motives woven into the score in a manner which foreshadows Wagner, instrumental music of considerable importance, several melodies of the *Volkslied* type and most importantly a German plot replete with German scenery and costumes. But Börne and Tieck, who was Weber's friend, knew that despite these characteristics, *Der Freischütz* did not meet their requirements for a German opera. The "Wolf's Glen" scene (Act II, sc. 2), described by Börne and Tieck as one of the noisiest scenes ever to be heard upon the stage, is sheer French spectacle and nothing more—here we have not an elephant, but a horde of ghosts, horses and what have you parading across the stage. Many of the vocal selections also show a kinship with Italian opera.

Good drama was one of the prime requisites of the German Romantic vision of a German opera and this is precisely what *Der Freischütz* lacks. Neither does Himmel's popular *Fanchon das Leiermädchen* (*Fanny, the Hurdy-Gurdy Player*, 1804) written in German by a German or Weigl's *Der Burgsturz* (*The Landslide*, 1812) present good drama. What we are really dealing with here are works which in one way or another pay homage to the German *Singspiel*, the form of which is derived from the eighteenth century French *opéra comique*. Even *Der Freischütz* used one of the most important characteristics of this type of French opera, spoken dialogue, a device Börne strongly criticized in his review of *La Vestale* because it destroyed dramatic unity. What the German Romantic writers insisted upon was good drama not light comic entertainment; in the end they had the upper hand, good theater was to become one of the chief hallmarks of German opera down to the present day:

> One must write such good music that good theater results in spite of it. When I decided to write an opera I had no other plan . . . than to render unto the theater what was the theater's due, that is, to build the music in such a way that it would never deviate from its function of serving the drama . . . it is only through music's deep concern with the drama that operatic music really becomes pure music.[27] [ALBAN BERG]

This is the reason for the great amount of attention the German Romantics gave to the operas of Gluck and Mozart, whose works were considered by Tieck and his circle as truly German although Gluck's musical idiom, as mentioned earlier, is basically French, and Mozart's is derived from Italian opera. Again it is a question of the drama and from a historical point of view Gluck had done much to elevate the position of the drama from its previous subordinate role in eighteenth century opera. Brentano in his review of *Achille* had included Gluck's works in the first category of opera, the true rarer type wherein the poem is all powerful. Mozart's popularity in the German Romantic era rested almost entirely on one opera, *Don*

Giovanni, in which the music and the drama combine to create superior theater.

I have never been able to accept the view that at certain moments in the history of mankind suddenly without warning there appears on the scene a creative artist of such extraordinary vision, of such remarkable talent, that the entire course of western culture is changed overnight. This is the way we tend to view the achievements of Wagner. But Wagner did not erupt like a volcano, his concept of the music drama is but the end result of a philosophy of opera that was in the making long before him. I see no difference between Wagner's supposedly unusual attention to the requirements of good theater and that of the German Romantic writers. I see no difference between Wagner's concern, for example, over the size of the dragon in *Siegfried* and Börne's criticism of the poor stagecraft in *The Magic Flute.* And is Tieck's, Börne's and Brentano's abhorrence of the singer who has no acting ability any different from Wagner's demand that the singers act?

In *Musical Sorrows and Joys* Tieck gave considerable attention to the problem of the popular Italian style of singing, a style which if German opera was to become a reality must be abandoned by German composers and replaced by a manner of singing more suitable to the German language; the translations of French and Italian librettos into German must also come to an end, translations which Kleist points out in the first paragraph of his review of *Cendrillon* are never satisfying either from a musical or linguistic point of view. Despite their love of Mozart's *Don Giovanni,* Italian methods of vocal execution and the Italian concept of melody were contrary to every theory the German Romantics held about singing and song. In Italian opera poetry was assigned a most insignificant role, dominated as it was by the ever present exhibition of the singer, whose shapeless melodic lines consisted primarily of ornaments.

The German Romantics envisioned a different type of operatic melody, one which first must be in keeping with their love of the folksong. As early as 1796 Herder, while in Paris, had written about his wish to see the development of a "new German opera

with music of the people."[28] The popularity of Martin's *Lilla,
Fanchon* and especially Weigl's *Swiss Family* is directly related to
the German Romantic taste for simple folklike melodies. But
Tieck and his circle demanded more than just a similarity to folksong, melody to them must secondly express the innermost heartfelt emotions of the soul. This is the whole thrust of the Count's
dissertation on singing in Tieck's novella. Third, the voice must
serve the drama. In Italian opera as mentioned before the singer
was paramount and the music was designed as a showcase for vocal
virtuosity. In Germany, however, and this is carried to an extreme
in Wagner's operas, the drama and the music are of the highest
importance and the singer is frequently sorely taxed by these new
demands. Weber recognized as early as 1817 that what the German
Romantics envisioned constituted a major difference between Italian and German opera. In the following passage he pokes fun at the
high expectations the Germans had of their singers:

> What monstrous demands one makes upon a good German singer.
> She must possess the Italian supple, delicate style of singing, sec-
> ondly, the most sublime style of French declamation coupled with
> an effortless, passionate performance and, lastly, the German man-
> ner of singing which is simple, natural, heartfelt and demands the
> greatest accuracy. How easy it is for a female singer in Italy.
> Throughout her life she moves within one sphere. The composer
> must accommodate his music to her voice, her talent, disguise her
> weaknesses, elevate her beauty and natural gifts.[29]

Whether or not Weber accepted this style, it was to dominate
future German opera, in the works of Wagner, Richard Strauss and
Schoenberg's school the ornate Italian style of singing is replaced
by one of even greater difficulty. What Tieck and his school were
working towards was the development of what might be called
lyric recitative, a type of melodic line which would grow out of and
be shaped by German speech, which would emphasize clear declamation as French opera did and yet at the same time pay homage to
the folksong and express the inner mood of the poetry. This style so
bewilders the old Italian that he calls it the "soul method."

The voice of Julie *(Musical Sorrows and Joys)* represents the German method of singing at its best. Tieck's heroine had been taught by her father, Hortensio, who in explaining her training to the novice makes these important remarks:

> A tone if it is correctly produced must rise like the sun, clear and majestic, the listener must feel the infinitude of music, the tone must be sustained to the end . . . what I want to hear in a musical sound is the rapture.[30]

These words as well as those of Count Alten bring to mind once again that concluding scene of Wagner's *Tristan* to which I referred in the first part of the Introduction (p. 4). Here I have in mind a very particular passage where Isolde sings, "Welten entronnen, du mir gewonnen, Tristan. . . . Du mir einzig bewusst, höchste Liebeslust!" ("There is no world now, I have won you, Tristan. . . . You alone I require, you, my heart's desire!"). With these words the voice of Wagner's heroine soars higher and higher until at last it reaches "that region above the earth" which Count Alten describes (Isolde holds a high 'A' for three measures at the conclusion of this passage); the "infinitude of music" being accomplished by this device and Wagner's endless melody. It is remarkable how closely Isolde's singing resembles the voice of Julie.

The Romantic composers were superb arrangers: whether this is good or bad we cannot debate here, let it suffice to say that no other age witnessed such a veritable obsession for meddling with original scores. Opera because of its very nature was a prime target for the enthusiastic reviser as any change in the original score could be easily justified purely on theatrical grounds. I suppose an eager arranger such as Franz Liszt would call Tieck and his fellow authors "purists" in this regard, but "purists" or not this group of writers performed an invaluable service to the history of music; they fought a courageous battle to preserve the original intentions of each and every one of their favorite composers. Any license with their music, no matter how small, was unacceptable to them. "*Fidelio* is dreadfully hard," wrote Brentano, "it is not at all easy to perform."[31] Yet Brentano never once suggests in his review of Beethoven's opera that it be made easier by deleting or changing certain passages. The whole *raison d'etre* for Hoffman's *Ritter Gluck* was to point out the abominable performance practices connected with Gluck's works.

No composer probably was subject to more abuse than Mozart; it was common in this period to arrange, adapt, revise and delete passages from his operas, even to insert additional numbers written by someone other than Mozart. In this connection I cannot help but quote a remark of Börne, "To desecrate the holy ashes of Mozart in such a way!"[32] Tieck in *Musical Sorrows and Joys* strongly condemned meddling with the original scores of Mozart and Gluck.

The influence of German Romantic literature on the development of opera, singing and song in the nineteenth century in Germany is a topic of considerable importance and one which deserves more attention than I have given it in this Introduction. In 1822 when Tieck wrote his novella and Börne a great many of his reviews, German opera was only in the theoretical stage and the German Lied, that most beautiful flower of German Romanticism, had also not yet reached its full bloom. It was only in the later decades of the nineteenth century that the musical theories of the German Romantic writers really began to bear fruit, in the music of Schumann, Wagner, Wolf and Mahler, for example, whose souls were nourished by the musical-literary works of Tieck and his fellow authors. In the music of Schoenberg I can still sense the influence of the German Romantic theories regarding opera, singing and song, in Schoenberg's Lieder which preserve the spirit of the folksong, in the way he wrestled with the problem of the drama in *Die glückliche Hand* (*The Lucky Hand*, 1913) which is a true poetic-musical form as the composer wrote both the text and the music, in the enormous burden Schoenberg placed upon the singer-actor and in his experiments with *Sprechgesang* (speech-song).

We may not entirely agree with the musical taste of Tieck and his circle: fans of Rossini, for example, might have the urge to "push the novice into a corner" like the Baron and his daughter. But one has to admit that the German Romantic writers knew exactly what they wanted to hear and they were absolutely clear on this point:

> But what is music? This question occupied my mind for several hours before I fell asleep last night. Music is a strange thing. I would say it is a miracle. We do not know what music is. But we do know what good music is and we know even more what bad music is; concerning the latter our ears hear a far greater amount. [HEINRICH HEINE][33]

NOTES

1. Börne, *op. cit.*, p. 1066.
2. Richard Wagner, *Sämtliche Schriften und Dichtungen*, 10 vols. (Breitkopf und Härtel, 1911), V, 109.
3. Tieck, *op. cit.*, II, 355.
4. Some of the more important essays on instrumental music by the German Romantics include: Tieck's "Symphonien," Wackenroder's "Das eigentumliche innere Wesen der Tonkunst und die Seelenlehre der heutigen Instrumentalmusik" ("The Strange Inner Substance or Music and the Spiritual Lesson of Contemporary Instrumental Music," in *Fantasies on Art),* and Hoffmann's "Beethoven's Instrumentalmusik" (1813).
5. Börne, *op. cit.*, p. 138.
6. Clemens Brentano, *Werke,* Friedhelm Kemp, ed., 4 vols. (Munich: Carl Hanser, 1962), II, 473.
7. Jessie Joskam Kneisel, "Mörike and Music" (Doctoral Dissertation, Columbia University, 1949), p. 34.
8. Tieck, *op. cit.*, p. 345.
9. Kneisel, *op. cit.*, p. 34.
10. Walter Salmen, *Das Erbe des Ostdeutschen Volksgesanges, Geschichte seiner Quellen und Sammlungen* (Würzburg: Holzner Verlag, 1956), p. 20.
11. These views of Herder were expressed, for example, in the philosopher's *Stimmen der Volker in Liedern* (1778) and are summarized by Salmen (i.e., n. 10).

12. Walter Salmen, "J. F. Reichardt und die europäische Volksmusik," in *Festgabe für Joseph Müller-Battau* zum 65 *Geburtstag* (Saarbrücken: Universitäts und Schulbuchverein, 1962), p. 98.
13. *Ibid.*, p. 92.
14. Salmen, *Johann Friedrich Reichardt*, p. 317.
15. Georg Kaiser, ed., *Sämtliche Schriften von Carl Maria von Weber* (Leipzig: Schuster und Loeffler, 1908), p. 176.
16. Kreisig, *op. cit.*, II, 147.
17. *Ibid.*, p. 168.
18. Benno von Weise, ed., *Schiller's Werke*, 42 vols. (Weimar: Hermann Bohlaus, 1963), XX, 99.
19. *Jean Paul's Briefwechsel mit seiner Frau und Christian Otto* (Berlin: Weidmannsche Buchhandlung, 1902), p. 255.
20. Heinrich Heine, *Werke*, 4 vols. (Frankfurt: Insel Verlag, 1968), II, 27.
21. Forbes, Elliot, ed., *Thayer's Life of Beethoven* (Princeton University Press, 1973), p. 956.
22. Tieck, *op. cit.*, p. 364.
23. Wagner, *op. cit.*, VII, 141.
24. Edward J. Dent, *The Rise of Romantic Opera* (Cambridge University Press, 1976, reprint), p. 111.
25. Brentano, *op. cit.*, p. 1127.
26. *Ibid.*
27. René Leibowitz, *Schoenberg and His School*, trans. from the French by Dika Newlin (New York: Da Capo Press, 1975, reprint), p. 169.
28. Blume, *op. cit.*, VI, 204.
29. Kaiser, *op. cit.*, p. 330.
30. Tieck, *op. cit.*, p. 379.
31. Brentano, *op. cit.*, p. 1127.
32. Börne, *op. cit.*, p. 1197.
33. Heine, *op. cit.*, III, 234.

4

German Romantic Musical Themes

AS A PIANIST I have never ceased to marvel at the unusual musical figure which Schumann used as the main motive in that part of his *Waldszenen* (*Forest Scenes,* op. 82, 1848) entitled, "Vogel als Prophet" ("The Prophet Bird"). I have never seen anything quite like it in the history of piano music before Schumann, it seems to elude the fingers, to fly out of the hands; beginning in the low register of the right hand it soars upward until it reaches its destination, then plummets downward, but never too low to begin its flight again, gaining more and more momentum as it expands, turns, twirls. What I am describing here is only a musical manuscript, but one with uncanny descriptive power, the musical notation ceases to exist and in its stead is a bird in flight, a strange bird which like that in Wagner's *Siegfried* or Tieck's *Der blonde Eckbert* (*Blond Eckbert,* 1797) speaks and sings and is understood by its listeners, filling their hearts with longing and enticing them into the mysterious world of primeval nature. This same bird reappears in splendid array in Eichendorff's *Magic in Autumn* and its song causes an inconquerable lust to grow in Raimund's heart.

It does not matter whether we are dealing with music or literature here, the experience is the same, the world of nature is translated into musical tones. I hear the fearful gusts of wind in the Overture to Wagner's *Die Walküre* no more distinctly than I hear the sinister tones of the whispering wind as it carries the magic sounds of the horns past Ubaldo's window like a mysterious breath, calling to Raimund, beckoning him to return to the ghostly world he has momentarily escaped, engulfing his soul in the indescribable sweetness of these tones until he can resist no longer.

Throughout German Romantic literature is a conspicuous group of musical *leitmotiv,* some of which already have been mentioned, such as music as the voice of the people, music as a divine powerful being; to these may be added certain other themes which play an important role in many of the selections included in this volume. One of the most important of these leitmotiv is the concept of "Naturmusik," i.e., the belief in nature as a mysterious force which expresses her inner world and her ceaseless activity through musical sounds. "There is no space in nature which is silent, everything resounds," wrote Börne.[1] "Music is nothing else but the rhythm of nature," Schelling once stated.[2]

German Romanticism rings with the voices of nature's realm, her poet-musicians listen to her secret song with all their hearts and souls and recreate it for us in a totally new and unique manner, describing her benevolent (harmonious) as well as her demoniac (dissonant) sides in terms of music. We sense a feeling of peace and oneness with the universe, of the unity of music with nature, as Edward (Körner's *Edward and Veronica*) does when nature's tranquil spirit is reflected in the whispering beech trees and the soft tones of a cricket. But we are overcome by a fear of sinister dark forces, of the night side of nature[3] as the sounds of the forest horns cause Raimund's falcon to fly away from his master, circling wildly in the air.

A second important leitmotiv is the German Romantic belief in the cosmic origin of music. "Music," wrote Wackenroder, "originated from the world beyond." This leitmotiv is directly related to and derived from the Greek doctrine of the music of the spheres.[4] The sounds which Tieck and his circle heard as the wind blew, as the waves pounded against the shore and which they translated into musical sounds such as those of instruments or a voice

59

singing they equated with the ethereal tones of the music of the spheres. This is beautifully expressed by Kleist in his letter quoted on page 12 and in the following passage from Hoffmann's *Die Automate* (*Automata,* 1814):

> An echo from the mysterious depths of primeval times has survived in the splendid legend of the music of the spheres which filled me with ardent feelings when I first read about it as a child in *The Dream of Scipio;*[5] enraptured by this tale I often tried to see if those wondrous tones would resound for me in the whispering of the wind.[6]

Several references to the music of the spheres *(Sphärenmusik)* occur in German Romantic literature. Novalis, for example, in "Klingsohr's Fairytale"[7] wrote: "Simultaneously a soft but deeply moving music was heard in the air, it seemed to issue forth from the stars that were wondrously interweaving themselves in the hall and from other strange movements."[8]

Tieck and his fellow authors were quite possibly introduced to the Greek theory of celestial sounds through the writings of Cicero, particularly, *De re republica* (*On the Republic,* 51-52 B.C.), the sixth section of which contains "The Dream of Scipio" mentioned by Hoffmann. This passage from "Scipio's Dream" appears especially significant not only because of its mention of the music of the spheres, but because of its relation to the imagery of Körner's *The Harp.*

> As I gazed rather intently at the earth my grandfather said: "How long will your thoughts continue to dwell upon the earth? Do you not behold the regions to which you have come? The whole universe is comprised of nine circles or rather nine spheres. . . ." I stood dumbfounded at these sights and when I recovered my senses I inquired: "What is this great and pleasing sound that fills my ears?" "That," replied my grandfather, "is a concord of tones . . . caused by the rapid motion of the spheres themselves . . . gifted men imitating this harmony on string instruments and in singing have gained for themselves a return to this region . . . the ears of mortals are filled with this sound, but they are unable to hear it."[9]

The main events of Körner's short story all take place at nine o'clock in the evening (the deaths of Josephine and Sellner, the magical performance of the harp), this hour being usually announced by the chiming of the nearby tower clock. Körner, in whose works an unusually large number of references to the Greek world are to be found, probably chose the number nine because of its relation to the music of the spheres and all that this theory implies.

The ancients believed not only that music originated through the movements of celestial bodies, but that the processes of life and death were also associated with the music of the spheres. The soul when it enters the world, for example, was thought to carry with it a memory of the music it knew in the region of the nine spheres.[10] This concept, incidentally, is stated by the Kapellmeister (*Musical Sorrows and Joys*) as he tries to explain why the novice returned to music despite his early unsatisfactory musical experiences. In addition the soul after death returns to this celestial region wherein it originally heard the music of the spheres.

In Körner's tale the chiming of the clock, like the sounding of the Euphon in Hoffmann's *Ritter Gluck,* is an announcement, a calling forth from the region of the nine spheres to the soul to return to its original home. Thus the clock chimes nine times when Josephine dies and Sellner also instinctively knows that when the ninth hour is announced he too will die. In Körner's story the chiming of the clock is accompanied by the appearance of the moon which in Greek literature is the demarcation line between earth and the spirit world. We may find this all rather difficult to accept, but to quote Hegel:

> In the Romantic, we have two worlds. The one is the spiritual realm, which is complete in itself—the soul, which finds its reconciliation within itself. . . . The other is the realm of the external . . . which, shut out from a firmly cohering unity with the spirit, now becomes a wholly empirical actuality, respecting whose form the soul is unconcerned.[11]

The theme of music emanating from a world beyond echoes not only throughout German Romantic literature, but German Romantic music as well. There is, for example, a particular phrase Schumann and his school are fond of using in their music, i.e., "wie aus der Ferne" or "aus der Ferne" ("as if out of the distance"). This expression occurs, for instance, at the beginning of one of the *Davidsbündlertänze* (*Dances of the League of David*, op. 6, 1837, no. 17) of Schumann and in the last movement of Mahler's Resurrection Symphony (thirteen measures from section 7). In Schumann's piano piece the melody in the right hand soars above all the other parts, its 'musical distance' suggesting a voice from beyond. Mahler significantly instructs his horns and trumpets to play "aus der Ferne" just before the entrance of the "faith motive" as if a voice were crying out to the soul to believe. One cannot help but notice the similarity of these passages to Eichendorff's musical imagery: in *Magic in Autumn* we are constantly aware of the sounds of the horns issuing forth from some mysterious region beyond the mountains. Similarly the music of the flute in Jean Paul's *Titan* (cycle 69) comes from a celestial source.

Wagner also experimented with creating the illusion of sound from another world in the Rhinemaidens' scene of *Die Götterdämmerung* (*The Twilight of the Gods,* Act II), by placing one harp offstage, the other on. The twentieth century device of placing instruments of the orchestra "off-stage," although not for the same reason as Wagner or Mahler owes a debt to German Romanticism.

The German Romantic writers also had a particular fondness for musical instruments which would reproduce or at least evoke in their minds the sounds of the music of the spheres, thus the vogue of the harp, the glass harmonica (Hoffmann's *Ritter Gluck*), the double mouth harmonica (Jean Paul's *Hesperus*), the flute (Jean Paul's *Titan, Die Flegeljahre,* Körner's *The Harp, Edward and Veronica*), and particularly the Aeolian harp.[12] Describing the voice of his heroine, Isidore *(Die Reise nach Schandau, The Journey to Schandau),* Körner wrote: "Her voice sounded to me like the tones of the Aeolian harp . . . endlessly sweet."[13] Note also this passage from

Lebensansichten des Katers Murr (*Memoirs of the Cat, Murr*, 1819) in which Hoffmann described the birthday celebration of Princess Maria:

> I persuaded them to restring the Aeolian harp[14] . . . and the storm, an excellent virtuoso, drew from it the most wondrous effects. . . . The chords of a giant organ resounded frightfully amidst the howling of the storm and the roaring of the gale and the bursts of thunder . . . the tones followed each other more and more rapidly . . . and one would have thought we were witnessing a ballet of the furies.[15] After half an hour the concert was over. The moon peeped out from behind the clouds. . . . The Aeolian harp, however, could still be heard . . . like the merging of distant, muffled bells.[16]

From a practical point of view the German Romantic composers could not utilize all these instruments in their music, but their new emphasis on woodwind color, particularly the flute, reflects their interest in recreating celestial sounds. The flute, for example, has a most unusual cadenza in the finale of Schumann's *Spring Symphony*. In Weber's opera, *Euryanthe* (Act III), the mysterious voice of a flute floats across the stage consoling the unhappy heroine and in the composer's *Peter Schmoll* (Act I) the same instrument echoes the misery expressed in Minette's sorrowful love song. The glass harmonica,[17] incidentally, was employed on one occasion by Reichardt and in Beethoven's incidental music to Duncker's drama, *Leonora Prohaska*.

The passage cited above from Weber's *Euryanthe* is an example of another German Romantic musical leitmotiv, music as a means of relieving the passions of the soul. Aristotle once wrote, "the proper time for using the flute is when the performer aims not at instruction, but at the relief of the passions."[18] When Sellner plays the flute following the death of his beloved it relieves the terrible grief which has engulfed his soul. In Börne's *Letter from Frankfurt* the performance of Mozart's *Requiem* "eases the grief associated with the loss of this great artist."[19]

Music as the mediator between the spirit world and man is

another leitmotiv illustrated by Körner's *The Harp*. In Greek literature the harp is the instrument of the spirit world. Wackenroder restated this theory when he described music "as a divine language which issues forth in the vibrations of beautiful harp strings."[20] In Körner's tale, the only way Sellner can communicate with Josephine's spirit is through music. The harp, which is her spirit, sounds only when Sellner plays his flute, and stops when the tones of his instrument cease.

The concept of only certain gifted persons being able to hear the music of the spheres which is expressed in "The Dream of Scipio" takes on various forms in German Romantic literature, the leitmotiv of "inner music" being, perhaps, the most important. Wackenroder's Berglinger, Hoffmann's Kreisler and Tieck's Kapellmeister, who often feels something of the divine permeating his soul, and many of the heroes and heroines of Jean Paul have the ability to hear mysterious music inside themselves in contrast to the common person who cannot. "Don't you hear anything?" Gluck asks his friend *(Ritter Gluck)* as the chiming he heard earlier has come back once again, to which the acquaintance (i.e., Hoffmann) replies, "No."[21] In Jean Paul's *Titan* the "hearing" Liana is contrasted with the uninspired Count:

> Liana suddenly said to the Count that she heard flutes. But before he had barely time to answer that all he heard was the sound of distant turtledoves, she pulled herself together as if preparing for some wondrous event to take place and gazed upward toward heaven, smiled and then blushing suddenly turned toward Albano and said: "I will be truthful with you; at this moment I hear music inside myself."[22]

In a footnote to this passage Jean Paul described Liana's strange ability to hear inner music (Richter uses the term, "Selbst-Ertönen") as some sort of an illness: "This sounding of music within one's self, which is similar to the sound of the Aeolian harp," he wrote, "is a common malady, like a headache and other sicknesses. . ."[23] In *The Harp* Josephine's unexplainable nervous disorder is characterized by headaches and is further aggravated by playing her harp. Jean Paul's Victor also appears to suffer from this strange malady. Is there any wonder that Robert Schumann to whom Jean Paul was like the Bible also had the same affliction:

> Schumann was speaking today of a curious illusion of which he has been conscious for several days. He hears inside himself exquisite musical composition, perfect in form. The sound is generally that of distant wind-harmonies, playing particularly beautiful melodies. His inward concert actually began while we were sitting at Junge's forcing him to put away the paper he was reading. . . . So it would be, he said in the other world. [FROM THE DIARY OF SCHUMANN'S FRIEND, RUPPERT BECKER][24]

This ability to hear music inside one's self, to experience a private concert of celestial tones, has contributed in great part to the popular conception of the Romantic artist as some sort of an inspired madman; thus the theme of music and madness is commonly referred to in several sources discussing German Romantic literature.[25] But this leitmotiv needs further amplification. To borrow a phrase from Tieck *(Musical Sorrows and Joys)* history has shown us that what one age considers insanity, another may not. To the German Romantics whose musical aesthetics are so intimately bound up with Greek thought, hearing celestial tones from above was not considered madness, but rather a manifestation of divine inspiration which sets the gifted artist apart from his fellow man. In Plato's *Phaedrus* this subject is discussed at great length, and the following quotation from this work gives one considerable insight into the German Romantic concept of what constituted divine madness:

> There is a madness which is a gift, and the source of the highest blessings granted to men . . . this madness is superior to a sane mind for it is . . . of divine origin. . . . The third kind is the madness of those who are possessed by the Muses, which taking hold of a delicate and virgin soul and there inspiring frenzy awakens lyrical and all other numbers . . . . But he who, having no touch of the Muses' madness in his soul, comes to the door and thinks that he will get into the temple with the help of art—he, I say and his

65

poetry are not admitted, the sane man disappears and is nowhere when he enters into rivalry with the madman.[26]

The restless, frenzied, possessed Count Alten, who has come under the spell of the Muses, and the old Italian depicted in Tieck's novella who, along with his wife, hears the music of King David and other musical ghosts from the past represent the two types of 'madness' described by Plato in *Phaedrus:* "And of madness, there are two kinds; one produced by human infirmity, the other a divine release of the soul from the yoke of custom and convention."[27]

What Plato is in effect referring to in his description of the second type of 'madness' is what the German Romantics would call the redeeming power of music. The ability of music to carry man away from the trivial cares of earthly existence, to ennoble his soul by revealing to him higher truths is a theme which is expressed in many German Romantic literary works. Notice, for example, this passage from Tieck's "Tones":

> When the present oppresses us like the walls of a prison, then music carries us to a new land, a paradise . . . and delivers us from the darkness here below . . . our heart rises from its terrestrial sphere . . . our thoughts move towards a finer nobler element.[28]

But for those whose souls catch a glimpse of this higher reality, who hear these celestial choirs, the payment is often quite high. Once one has tasted the forbidden fruit and fled from the prosaic duties of everyday living, one becomes like Tieck's Count Alten, a spirit in exile, tossed like a ship upon the waves, elevated at one moment to sublime heights by the tones of the Muses and the next set down to earth with a jolt when the song ceases. Count Alten, like Wackenroder's Berglinger and Hoffmann's Kreisler and the whole group of German Romantics, both fictitious and real, who have experienced the redeeming power of music, find that life on earth with its imposed responsibilities is often intolerable to bear. "It often appears to me," Schubert once wrote, "that I do not at all belong to this world."[29]

What then is the answer to this paradox, how can life on earth become tolerable if music can produce this type of madness which involves a separation from life? To reconcile the discordant principles which are inherent in this view of music, to restore harmony as it were to the dissonant soul, the German Romantics introduced the element of love which when combined with music and when nourished by music bridges the gulf between the enraptured artist and earthly life which music itself has caused. "Artists when in love create magnificent works with the inspiration of heaven and neither die miserably of consumption nor do they become insane," wrote Hoffmann in *Memoirs of the Cat, Murr.* [30] The anguish of the Count is ended when he finds Julie in whom Tieck has embodied the spirit of love and music. Music and love is a very much overworked theme by the time it comes to Wagner, but, nevertheless, it is impossible to think of *Tristan* as anything but a glorification of this leitmotiv. Körner incorporated the theme of love and music in several of his works, but no passage is as moving as that in *The Harp* in which the love of Sellner and Josephine is symbolized by the tones of the flute and the harp melding with each other as they merge in unison.

During the foregoing many comparisons have been made between German Romantic and Greek musical aesthetics. But on one point we may have to draw a line between the two eras, i.e., when it comes to the critical analysis of a work of art. The German Romantics believed that artistic genius which is divine and intuitive descends to a lower form of talent when reason is applied to it. Greek literature appears to refute this idea, the subjective and the intellectual, science and mysticism, although contrasting qualities are not kept apart; despite the Greek belief in the divinity of creative power the critical faculty was still considered an important and indispensable element in the artistic process. To the German Romantics, however, a creative work of art could not because of its divine nature be subjected to any form of intellectualizing or as Tieck stated in "Symphonien:"

> If we seek to intellectualize that which is divine, like art, then we shall only become entangled in a web of rambling rhetoric . . . one

67

comprehends art in a manner which is quite different from intellectual understanding.[31]

We see this philosophy expressed in Wagner's opera, *Die Meistersinger von Nürnberg (The Mastersingers of Nuremberg,* Act II, scene 2) in which the young poet, Walther, tells Hans Sachs that the song he heard in his dreams will be destroyed if it is subjected to rules. Schumann expressed the same concept in his essay, "On the Inner Relationship of Poetry and Music": "Those whose inspiration is derived from the highest beauty and not mere rules create works which are truly divine," he wrote, "it is inspiration which elevates the song of the singer to the clouds."[32]

This concept that music cannot be comprehended through intellectual processes dominates German art criticism which is for the most part neither scholarly nor analytical although Tieck and his circle certainly had the knowledge to write in a highly erudite fashion: music which they believed was an expression of divinely inspired emotion must in turn be described in terms of feeling. This aversion to intellectualizing contributed to that certain quality of German Romantic music which sets it apart from previous periods, i.e., heartfelt spontaneity, spontaneity which arises from the belief that one must capture the moment of divine inspiration before it is gone forever.

In Arnim's essay, *On Folksongs,* the poet discusses the effect of music on man's character, a theme which appears frequently in the writings of Aristotle and Plato. German Romantic literature often interrelates man's moods and music, a literary device often referred to as the symbolism of tones. Thus the low tones of music and the minor keys, for example, are symbolic of and produce sorrow, melancholy and other related states of mind, the major keys and the higher tones evoking happier moods. Tieck in *Musical Sorrows and Joys* tells us, for example, that the novice as a child had a particular fondness for the popular tune, "Here Slumber My Children," because he could play it on the low strings of his violin and thereby produce melancholy feelings in which he enjoyed indulging himself. The simple light songs of Schulz also caused pleasant warm feelings in the novice. In Körner's *The Harp* the low tones of the flute and the harp are associated with death. Weber in his projected novel, *Tonkünstlers Leben (The Life of a Musician)* had planned to place a certain note at the end of each chapter, each of which would be in keeping with the mood previously expressed. And the tones of the forest horn, what a multiplicity of feelings this instrument evokes in Eichendorff's *Magic in Autumn.*

A particularly interesting aspect of the concept of the symbolism of tones is the German Romantic belief in the interrelationship of the sounds of instruments and colors which seems to have originated with Tieck. As early as 1799 Tieck had written in *Fantasies on Art:* "Every single sound of a particular instrument is like the shade of a color, and as each color has a related primary color so every instrument has a single specific timbre all its own."[33] This statement is the very foundation of the German Romantic composer's concept of orchestration in which the instruments of the orchestra were considered like the colors of an artist's palette; the low tones of the clarinet which Weber exploited for the first time in *Der Freischütz* have all the sombre qualities associated with the dark hues. There are several passages in Tieck's writings in which color and sound are brought into one focus. The flute, for example, in *Franz Sternbald* being associated with the color blue; the songs of Schulz *(Musical Sorrows and Joys)* brought to his mind the colors of the blue sky and the green grass.

Concerning the fusion of musical sounds and colors I do not think, however, that anyone could equal the originality of Hoffman's description of Kreisler's coat in *Brief des Kapellmeisters Kreisler an den Baron Wallborn (Letter of the Kapellmeister, Kreisler, to Baron Wallborn):*

> When I find myself in that kind of unusual situation in which some supernatural power has cast a spell over me, I often resort to making funny faces, as I am well aware. I also happened to wear a frock coat which I bought once when an unsuccessful trio caused me to be in a bad mood, because its color was in C minor I had to have a collar of

the color of E major sewed on in order to appease the spectators. I hope your Majesty was not irritated by this.[34]

It is difficult to know precisely what Hoffman was symbolizing by these two keys, but I think that Weber who was a close acquaintance of the poet sensed the subtle meaning of Hoffman's musical imagery. In Weber's *Der Freischütz* the theme associated with the devil is in C minor, whereas that associated with the angelic Agathe is in E major. Thus Kreisler's coat in C minor conjures up the image of the sinister evil forces which are allayed by the bright collar in E major. Following Tieck and his school the correspondence between color and sound was more and more exploited, i.e., the color organ of Scriabin, for example.

In this part of the Introduction I have attempted to discuss many of the important musical themes which appear in German Romantic literature and which ultimately influenced the development of German Romantic music. This list is not meant to be all-inclusive, rather its primary purpose is to shed some light on the musical imagery which appears in the selections in this volume.

"Without music the world is like a dingy unfinished house."[35] This sentence, which was written by Tieck in 1799, might well be considered the motto of German Romanticism. I can imagine the Greek civilization without music, for I rather think the Greeks loved knowledge more; I can even imagine all civilization without music, dreary as it would be. But I wonder if German Romanticism could have existed without it. Music is German Romanticism, German Romanticism is music and I can find no way to separate the two. Not that the German Romantics had little to contribute to the history of culture, but what they said was uttered with the aid of music, inspired by music; music was their sustenance, their national life, their source of beauty and truth.

NOTES

1. Börne, *op. cit.,* p. 435.
2. Walter Wiora, "Die Musik im Weltbild der deutschen Romantik," in *Beiträge zur Geschichte der Musikanschauung im 19. Jahrhundert* (Regensburg: Gustav Bosse, 1965), p. 27.
3. Gotthilf Heinrich von Schubert in his popular book, *Die Nachtseite der Naturwissenschaft* (*The Night Side of the Science of Nature,* 1808) attempted to prove the existence of a "night side" of the universe, a side that is turned away from the sun where the objects of the world take on a sinister appearance.
4. This term was used by Pythagoras and other Greek mathematicians to refer to those ethereal sounds which were produced by the movements of celestial bodies.
5. Scipio Africanus, the younger (i.e., Publius Cornelius Scipio Aemilianus, 184-129 B.C.), Roman soldier, orator, consul.
6. E. T. A. Hoffmann, *Poetische Werke,* 12 vols. (Berlin: Walter de Gruyter, 1957), VI, 106.
7. This work dates from the early part of the year 1799; it appears to have been written prior to or concurrently with the *Hymns to the Night.* Later Novalis incorporated this story in the ninth chapter of *Heinrich von Ofterdingen.*
8. Novalis (Friedrich von Hardenberg), *Dichtungen* (Hamburg: Rowohlt Taschenbuch Verlag, 1963), p. 173.
9. William Harris Stahl, *Macrobius' Commentary on the Dream of Scipio* (New York: Columbia University Press, 1952), pp. 72-74.
10. *Ibid.,* p. 197.
11. Carl J. Friedrich, ed., *The Philosophy of Hegel* (New York: The Modern Library, 1954), p. 364.
12. The Aeolian harp was little more than a box with a hole in it with strings stretched across it, the sound being produced by the wind blowing across the strings. The name is Greek in origin being derived from Aeolus, the god of the winds in Greek mythology.
13. Körner, *op. cit.,* II, 326.
14. Hoffmann in this passage uses the term "Wetterharfe," but the Aeolian harp is clearly implied here.
15. Ballet of the Furies in Gluck's *Orfeo* (Act II).
16. Hoffmann, *op. cit.,* IX, 23.
17. Glass harmonica, a set of musical glass tubes (or glasses) played by moistened fingers.
18. *Aristotle on Poetry and Music* (New York: The Liberal Arts Press, 1956), p. 47.
19. Börne, *op. cit.,* p. 1117.
20. Tieck, ed., *Phantasien,* p. 88.
21. Hoffmann, *op. cit.,* I, 18.

22. Richter, Jean Paul, *Sämtliche Werke,* 30 vols. in 17 (Berlin: G. A. Reimer, 1860-1862), XXII, 231.
23. *Ibid.*
24. Stock, *op. cit.,* p. 285.
25. See, for example, George C. Schoolfield, *The Figure of the Musician in German Literature* (University of North Carolina Press, 1956) or Walter Wiora's article (p. 71, n. 2).
26. Irwin Edman, ed., *The Works of Plato,* trans. by Benjamin Jowett (New York: The Modern Library, 1956), pp. 284-285.
27. *Ibid.,* p. 310.
28. Tieck, *op. cit.,* pp. 87-88.
29. Karl Kobald, *Franz Schubert* (Leipzig: Amalthea Verlag, 1948), p. 208.
30. Hoffmann, *op. cit.,* IX, 151.
31. Tieck, *op. cit.,* pp. 91-92.
32. Kreisig, *op. cit.,* p. 174.
33. Tieck, *op. cit.,* p. 89.
34. Hoffmann, *op. cit.,* I, 349.
35. Tieck, *op. cit.*

5
Concerning the Present Translations

AS STATED in the Preface the works included in this volume have not been previously translated into English, although selected short excerpts from some of them appear in English in various sources dealing with German Romantic literature (see Bibliography under Coeuroy, Schoolfield and Wernaer, for example). The two exceptions to the above are Körner's *The Harp* and Kleist's *Holy Cecilia*. The translations of these two tales listed in B. Q. Morgan's standard index, however, date back to the early nineteenth century and are not readily accessible; the English renditions of these two stories contained herein are my own.

In the translations to follow I have attempted to retain the original literary style of each selection rather than to "modernize" them. The flowing lyrical quality of German Romantic sentence structure, for example, is a characteristic which I tried to preserve. I have therefore adhered to the original punctuation, maintaining the many colons, semicolons, commas and dashes rather than to subdivide the long sentences with their wealth of subsidiary clauses into smaller units. Only on rare occasions did I find it necessary to break up a lengthy statement into shorter sentences. In the case of the poetry included in this volume I found it necessary to use the more modern method of free verse in order not to lose the essential meaning; however, the number and division of the lines of the original poems have been retained.

I have also tried to preserve the original tense used in these selections although the English rendition of certain verb forms may seem unfamiliar and obsolete now. I have retained, for example, the use of the present tense in certain passages in which Kleist and Schumann adopt the so-called flash-back technique which is a conscious attempt to transport the reader back to some earlier episode in the story. As for the notes, many are my own, but in the case of those that are not, I have placed the abbreviation, "ED.," (i.e., editor) after the notation. In cases where I consulted more than one edition of a work, I have given proper credit to the appropriate source. As these selections are intended for those interested in German literature as well as German Romantic music, the notes provide both musicological and literary data.

Throughout these translations my one guiding principle was to make these selections as readable as possible without destroying the author's original intent and meaning. Most of the selections lent themselves to this kind of treatment, but I have to admit that Arnim's essay, *On Folksongs,* was especially difficult to render in a proper English translation because the poet's verbiage often obscures his meaning. In this essay I often had to resort to poetic license; I also felt it necessary to select only certain passages which I felt could be understood without a great deal of background information. There are several German editions of each of the selections included in this collection and I have tried to choose the most reliable. A list of these editions follows the Bibliography.

PART II

Translations

Ludwig Tieck
[1773-1853]

MUSICAL SORROWS AND JOYS [1822]

THE TWO FRIENDS alighted from a carriage before the entrance to the city in order to walk through the lanes and avoid being questioned at the gate. It was still early in the morning and an autumn mist covered the landscape. Along the way they noticed a little house, somewhat removed from the road, out of which came in these early hours the beautiful sound of a woman's voice. Astonished by the incomparable discant as well as by the unusual hour they walked closer to the house. They noticed several persons with lutes and notebooks approaching the dwelling and when the small door opened the older traveler, no longer able to contain his curiosity, remarked to a passer-by, "Most likely my friend, a musician and a female singer, live here."

"The devil and his grandmother live here!" resounded a croaking voice from out of the open window on the top floor and at the same time a lute case fell on the head of the questioner. At this moment the singing stopped and the older traveler saw a small old man standing in the window who made the angriest gestures and whose sparkling black eyes shot out furious glances from beneath a thousand wrinkles. The traveler did not know whether he should laugh or become angry, yet he was so touched by the strangeness of the old man that he lifted his hat in embarrassment and withdrew silently with a polite bow.

"What was that all about, Herr Kapellmeister,"[1] said the younger traveler, who was himself a singer, when they walked some distance from the small house.

"I don't know," replied the former, "perhaps it was merely some mad old man or maybe some ghostly figure appearing here in the vicinity of a lonely fir forest."

"You joke," said the young singer, "I do not understand how you could take the old man's insults so calmly."

"Leave it be," said the Kapellmeister as he walked down the small quiet street of the city, "there was something strange in the sound of the woman's voice which deeply affected me; it was as if I were in a dream and for this reason the old fool could not make me angry."

"Again the old ecstasy and patience," said the younger traveler, smiling, "for one thing we heard very little and secondly in that little bit we heard nothing special, there was neither method nor schooling in the melancholy voice of the singer."

As the two companions now went around the corner towards the inn, they heard a song being whistled from the top floor of a nearby house. A round, young face with a nightcap peeped out of the window and as soon as he noticed the two travelers, he exclaimed, "Wait a moment friends, I will be right down. Dear God! What a sight for sore eyes!" He pulled his head back so quickly that he hit it violently on the low window frame and the clothing on his head slowly floated down to the feet of the Kapellmeister.

"Wonderful," said the older traveler while he picked up the nightcap, "do these peculiar omens prophesy something good or bad?"

"It is our enthusiast, Kellermann," replied the young singer, "listen he is already rattling the front door with his key."

At this moment the admirer rushed out of the house in his robe and embraced both musicians in a theatrical, affected manner; he did not tire of pressing and hugging each one to his breast and then stretching out his arms strangely in the air until finally the young man said, "That is enough, you are overdoing it. It is lucky that no one is up yet otherwise your capers would incite all the street urchins."

"Well, now you are really here, you wonderful people," exclaimed the enthusiast, "It would not matter to me if the entire magistrate would be scandalized or share in my delight. For three months I have not been able to understand why this lane was truly built or even less why the houses upon it have so many windows to open and close until now finally their destiny is fulfilled, you came walking down this lane and I peeked out of the top window of that house with my lost nightcap in order to greet you in the name of future generations. Well, most esteemed sir, will your opera be performed after all?"

"Are your singers still in good health?" asked the lively Kapellmeister.

"So, so," replied Kellermann, "depending on their whims. Actually the way it is these singers live in their own world. The addition which is growing at their throats together with their arms and legs makes it difficult to stand them; the unnatural swelling, however, up above, which they call, head, is like a piston into whose receptacle the most incredible stupidities are absorbed. As far as I know they are all well, that is, if they want to be. However, if this or that aria does not please them, if one singer has too much, the other too little, if the aria is in the key of A minor rather than G flat major then, perhaps, within three days they will all fall down like flies."

"Put on your clothes," said the singer, "and join us in the inn over there so we can talk more. Also you ought to accompany us on our visits."

Without an answer, Kellermann ran into his house and the travelers went to the hotel where their carriage was waiting for them.

In the evening a large party had assembled in the house of the music lover, Baron Fernow. The rumor that the popular Kapellmeister and his first tenor had finally arrived brought everyone who was interested in the new opera into the residence of the Baron: they hoped to hear some of the best parts of the opera performed, and many persons crowded in only for the purpose of being able to discuss the music afterwards with their friends at other parties. Amidst this tumult, which was cleverly controlled by the Baron, his wife and daughter, the nimble enthusiast swam around like a fish in a stream whispering into the ears of everyone present how splendid the new composition was, how magnificent its style, how lovely were the melodies and how excellent the expression, although he himself had not yet heard a note of it. His round, red face bounced like a ball from one listening head to the other, most of the people, however, merely nodded out of politeness. Meanwhile the attention of part of the gathering was directed to another subject, a young girl had just entered, whose glowing beauty, expressive head, noble bearing and fine manners made them greet her with respect despite the fact that her attire was of the plainest sort. The Baron's daughter rushed up to her while she exclaimed, "Oh my dearest Julie, how happy I am that you were able to come, but what about your father?"

"Well you know," replied the beautiful girl, "how unsociable he is and how little his melancholy and poor health fits in with society; and I confess, I would also not have come if I could have imagined that your party would be so large."

The guests spoke about the extraordinary beauty of this young woman and upon inquiring they learned that she was the daughter of a poor musician. She lived in a distant city and communicated with the Baron's daughter through a friend. The performance of the Kapellmeister's opera had not yet begun because the host was waiting for one more guest to arrive, a young Count who was said to be one of the greatest music enthusiasts. "Imagine to yourself," the Baron said to the Kapellmeister, as he tried to describe the young Count, "the most strange and restless of men, nothing interests him but music, he runs from one concert to another, travels from one city to another just to hear some particular singer or musical composition, he avoids all other associations. He speaks and thinks only of this art and rarely is he calm enough to listen with complete attention to a piece of music for he is as distracted as he is over-excited. In addition he seems to have the most stubborn and most restricted taste for rarely is he pleased with anything he hears. He is never satisfied with the way music is performed, yet he remains an enthusiast all the same. Our young Count comes from a large rich family and was for a period of time in the diplomatic service at a distinguished court. However, he gave up everything for music which paradoxically it seems he often detests if one listens to his conversations." After this portrayal the close friends of the Baron were anxious to see this young man who seemed to be pursued and tormented by angry and good spirits. Therefore, when Count Alten finally entered everyone looked at him with great curiosity. He greeted the party hastily and his dark eyes quickly scanned the guests; then he lowered his glance and continued his conversation with an old haggard and shriveled-up Italian who had come with him. But suddenly he broke off his conversation and exclaimed half audibly, "Heavens! who is that?" He stood directly behind Julie. The tenor now sang an aria from the new opera and everyone seemed enthusiastic, the Count, however, was deep in thought.

"Now your excellency," the Italian asked at the conclusion of the song, "are you not content?"

"I have heard no sound," answered the Count, while he raised his head and pushed his black locks away from his thoughtful, melancholy brow.

He took advantage of the intermission and while the guests pressed themselves around the Kapellmeister, praising and admiring him, the Count stepped forward and seated himself next to Julie. He wanted to speak to her, but when she turned her face politely to him, he recoiled in fright. "No, surely, I had not expected anything like her!" he said to himself. The young girl was astonished and embarrassed. "Forgive me," the Count addressed her more cheerfully, "you probably thought me peculiar when I stood behind your chair a few minutes ago; I thought I had met you somewhere before, but now I have been so dazzled by your extraordinary beauty that I must have time to pull myself together. True genuine beauty can indeed frighten a person, for there is something superhuman about it which overwhelms our senses and our mind. Heavens! How you must be able to sing!"

"I do not sing at all, Count, I do not have any voice nor any knowledge of music," Julie replied with a pleasant voice.

The Count looked up at her with a penetrating glance, shook his head in doubt and crossly muttered inaudible words to himself. Now a duet was being performed and everyone was attentive except the Count who continuously looked at Julie. The duet was difficult and the first singer expressed her irritation, the Kapellmeister became upset and showed her the way it should be performed, but his efforts were in vain, they had to stop because the singer insisted that the passage did not suit her voice and should be changed; the Kapellmeister believed he could not allow expression and power to be sacrificed to such willfulness, for the excellent singer he knew could if she wanted to exert herself a little perform this passage and even more difficult works with ease. In the meantime the opera was interrupted because of the argument and while the Kapellmeister tried to substitute another selection, the Count said to Julie, "I wager if you wanted to, you could sing this difficult aria at sight." As Julie continued to insist that she could not sing, the Count said, "Your blushing and the expression in your eyes contradict your denial. How can you tell me that the soft, soul-filled swelling which I see in the middle of the lips of your round mouth has not been formed by pure full tones which soared over this hill many times. For only the sound of music can form such an expressive elevation when it travels across the red street and lovingly blows its tones over it. Completely opposite are those furrowed corners of the mouth which that famous singer over there has, whose lips which are tightly pressed and pinched squeeze out such poor shrill tones."

"You are too clever," replied Julie, "but I regret to say that you are still wrong."

"You also speak just like a singer," the Count continued, "in your speech I sense a lovely, but hidden tone which like a bird does not dare unfold its wing. But if you would sing just one single note! The happiness of my life depends on your ability to sing!"

"You torment me, Count," answered the embarrassed girl sensitively. "I assure you most sincerely I will not sing because nature denied me this splendid gift."

"Oh your excellency," said the small brown Italian, "everyone is said to have virtuosity, but not everyone can sing just because they have a beautiful fine mouth. On the contrary many a divine prima donna who sings heavenly sometimes and at other times seems to scream often has a mouth like Signor Cerberus[2] who they say has the talent to sing three parts like one solo."

The earlier cheerful spirit of the musicians was disturbed, the Kapellmeister annoyed and the first singer displeased beyond words. The enthusiast was in a dilemma over whether he should say something or not, on one hand he did not want to spoil his relationship with anyone present, but by the same token he also did not want to be a quiet, indifferent observer. Since they saw that nothing more of importance would happen this evening, most of the guests little by little withdrew along with the musicians, and only the Kapellmeister remained whom the enthusiast stayed with without waiting for an invitation; the Count, deep in thought, and his Italian friend also stayed in order to join the Baron's family for a glass of wine and some light supper.

"As usual, it happened again," began the Kapellmeister, as they sat around the oval table, "one works very hard, one studies, one torments oneself and finally then one is happy when the work is finished and appears well-done, but then the creation has to be given over to those rotten miserable artisans who have learned nothing and with the little they know act as if they want to keep the wondrous achievement in the dark. Can there be any sadder profession than that of a composer? Even when finally this misery is overcome through pleas, threats, jokes, adoration, lies and false-hoods, through small changes, additions and deletions, the mar-tyred work is subjected to the mercy of the whims of the public and blind chance, its almighty ruler. However, now there are other things with which to contend, it must not be either too hot nor too cold, the hall must be neither too full nor too empty, and in order to receive the necessary applause from the audience and to excite some enthusiasm no great political news or the name of some tight-rope walker or leaper can be announced. And yet one cannot help getting excited during the performance and start another new work which will be just as ungratefully received."

Suddenly the Count got up and asked, "Where did the young woman go?"

"Do you mean the person by whom you sat for so long?" asked the daughter. "If so she left some time ago, a servant came to get her for she lives quite far away."

"She should sing your splendid work," said the Count, "then we would hear something quite different."

"You are mistaken," corrected the daughter, "I know that the young lady about whom you are talking is definitely not musical. However, she sews and performs other womanly tasks quite well and her father, a poor old musician, has also allowed her to learn some drawing."

"Oh, you old sinner," exclaimed the young Count in a most irritated manner, "do you mean to tell me that those lips never sang a song, that no musical sound ever came from that rounded mouth! Is it not as if one would rob the rose of its aroma, which nature has already provided for it, before the rose begins to bloom?"

The daughter who believed herself to also be a singer was some-what annoyed by the Count's remarks, but her curt answer was ignored because in the meantime the Kapellmeister continued re-lating his grievances. "Aside from these poor incidents," he com-plained, "when the work is performed for the public the composer is suddenly confronted by the shortcomings of his composition,

84

inadequacies of which he had not previously dreamt while working in his room. For no matter how many times we sing through a work and study it, examining it from all sides, and listen to the judgement of friends and scholars, so many things, sometimes the best, sometimes the worst, reveal themselves for the first time during the performance. Surely, isn't the destiny of the artist a sad one? I never begin a new task without being sincerely convinced that now I will create something completely and totally first-rate, perfect, which will equal the works of my great predecessors and might even, here and there, surpass them. But in the midst of my composition I soon begin to lose this heavenly peace and my confidence vanishes, the rapture I experienced when I began changes into the most bitter doubt. Then I often begin to feel deep inside me that something of the truth, of the divine, has found its way into my work and that my notes will reach the unknown listener in the adjoining room. It seems to me that it should be so easy, that I only have to move my head this way or that and genius would appear, but he never does. My spirit, trying to find this distant path, tortures itself and so I work on miserable and resigned. The whole thing seems to me to be comparable to the state of the ape with his sad restlessness and his annoying facial expressions, perhaps, the ape has each moment a glimpse of reason, sometimes it is vague, sometimes it is clear, but when he wants to snatch that which is almost within his grasp, it eludes him and he finds himself back where he started again. Or to put it another way, you have an idea, cannot formulate it, know that it is there, but the harder you try the further it eludes you, just when you think you have it, it disappears and like a frustrated ape you return to your task."

But now a middle-aged man, a scholar and close friend of the host, who almost daily visited the Baron and who avoided large social gatherings, joined the party.

"I see you have avoided our concert as usual," the Baron addressed him.

"I am only a novice," replied the friend, "and as such I avoid mingling with scholars. Should the unmusical spoil the pleasure of the cultured by his dull presence?"

"We are well acquainted with this rogue," the Kapellmeister called to him while he greeted his old friend. "You have done the right thing, for our singers have been up to their old tricks again, sung poorly, appeared superior, criticized the music and finally ended the performance burying the music in discord and obstinacy."

"Are you really unmusical?" asked the enthusiast. "And you make no secret of it?"

"Why should I?" answered the novice. "No one can do everything nor can he awaken and cultivate all his slumbering natural abilities."

"You have a great deal of character to confess it so boldly," replied the enthusiast, who had become so over-excited by the music and the hearty enjoyment of the wine that he didn't even notice his own strange behavior. "Look," he continued, "I have already gotten myself in a great deal of difficulty because I did not have the courage to admit I was unmusical. Originally, it appears, nature created me without any feeling, subsequently I avoided all concerts and operas and if in social gatherings songs were sung or cantatas were performed I either found someone with whom I could talk or tried to get hold of a book for there is nothing like a hearty lasting conversation about local news or some interesting slander to totally distract yourself from music. 'Look at the stick,' I heard them say about me, 'has the thin person over there a human soul sitting in its spacious flesh? Imagine not to be able to understand anything about music, this most divine of all arts! Is there a rock or a stone which would not be moved by heavenly harmonies?'[3] Now a certain woman at that time greatly attracted my attention: she was in the habit of crying heartily as soon as the singing began because of her excessive feeling. I with my cold heart was an abhorrence to her. 'How can you love anyone, you who have not the faintest notion of this rapture which stems from heaven and is so closely related to love?' she asked me. Then, friends, I came to the conclusion that I had better change my opinions and become appropriately inspired by music. All my friends and acquaintances were astonished when my newly created, unspoiled rapture poured forth from my eyes to them. There was no holding back now, I outdid every type of ecstasy which I had been able to observe in social gatherings. My whole being wiggled from joy; as soon as the clavier had struck, my legs beat, my arms swung, my eyes wobbled, yes, I even used my tongue to help and occasionally licked my lips which I opened wide to show how astonished I was. Then I had to clap my hands, my eyes, if it was possible, had to cry and with outstretched arms I had to press friends as well as strangers to my heart which beat with powerful strokes in the most wild enthusiastic manner. I was so unnerved, so tired and faint, that I now wished art and artists, love and harmony, in any case all the enchanted feelings I was supposed to have, to go to the devil."

"But did you really feel a lot?" asked the novice laughing.

"That is a serious question," replied the enthusiast, "if a person wants something very badly, surely some trace of the desired object must penetrate his being; it is hard to believe that if a person consciously imitates certain feelings many times, those feelings should not at some period in his life re-echo in his heart. But to be quite truthful, all my efforts to win the admiration of my friends left me with a feeling of intolerable emptiness, I was indeed what the crowd calls, bored, and if I had not at that time so diligently employed my hands and feet, I would probably have yawned heartily. However, the worst part of the whole thing was that all my efforts were in vain for my malicious friends believed that in trying so hard I resembled a person who mounts a horse too high and subsequently falls off from the other side. If at first I appeared like a stubborn animal I soon seemed like an unruly coward, my enthusiastic gestures looked like I was having a spasm, one would almost have to believe that I made these exaggerated motions because my doctor recommended them to me to help me to lose weight.

"Oh and the musicians, they have caused me to suffer the most. Eight months ago two famous composers performed their works here in the hall. When the first finished, I fell upon his neck with flowing tears and this composer, so moved by my enthusiasm, patted me kindly on the back. We hugged each other warmly and he said that he had never met anyone so thoroughly knowledgeable in all the kingdoms of the musical world. Now it was the other composer's turn to conduct his work. When it was finished I had no more tears, but, however, managed to sob magnificently, sobbing is of course on a much higher plane than tears. The ordinary gestures of admiration were not enough of a reward for this composer, I had to let myself go completely, hold back nothing, I had to dissolve my entire being as it were and thus fell as if dying into his arms, it had to appear as if I had come close to real death. The coarse rascal, however, actually allowed me to fall down upon the floor without making an effort to catch me and as I lay there in my artistic swoon he scornfully said to me, 'In the name of heaven stay where you are, for any person who is able to cry over the shoddy work of that composer over there does not in the least deserve to hear one note of my music.' So I got up and went to seek comfort from the other composer, my great friend, who said I was such a scholar. But as I cried out to him, he also jumped away from me so abruptly that I almost was pushed with my nose against the wall, he excused himself by saying that whoever possesses so little genuine feeling that he can so excessively admire at the same time both miserable as well as noble music is no friend of art, but a misformed monster. Now when I wanted to seek solace from my beloved she also was furious with me because I had cried at all the wrong places and had expressed my feelings at the liveliest places in the music, passages where only the smallest amount of sentiment should be shown. Oh, dearest, most revered one, a person feels almost compelled to take an oath not to move during the arioso, the cavatina, the finale, the overture, the adagio and the presto,[4] but just to sit there with one's legs slightly apart, only allowing himself to beat the time now and then; for if all the hammering and puffing, this wearing out of our mortal enraptured soul, these prophetic flowing tears which mirror the reflection of the invisible, if all this is of no use and causes infernal antipathy instead of heavenly sympathy, I say once again to you I would prefer to be the person who works the bellows of the organ or the blacksmith rather than be a genuine enthusiast. Therefore do not be surprised if I turn my back again on that ungrateful art."

As they laughed over these confessions, the novice said in a happy mood, "The sorrows of music also belong to the most painful part of my life, absurd events which I suffered as a youth and which even now cause me some fright, when I think about them, resulted from music."

"Let us hear about them, my old friend," exclaimed the Kapellmeister, "Indeed I have complained enough about my own sorrows to which of course no one paid any attention."

"I was about twelve years old," the novice began, "things were going well for me, I progressed quickly in school, my teachers and parents were satisfied with me, when suddenly an evil spirit angrily planted his weed among the sprouting wheat and spoiled the harmony and comfort of my life. My father, a strict but cheerful man let me choose my vocation; he was a friend of music even though he had no talent. One afternoon he asked me whether I would, perhaps, like to play an instrument. The thought had never occurred to me. He told me that he would not demand this of me and that I should think it over, but if I made up my mind to study an instrument, I would have to be serious about it. I knew my father quite well, I realized that he would not be surprised if I did not devote myself to music, but if I started taking lessons, he would not allow me to discontinue them. Until this time music seemed quite boring and of little consequence to me, perhaps, because I did not know how to listen with concentration. I downright hated opera because during the arias and duets, which I did not understand at all, the action, the only thing in which I was interested, stopped. Music was never a part of our home life, with the exception of the time I spent with the dancing teacher, who felt I was one of his best students, but who, however, could never make me realize that the music he played upon his violin had something to do with the dance. If I hit upon the beat by accident at the beginning I danced

89

the minuet, *Kosak* or whatever it was. However, if I missed the beat, no increase in volume, no stopping or speeding up, nothing could help me get the rhythm. I felt that dancing was like a superstition. If you think that dance music frightened me, the music I heard in church, which I never liked, drove me to despair. My nerves were never strong and the roaring organ with its crashing tremolo stops numbed my brain and I found the shrill unison singing of the congregation unbearable. Even to this day I have not learned to put up with either of them: it frightens and alarms me to be near an organ, although it may be a noble invention, and the singing of the choir, which drags itself along the floor so humbly like a chained penitent criminal, takes all my courage away even if the music is performed well; all poetry and music dies out, down to the last spark of my soul and an emptiness comes over me and I feel sick of life."

"One could say a lot about this," thought the Kapellmeister, "in addition the novice probably has some strange peculiarity."

"I had not the faintest notion of what music was as a youth," began the novice again, "nor had I exhibited even the slightest trace of any talent when suddenly the evil spirit put the idea in my head that, perhaps, hidden inside me was the soul of a great violinist. The violin was bought, a teacher hired. But what a combination, the strangest teacher, who taught me as if I had been playing for years, and myself, the strangest scholar. During our first lesson he only let me draw the bow across the strings of the violin, the sounds of which tormented my delicate nerves. Then he made me a music book in which he had written a few easy songs for me to play. 'This piece,' he said, 'is in D major and is called, "Bloom, Lovely Violet".'[5] I did not worry about the two crosses I saw on the music or what D major meant or whether these things meant one or many sounds or what the bar-line or strokes on the notes meant, we did not trouble ourselves about these insignificant things and played cheerfully through the song, I merely imitated him, memorizing the position of the fingers and everything. We followed the same procedure for the second and the third song which was in C major. I

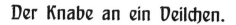

Bloom Lovely Violet by Johann Abraham Schulz.

LUDWIG TIECK

noticed, however, that in the third song the two crosses were missing; each time I played a wrong note he told me the name of it but he did not find it necessary to say anything else or to explain to me how long each note was held. This whole thing sounds like a fairy tale, but it is really true that for six to seven years I played the violin in this manner without having the slightest desire to get to the core of the thing or my teacher thinking it important to add some theoretical knowledge to our practical method. Moreover, you would think that he would have shown me the way music should sound. It is not hard to understand what discordant sounds I made on the violin if one considers that I played everything by heart, the length of the notes, their variation in minor and everything else. I only knew the notes according to where they stood on the lines and nothing more, moreover, I had no ear at all and my bowing and finger positions were frequently poor. My teacher, who was truly a capable violinist, complained about his ears during each lesson. I myself suffered true torments of hell every time I put the violin under my chin. This rattling, wheezing, squeaking and cooing was unbearable to me, if one listens closely to even the best violinist one can hear a harmonic produced; if one places a finger lightly in the right position, especially in the high register of the violin, an overtone or harmonic is heard, but I could never produce a harmonic, only the most abominable discords. My serious teacher often shook his head and said that of all his pupils none had so little talent as I. Indeed while I played my violin I had more mishaps than any violinist I had ever seen. Once, for example, when my teacher and I, after I had studied with him for some time, became really enthusiastic over a lively passage we were playing, suddenly during the Allegro my bow screeched as it slid past the bridge and over the tailpiece and to my terror my teacher lowered his violin because of the sound I produced, a sound which can only be imagined by those who have produced it themselves. More than once the tailpiece fell off as if in sympathy and a violent pop sounded in the middle of the note which ended a languishing Largo. Once even, and I thought at the time that death had surely come to claim me, the clamp

92

broke off which holds the tailpiece and sprang mercilessly against my nose. During this lesson our harmony came to an end for my violin had to be taken to the repair shop. After some time had passed, my father was curious to hear how I was doing. I performed several of the songs for him which I felt I knew best. He was frightened by what he heard and even more astonished by what he saw. He believed that in the art of making faces I had progressed beyond all imagination and that my music could be of use to drive away rats and mice; he warned me to confine my facial expressions to something else otherwise I certainly would soon look like an ape. That was my reward for performing for him, with little success, my favorite aria, the then popular song, 'Here Slumber My Children',[6] which I believed I could do well and which had many lingering melancholy and sedate passages on the low strings and I did not have to climb up to the high register which I detested once and for all."

"But didn't you have any happy times during your musical studies?" asked the Kapellmeister humorously.

"Few," replied the novice, "my teacher now found it necessary to buy a mute because of my facial expressions, which I attached with joy to my violin because suddenly it produced another sound, moreover, the mute, like a Spanish rider,[7] made it impossible for my bow to spring across the bridge in rapid passages. It also gave me sincere joy for now for the first time we could progress faster playing at sight the 64th notes in the overture like one and the same note thirty times in a row, an effect which generally occurs towards the end of the piece shortly before the curtain falls.[8] I liked to repeat this passage when I was alone because it posed no difficulties for me and the repeated 64th notes, moreover, made me feel as if I were sitting in my beloved theater."

"But at that time," asked the Kapellmeister, "didn't you have some clear conception of music?"

"Very little, no more than I had in the very first lesson," answered the novice, "I understood nothing about rhythm, execution, tone production, I played sonatas and symphonies still from

LUDWIG TIECK

memory, just the way I heard my teacher play them. I understood
neither melody nor phrasing, once in a while a pair of beats seemed
to have some relevance, but I never could connect them to anything
else, I was so far away from any idea of what music was that one
time I imagined that every letter in the alphabet was a note because
my teacher had named such letters as g, a and b, so it seemed to me
that all I had to do was to take the notes and make words out of
them and then play them more quickly or more slowly. When I
asked my teacher where the m, r, or p were, he laughed at me, but
didn't bother to correct my ignorance, he was always surprised over
my frightful naivety and constantly wondered why I did not know
what seemed to him to be self-evident. Do you know that even
though all music seemed like a din to me, I tried once to compose.
The beat seemed to me to be like a prejudice and I could care less
about key, and never will I forget the joy which I brought my
teacher when I delivered to him my first composition, a group of
wild jumbled up notes. He wanted to split his sides with laughter
and did not tire of playing my fantasy with pleasure and joy. To me
it sounded like all other music."

The old brown Italian heartily enjoyed this tale and even the
brooding Count laughed. "It is inconceivable that you endured it
so long," said the Baron.

"I had to," replied the novice, "on account of my father for I had
promised him that if I began to study an instrument I would stick
to it. Otherwise he took no further interest in my music and when I
was supposed to play for him on Sunday afternoons he always said
that he had a toothache and excused himself. Once I suffered a
terrible humiliation when I was studying the violin. The lady who
owned the house in which we lived had invited several pretty girls
to a birthday party she was giving for her grown-up daughter. In
order to make the occasion a special one the good woman had con-
spired with my mother to have me secretly come up the stairs with
my violin, tune up suddenly in the next room and then surprise the
pretty girls with some English dances to which they could dance
merrily in the hall. Subsequently I was led into the next room with

94

all secrecy. Through the curtain I saw the most lively gathering, but now to tune the violin. How mean! I had never tuned a violin in my entire life because my teacher did it for me, moreover, I could not tell whether it was out-of-tune or not, so avoiding making matters worse, I never said anything to him one way or the other about it. It appeared to me more noble as well as more cautious to announce myself to the gathering with my favorite aria and so suddenly I charmingly played 'Here Slumber My Children.' The joy of these non-sleeping girls was indescribable, with loud rejoicing I was pulled into the hall where I stood as if dazzled because I had never in my life seen so many charming creatures in the same place. I was beseeched with requests. I showed them the English dances which my good teacher had written for me in my notebook. I played one, but it was not suitable. They asked me about the number of turns and other questions relating to dancing which I could not in the least understand. I tried a second English dance and a third, but in vain. My performance came to an end because we could not communicate with each other. I, who they had pulled in with the greatest triumph, now had to leave amidst the greatest humiliation and their annoyance lasted the rest of the afternoon, I had ruined the party. When my mother asked me how it went, I told her that the girls could not dance, and so it appeared to me because the young ladies did not know how to react to my music. Finally my teacher was assigned to a distant foreign orchestra and I believed now that my torment was at an end; but my persistent father had already procured another teacher, who, after I had played for him, felt I must start all over from the very beginning. I, who had played symphonies and the most difficult works, now had to hammer into my head those detested chorales and church melodies, moreover, everything had to be slow, I could only play half and whole notes because my new teacher insisted that I had no bowing technique nor any concept of how to place my fingers on the strings. This teacher had such a delicate sense of intonation that the grimaces he made over my bad sounds were worse than my own. He also never laughed at my clumsiness and lack of talent like my first teacher, but took my musical education very much to heart and many times he was almost close to tears. Fortunately, this new torment only lasted a half year for me for at the end of this time I had to leave for the university and since then have never played a musical instrument. These confessions, gentlemen, describe in short only the smallest part of my musical sorrows, for if I would have wanted to describe them all to you, I would lack the time and you would lack the patience."

"Now it is your turn," said Baron Fernow turning to the old Italian. "You have experienced a special joy while listening to these tales and it is only fair that now you share with us some of your own musical sorrows, which you as an old virtuoso must have undergone."

"Oh gentlemen," said the old man with a strange expression on his face, "my sorrows are too tragic to give you pleasure, also, because I am an Italian, I cannot express myself very well in your native tongue and for this reason I must ask your indulgence if my confessions should be combined with confusion. Since I was a child I have been a skillful singer, a good tenor and an accomplished pianist. When I sang in the theater in Naples for the first time I was successful and well-applauded. Then I went to Rome, but unfortunately, I did not make such a hit there for the gentlemen of Rome are very critical and think that they have the finest ears in the whole of Italy. Oh, but in Rome I saw a young woman in the carnival who later took lessons from me in order to better prepare herself for a position as a singer in Florence. Oh, what tone! What talent! What eyes! She was my beloved, my favorite, my heart, and before we knew what happened we ran away together to Florence where we were married and where we sang together in the theater with all the passion of our love. There was much tenderness in our marriage, but also much discontent, for my dearest one was a jealous person, for, if I must admit it, but in a humble way of course, I was quite a handsome youth and women easily stirred my heart. Nevertheless, everything went well for us until we were employed in a German town. Here there lived a certain composer, a maestro, a true theoretician, full of pretension, but clever, furthermore, a handsome man. Hortensio, as was his name, pleased my beloved and she wanted to become one of his pupils, to learn to sing, as he said, in a great noble manner, not from the throat, but as the Germans believed from the soul. Soul! An extra German invention known to no other country. Up to that time, my wife had a beautiful tone, a superhuman high register, bright as glass, sharp, loud; a composer could compose any way he wanted and require the highest pitches, but we never lost control, correctly we sang these difficult passages, our voices climbing higher and higher in the cadenza and then as we reached the highest tone our voices descended down again—bravo, bravo, bravissimo it was screamed from the theater boxes, the audience clapped and beat their fans especially applauding my wife who bowed with hands crossed across her heart and it never occurred to anyone during the music that the composer had wanted to squeeze in thoughts or special feelings, the singing, the technique was everything. But Hortensio, Hortensio, damned beast. I almost dropped dead when I heard his soul method for the first time. No passaggio,[9] no transition, no trills, she sang like a calf being led to the slaughter, not a trace of style or method. I was the first tenor then, but I could not break the habit of vigorously pinching the round arm of my prima donna during the love duet. She screamed dangerously, the audience thought it was part of the new manner and began to laugh. From that day on there was dissension between us, the public no longer applauded us. Hortensio was a great theorist and enthusiast, but he did not want to be a lover for he was married to a good woman who, according to the German manner, was all soul. Now malice began to grow more and more in my delicate Isabella. She wanted to return to the old brilliant style, cursed soul and heart, but when she sang it sounded as if she screamed like a possessed person, she raged and often twisted her throat, grumbled and puffed as if her small throat was like a chimney out of which Satan's breed were trying to escape on pitchforks and broomsticks to fly to the Brocken.[10] So the misery was complete, all that was missing was that she laid the blame on me for she truly believed this was the case; I sang so badly, I had regressed, to make a long story short, we were finally dismissed with a small pension. We travelled the entire province to find the cheapest accommodations, but we always ended up with the most expensive, we gave concerts, I gave private lessons, but dear Isabella could not give up her music and the worse she performed the more she wanted to sing, at last when no one wanted to listen to her anymore we continued the spectacle privately in our room. Indeed I had to be superhuman to endure the battle cries and many times I thought I could have died. We had a big powerful cat who always liked to lay on our piano, the chap feared neither rat nor mouse, never ran from a big dog and one time had a fight with a ferocious bulldog; but as soon as my wife just opened up the lid of the piano in order to strike a few chords, the cat ran as fast as it could up to the highest floor. We raved so intensely that no innkeeper would accept us any longer as tenants. Naturally no one wanted to hear our concerts for the human ear is delicately constructed for the most part and very few people can bear singing which is out of tune and annoying. One day my wife said to me that I should put on my best clothes for a large respected number of people had been invited to our home for a concert. We sang and raved, but there were no people there. When I talked about it with her that evening she said that the human race is so constituted as to be too insipid and coarse to appreciate her art, therefore, she had invited only celestial spirits who never complain about dissonance and I am but a fellow too thick-headed to be able to see the fine creatures with my own eye. Now the ghost gatherings continued on and she told me how her performances elicited such great applause from these connoisseurs. On another evening when the assembly of spirits was with us and we both had screamed enough, she suddenly said to me that I sang entirely wrong, it was unbearable and King David who certainly was a musical connoisseur did not want to come any longer if I did not sing more correctly and with more respect. I was supposed to go over to him at once and ask his majesty to forgive me. But where was he sitting? 'There, next to the oven, for the old gentlemen is always cold,' said my wife. Submissively I performed my act of devotion with polite expression and was pardoned."

"Poor man!" said the Kapellmeister, moved, "and how long did your wife live?"

"Please forgive me," replied the Italian. "I don't want to slander my departed wife, but at first I thought it was nothing more than madness, but soon I saw my mistake. For as time went on and the days became colder and shorter, my wife tortured me violently and I almost tore my neck apart while singing at a special concert at which all the celestial spirits paid us honor, at that time I saw, as I brought in the lamp, the whole room full of invisible beings, as one would say, dead spirits. My eyes have been opened up since that event and I have made many interesting acquaintances among the departed and no longer feel the need to associate with live people."

"That I believe," said the Baron, while he stared with a questioning glance at the narrator, the daughter moved away from the old Italian, the enthusiast was astonished, the novice laughed and only the Count who knew him already remained calm.

"We realized," continued the old man, "that our very extensive acquaintance with the spirits of the past was becoming somewhat annoying and later on we became more selective and confined ourselves only to famous musicians. Yes, gentlemen, from that time on I came to know the very foundation of counterpoint, tone production, performance and style, knowledge which cannot be found in any book. But my dear wife died soon and since her death I have not been able to communicate with the spirits of the past for these gentlemen would never reveal themselves to me again after my wife departed from this earth."

After a pause the Baron asked the Count whether, perhaps, he did not also have some musical sorrows to tell the group. "In part, gentlemen, your complaints were caused by your contact with music in the absence of a true love or deep feeling for this art. My misfortune stems from the very opposite. From my earliest youth the joy of my life was music, my desire for this art, which was over-exaggerated, caused many problems for my parents and teachers. I wanted to learn nothing else and often deplored any other occupation which kept me from becoming a musician. Wherever a tone or a song was heard, this is where I was with my whole soul and I forgot all my duties. My father, a serious and forceful man, was annoyed by my enthusiasm for music because it threatened all his plans for my future. I was a passionate youth and believed in my youthful eagerness that when it came to defending my love of music nothing was sacred and if my fanatic retorts were not sufficient I would often resort to insulting and offending my father in a most unbecoming manner and this struggle, this remorse and contrition which I experienced because of my passion and my ill-humour which attacked everything in the world including myself, this sad state of affairs which tore me to pieces totally ruined the serenity of my youth for the pleasure which music afforded me and which I could only achieve by force was still not capable of making amends to me for everything I had to endure. It may be that my expectations were too deeply strained, my conception of music and the demands I put upon this art were inclined to be too high, in short, performances of music, even if well-done, were for the most part spoiled for me. This is because quite often I believed that a great deal was put into performances of a musical work which did not belong there at all, that music was often degraded for mere pleasure, that this art generally had to compete for effects which are unworthy of her like a contestant in a contest and that only a very few singers know what execution and feeling really mean. A deep melancholy took possession of me and I believed that probably nowhere in the world could I find that particular indispensable mood without which music could not achieve its highest state of perfection. Finally I had to give in to my father's wishes and take part in his business. The work became easier for me than I had imagined and my father, who on account of my love of music almost took me for an idiot, was so satisfied with me that his affection for me returned. After some years had passed I was sent on important diplomatic missions to a great court. For a long time I had observed the new singers and was dissatisfied with almost all of them. If the voice is said to be the expression of human feeling or the enthusiasm of human passions, then it must raise itself to sublime heights, it has to swell mightily and soar higher and higher in order to reach and conquer the all-powerful, the strongest illuminated region above the earth. It is only in this region where composer and singer are able to express the divine quality of love, human sorrow, devotion and every impulse of the soul and yet I found that almost always the harmonious tones of music, the pleasure of these sounds, was employed only for the purpose of creating a petty type of art hardly different than some athletic feat like leaping or tight-rope walking which is characterized by virtuosity and exhibitionism and which should be excluded from genuine art. Yet what is even worse to me is the rather widespread method of expression which a certain group is encouraging—no crescendo, no portamento, rather a sudden shriek like a cry of anxiety or help alternating abruptly with an equally sudden puff, an unmotivated letting go of the song, a hollow moan instead of tone, this abrupt continuous change from one extreme to the other made me feel one time that I heard nothing one moment and the next was terrified by piercing tones, a disturbance which, however, greatly pleased the audience, but which appeared to me to be something so far away from all technique that I can only describe it as the vulgar antithesis of singing. Concerning the newest taste in opera I prefer to remain silent because I could complain endlessly about it. No sooner had I introduced myself to the foreign court then I was given the order that I would have to return to my country quickly with an important assignment. Before I left there was a concert in the evening at the home of the brother of the ruling Prince and a new female singer was to be heard for the first time. I went into the concert hall. The crowd was so thick that I could see only the nape of the singer, whose dazzling whiteness was enhanced by a wonderful curly brown head of hair. The girl began to sing and went from the first tone into the second and into the third with such power, and charm that I stood enchanted for it was more than I had imagined, it was what I had always wished for. This pure, heavenly discant was love, sublimity, delicate power, permeated by the most intensely noble celestial feeling. I did not hear all the offensive methods to which I had so often been exposed, the piercing dazzling glass tone which even overpowers the harmonica,[11] the numbness in the last dizzying tones of the upper register which offends and pierces the ear like spikes, the swoon on the edge of the voice which arouses in us one moment a feeling of pity and the next sounds like a cry for help and applause—all this was missing. No, her tone was itself, certainty, truth, love. Now for the first time I realized how Hasse[12] could have dared now and then to have the soprano trill on one and two syllables for many beats and then allow the voice to fall and then rise again. I was so astonished that I forgot myself and everything else. In this sublime moment I secretly vowed that only this creature with this wonderful voice and no other should become my wife. The councillor and the advisor of the Prince tried to get my attention for I was supposed to be present at a meeting. I went over to the ruling gentleman of the castle. It was difficult for me to pull myself together for this very important conversation. After the meeting was over I had to throw myself into the carriage this stormy night. I asked the old councillor, my companion, and the servants about the girl I had just heard, but no one seemed to know anything about her. I arrived in my country, tasks which occupied me far into the night urgently awaited me. I could not see my father very often for he was ill. When at last I had finished my assignment and wanted to devote my comfort and service to my suffering father, it was too late, I could only close his eyes for him. For the first time in my life I realized how dear to me the honorable man had been, but now I was free to follow my own wishes. I withdrew from the diplomatic service. As soon as my affairs were organized I journeyed back to that residence where I first heard her, but—and how is it possible to believe that no living soul at that court wanted to discuss her or that evening which I described, as if this singular heavenly voice was one of the most ordinary occurrences which one hardly notices and then forgets or as if I was mad or under a spell and had imagined everything. As my search for her at this court was in vain, I tried to find this miracle during my subsequent travels. Therefore, I missed no concert and no opera. I visited every musical gathering, but always without success. For two years I led this restless sad life and this evening I thought I would go mad for in this girl from a distant city who sat next to me I believed to have found my unknown love, the same curl on her neck, the same fine contour of her ears and mouth, the same facial expression appeared to me to be identical to those of the singer I heard."

The daughter of the house asserted again that the Count was thoroughly in error and that although some of his remarks were in good taste others were one-sided. "Do you think you will keep your strange oath?" the Baron asked afterwards.

"I have to," replied the Count, "for you may laugh and find it inconceivable, but that wonderful sweet sound has instilled love in me, true love. For why should we experience this emotion, this enthusiastic ecstasy, only through our eyes? I dream of this angel voice, I hear it always, everything reminds me of this sound. Oh heaven! If it were gone, if she were dead! I do not even want to imagine the immensity of this sorrow."

With the exception of the novice, the others seemed as if they could not understand this passion or want to believe it. Since it was late the gathering broke up and the Italian accompanied the Count in whose home he lived.

"Excellency," the Italian began in a lonely street, "do me a favor and accompany me the day after tomorrow to the gate which stands at the entrance to the forest for it is there that I want to kill myself."

"Fool!" said the Count, "of what are you thinking? Have I not promised to provide a living for you?"

"That is all very nice and I thank you for your generosity," said the Italian, "but I have had enough of life, I greatly long for my departed half."

"So that you may continue your cat concerts in the other world?"

"That is not the only reason," replied the old man, "I was so used to living with my Isabella and with Palestrina, Durante, Bach and all the great people including the royal Kapellmeister, David, that I can no longer endure the company of ordinary people. Please advise me, Excellency, how should I kill myself, by hanging, shooting or drowning?"

"I will have to lock up the fool," said the Count.

"Each method has something to recommend it," continued the Italian, without letting himself be disturbed, "air, fire, water— each is a good element. There is only one thing which would make my life better and give me a reason to life."

"Now what is that?"

"If I could meet Hortensio once more!"

"And why?"

"So I could give him a good thrashing for ruining her singing technique at that time."

"Dreamer," said the Count as they walked toward the gate.

"And what are you, Excellency," murmured the old man while the servants came to meet them.

The Kapellmeister was in despair. It had happened as he had feared. The leading singer was more irritable, she felt insulted and immediately came down with quite a serious illness which made it impossible for her to sing a note, let alone even to leave her room. The enthusiast walked in and ran to and fro, but his interference made the situation worse rather than better because he related each time faithfully to each party what the other person said, the Kapellmeister became more and more provoked and the leading female singer in the end went as far as to demand that the two most important arias should be completely rewritten and the duet in the last act must be put in the first act and of course immediately in the beginning, she also demanded for herself the great aria of the second female singer, without whose consent there would never be any peace. The Kapellmeister who was so beside himself because of these excessive demands swore that the prima donna should not sing one note in his opera even though he did not know how to replace her.

"If only my beloved were alive!" exclaimed the old Italian who also took part in the deliberations and now saw the Kapellmeister's despair. "Oh how brilliantly my departed wife would rise in the theater again. The role is written just for her."

"Perhaps you could take over the role yourself?" the Kapellmeister asked with tragic malice.

"Yes, Signor," exclaimed the old man. "If you cannot find another singer, I can startle everyone and sing falsetto."

"It really does not matter which way I am ridiculed," cried the Kapellmeister in desperation, "anyway at least no lover would applaud at the wrong time and no jealous person or the admirer of the second singer would hiss and make fun of the prima donna out of envy. Would you promise to behave yourself, old man?"

"If one has to, one can do anything," answered the Italian, who took the whole matter quite seriously. "Thirty years ago I was quite handsome and all the young men ran after me when I took the part of a woman in the carnival."

"Well, now we have a prima donna," said the enthusiast, "and if the setting of the opera could take place at night and the stage could thus be dark, it would be worth it to see what results our good friend could achieve."

"That is, if I am not dead before the performance," interjected the Italian. "I could, you know, get deathly ill just like the other singer got sick."

"I can see already," the Kapellmeister concluded, "that I have travelled here in vain; all the preparations I have made were useless. As long as it remains impossible, by order of the authorities, to put an end to and punish such insolence, as long as the public does not take revenge against such rudeness and contempt so that no second person would dare the same offense again, we remain the victim of this caprice of ignorant people who are rewarded much too much for their moderate talent and are spoiled by the directors and the public. I will pack up and go."

LUDWIG TIECK

The enthusiast cried from pain, but the Italian said, "You are totally correct; isn't it so that life with all its misery is not worth discussing?"

"I have had all I can take," answered the Kapellmeister.

"Well then, come along with me and keep me company," said the old man in a friendly manner, while he pressed close to him.

"Where to?"

"To the other world, to the great wide space beyond where one can enjoy oneself to his heart's content. Tell me, should we throw ourselves into the water or should we blow off our heads the way they do birds sitting upon a perch?"

"Go," exclaimed the Kapellmeister, "it is early in the morning, but you are already drunk."

"No," said the Italian, "I once took a holy vow to kill myself if I did not meet the lovely Signor Hortensio again; my whole situation would change if I found him, but if this joy is not fulfilled, I ask you, what kind of a shabby life is this? There you sit continuously, foolish maestro, and plunk upon the piano keys and write your music and worry about the ingenuity, character, melody, style, originality or as one calls these things, the substances of music, and who thanks you for it? Who notices it even a little? But let us talk like reasonable men. Isn't it more pleasant just to do away with oneself? Yes, fame, the afterworld! What we want is to reach the dear world beyond a little sooner and to look behind the curtain to see if it really exists. The day after tomorrow, dear friend, join the party. I will also bring along a pistol unless you would rather hang yourself, but the weather, however, is now windy and nasty."

"Stop the nonsense," said the Kapellmeister in a very serious manner, "or, old fool, you will be put into the lunatic asylum."

"And don't people live there also," said the Italian smirking. "You do not seem to use your brains very much, young man, they are still green and unripe. I, on the contrary, have become softened and lifeless because my mind has been worn out by constant use. I am not ambitious so you don't consider me sane or wise like the

106

Greeks. I have known different people from you, you poor modern, short-sighted man! And if Nestor or Phidias or Praxiteles,[13] with whom I have so often conversed would have said such a thing to me, I would have boxed each one of them in the ears."

He ran away raving and the Kapellmeister sat down sorrowfully; also the babbling enthusiast abandoned him because he realized that the Kapellmeister needed to be left alone in order to give way to his grief undisturbed.

"No," the novice said in the evening to Baron Fernow, "I have taken an oath never again to touch a violin, therefore, spare me." The father and daughter wished that he might play just one small song for them in order to have some idea of how he played his instrument as a youth."

"One should renounce nothing," said the Baron, "especially the practice of so noble an art."

The Kapellmeister came in and told the gathering about a particularly unreasonable request which the Count had asked of him. He related that the Count had visited him and asked him to accompany him and the old Italian that evening into the forest which lay outside the city where the Italian wanted to shoot himself; the Count wished to have one honest man to bear witness who afterwards would be able to verify that the old man had committed suicide. The Baron was of the opinion that one must immediately seize and imprison the deranged Italian; the rest agreed with him, the novice, however, questioned whether a person should be denied the right to do with his life as he wished. The opinion of the novice started a controversy over whether the state or other persons be permitted to control a person's actions; the Baron maintained, without reservation, that such control was necessary in this case for any person who decides to take his own life has to be considered insane.

"Then one must first determine what is insanity," the novice interjected, "for history has shown us how the law and its executors have condemned certain persons to death whose actions were considered contrary to the prevailing way of thinking, but which other generations have extolled or viewed with little concern or even considered laughable. Many liberal persons who deviated in the past from certain opinions were put to death, condemned as sorcerers or witches and now when we no longer consider such persons mad and put up with the great number of suicides which occur in our time, I don't understand how one can justifiably forbid the wretched and troubled the right to end their life especially when they have made this decision themselves."[14]

"It is paradoxical," exclaimed the Baron, "I don't know enough about philosophy to be able to refute you, but just from the standpoint of religion, you must know that you are defending an evil situation."

"I promised the Count that I would accompany him," said the Kapellmeister, "for I cannot imagine to myself that the old fool will carry out his intent. Moreover. it would not be at all surprising if a poor plagued Kapellmeister availed himself of this opportunity to keep him company."

With a disturbed and thoughtful frame of mind the Count now joined the party. They asked him whether something new had occurred; but he uttered that he had resolved to travel on after the old Italian killed himself because the memory of that voice had been revived anew through their conversations and he could not endure the longing which had overpowered his entire being.

"So then you take him seriously?" the Baron asked with surprise.

"If he does not kill himself," the Count replied, "I will take him along with me on my journey."

The Italian walked in and he seemed in better spirits than ever before. Everyone observed him with a certain awe, but he took no notice of their change in behavior and now as the enthusiast and the singer joined the gathering the conversation became cheerful and caused everyone to be in a good mood with the exception of the Count whose gloomy appearance did not change.

"Let us," said the Kapellmeister finally, "continue some of our recent conversations. How is it possible," turning to the novice, "that after your recent unusual confessions you could have become such a great friend of music?"

"Perhaps my unusual musical training actually increased my love of music," replied the novice, "because once this love had matured and suddenly awoke in me all on its own, without any prompting, I found that I could appreciate my favorite pastime without having to study music at all. I finally got to the time when I could understand small simple songs which remained in my memory; for instance, I could easily grasp the songs of Schulz which I often recalled, these songs, although not particularly poetic, cause a pleasant warm feeling and paint for us such a clear blue sky, green landscapes and light figures. Only the larger compositions, especially dramatic music, were offensive to me, even if I heard sometimes in them a small aria, it offended me just the same. Even those who have great difficulty hearing finally learn to enjoy the short melodies although the continuity of the large musical compositions remains unintelligible. When Mozart's *Don Giovanni*[15] was given for the first time I allowed myself to be persuaded to visit the theater. This opera was composed not long ago and in Germany the fame of its creator was still not established until shortly after its performance, the fact that Mozart was not well-known was brought out by an esteemed musician[16] who during and after the performance could not stop criticizing the work. But during the Overture I had the feeling that for the first time I heard and understood true music. During the course of the opera my delight rose, the intentions of the composer became clear to me, and the great spirit, the unending harmony, the magic of the splendor, the variety of the most conflicting sounds, which, nevertheless, united themselves into a beautifully organized whole, the deep expression of emotion, the bizarre and ghastly, the boldness and sweetness, the comedy and tragedy—all this, which makes this work unique, passed through my ears and into my soul. My rapture was increased by the realization that this understanding and appreciation happened so suddenly and I could hardly wait for *Belmont*[17] written by the same composer, whose passion greatly charmed me. I sought also to understand the work of other composers and was overpowered by Gluck's great style, noble rhetoric and profound spirit, I enjoyed Paisiello[18] and Martini,[19] Cimarosa's[20] bright spirit became clear to me and I tried to comprehend and assimilate the multiplicity of past and present musical styles. During my university years I forgot about music, but when I returned home, however, my enthusiasm returned with even greater intensity due to the conversations I had with some trusted friends which helped clarify my judgement and feeling. Now I became acquainted with the wonderful genius of the great composer, Sebastian Bach, who knew and was capable of everything and whose work which influenced the development of all future music I can only compare to the old revered German cathedrals whose sublime nature makes us realize most clearly the eternal inexhaustible powers of the divine and in which ornamentation, love and seriousness, diversity and charm unite in the highest necessity."

The Kapellmeister said, "One could become dizzy from looking at all the music which preceded and influenced Bach; it also truly requires a great deal of musical insight to be able to follow in the right manner and to understand polyphonic music such as the fugue, I never thought that a lay person could be capable of comprehending this type of music which is like an all-powerful spirit."

"After several years," the novice began again, "I was fortunate to make the acquaintance of a noble family whose members, particularly the women, cultivated music in a delightful manner.[21] The oldest daughter was a soprano and her tone which was so full and lovely, so heavenly clear, brings to mind, my esteemed Count, your recent description of the voice of your unknown love. Amidst this circle of new acquaintances I was introduced not only to many secular compositions, but the splendid eternal poems of the great exalted Palestrina, the wonderful works of Leo and Durante, the magic melodies of Pergolesi, which I must equate with the chiaroscuro of Correggio, the beautiful psalms of Marcello, the magnificent serenity of our Hasse and the dramatic *Requiem* of Jomelli. In addition I heard many works of Feo and Allegri and the *Miserere* of Bai.[22] This music is so pure, so unembellished, so simple, lacking all stylish affectation, it is unlikely that one will ever hear these masterpieces performed so faultlessly, so free of all decoration. The happy hours I spent with my friends transformed and elevated my spirit and were milestones in my life. I tried to set down my thoughts at this time, but only in a few meagre poems was I able to express my feelings.[23] At that time in my life my soul had so submerged itself in the sounds of this divine religious music that I did not want to hear any secular works, it seemed to me that music is deprived of its divine quality when it has to lower itself to express base human emotions. I believed that music's true destiny was to soar to heaven, to proclaim the divine and the belief in God."[24]

"What you have said," interjected the Kapellmeister, "proves that in those days your whole heart was permeated by the glory of your vision. It would be wrong to call such enthusiasm one-sided, for our soul, if it is truly moved and stirred in such a wonderful manner, feels during this new experience its own complete power and its immortality. The soul then finds the beauty which earlier had stirred it and is elevated and fulfilled through its new experience and rightfully looks down upon its earlier condition as something unworthy. Genuine rapture can never be experienced by people whose hearts are incapable of such a vision. The most exalted and beautiful mission of our art is accomplished by church music which of course is degraded by modern composers. But I am convinced that later on your own enthusiasm will lead you once again to your beloved Mozart and other composers."

"To be sure," continued the novice, "for love can never change to hate. I have always feared those persons who tomorrow tread upon what they adore and worship in excess today. Our development can and should only be a modification of one and the same power, one and the same truth, not restless exchanging, alternation and unquenchable demanding for the new and unheard-of which can never be totally satisfying. When later on I had the good fortune to hear many of the same works which I mentioned earlier performed by the Papal choir in Rome I felt that a unique traditional method of performing the old canti firmi was being practiced here, a method which made these chants simpler and different from what I had known, but I never heard again this indescribable discant neither in Rome nor here in the theater nor the music of Pergolesi or other more modern church composers performed with such perfection."

"From your descriptions," began the singer who was a friend of the Kapellmeister, "I have to conclude that you are probably rarely satisfied by modern singing techniques. But I confess to you that I do not share your opinion in this matter, too much simplicity is repulsive to me, what interests me is how the virtuoso controls his voice and the music. One might make an analogy here to the actor who does not merely read his lines, but through the rising and falling of his voice, through short pauses and rolling tones brings out those hidden meanings in the text of which the normal reader is not aware."[25]

"You are probably right," replied the novice, "if you mean by your remarks what I could call declamation in acting or diction in singing. I also have to agree with the Count's recent description of that type of musical expression which is false and inadequate. And is it any different in our drama? One cannot judge an age by its deficiencies or merits alone, art is a reflection of many things, both past and present, even the negative and positive qualities of history and government are part of this great intertwined web. The singer who moans and shrieks can rarely completely express the true meaning of an aria or a duet, which as an actor he should be able to do, in a similar manner, the actor who resorts to overemphasizing accents, stressing various words and strongly underlining certain passages sacrifices by these methods the meaning of the whole and as a result the scene like a musical passage becomes trivial and empty for the connoisseur. It is difficult in our time to find actors whose passion is sincere and believable, the majority deceive us, there is little truth in their hollow empty sounds. Our honorable friend, Wolf,[26] and his wife are, however, exceptions, and as such their talent is unrivaled in Germany even though from time to time an actor appears who opposes the now prevailing worthless hollow methods which have almost completely destroyed our theaters. I do not mean to imply that actors do not try to do justice to their art, but, unfortunately, the school which promotes these inappropriate methods both in singing and acting is now in vogue, and these methods which include the expression of feelings which are not in the text cast the meaning of the whole in darkness, if I wanted to be quite harsh, the purpose of art, yes, even the art itself is destroyed by this approach."

"You are completely right," exclaimed the Kapellmeister. "However, it is unfortunately the same with my own colleagues, the composers. Every song which they write has to be through-composed, that is to say, each verse must have new music, they accentuate forcibly, pause, suddenly break off a phrase and as a result each song sounds affected and is not easily grasped by the listener, the shadows they paint to emphasize certain lines are so strong, that it is impossible to overlook these places in the text, the song comes before our eyes like patches of black without any other colors. It should be up to the singer at any rate to create a certain amount of variation in the melody or the listener who through his love of music innately feels a slight alteration in the music."

"Very true," joined in the novice, "it is because of the composer's emphasis on variation that many a gifted great musician, like the splendid Beethoven, cannot create enough new ideas, rarely does he allow the listener to enjoy one musical idea for any length of time; before we scarcely understand the first, he over-powers us with a second and a third idea and thus himself destroys his most beautiful effects. This same tendency is even pronounced in his settings of Goethe's songs, what restlessness, what sharp declamation, what darting from one idea to the next is evident in these works. I do not want to do an injustice to this splendid composer or to any other for that matter, but I have become so accustomed to Reichardt's settings of Goethe's lyrics that I cannot envision these poems, particularly the early ones, done in any other way."[27]

"If it is your opinion," the daughter of the Baron began, "that the exaggerated improper singing technique along with the excessive expression which the singer imparts to the melody casts a shadow over the song as a whole, then you would agree with me that my beloved Rossini is totally free of these faults."

"Oh divine Maestro, oh, more than divine Rossini," the old Italian cried out with much enthusiasm and with a distorted face. "He is the true one, the undisputed magician of the century who leads us poor sheep who have gone astray back again upon the right path, who totally annihilates all the improper German efforts, who creates with heavenly inexhaustible genius opera after opera, art work after art work, and who erects for himself a pyramid or mausoleum under which afterwards lie buried forever all those soulful klinkers with their excessive expression and abundance of ideas."

"Oh how true," exclaimed the enthusiast, "I have often vowed that I would listen to no other composer but Rossini. However, the great delight I experience whenever I hear his music makes me feel, because I am a German, like a traitor to my own countrymen."

"What has nationality to do with it," said the novice. "There are many Italians who could easily form their own club for the purpose of defending the music of Gluck and Mozart whom they greatly admire regardless of their nationality. But if there is such a thing as a true German opera, then we would have to give this title to Mozart's *Don Giovanni,* regardless of the fact that this opera was originally written for Italian singers. Italy has demonstrated quite clearly that it neither admires nor understands the great, profound genius of Mozart. Mozart, Gluck, Bach, Handel and Haydn are genuinely German and we would not allow this to be disputed by anyone, their music, which is truly characterized by a national character, markedly contrasts with the Italian style."

"And then," interjected the Kapellmeister, "we can give Rossini his due and admire his talent and melody if at the same time we realize his defects, such as his lack of drama which arises out of the way he writes so hastily. He composes without following any rules and for him neither dramatic continuity nor character portrayal are of any importance. Yes, I fear his style, like that of many a dramatic writer, lacks substance and training and to force him to become consistent and pay attention to content and quality would only mean prohibiting him from composing altogether."

"His quick fame," said the novice, "is probably due to the fact that genuine feeling for music is threatening to perish. However, how is one to bear the low inferior character of his melodies which results from his total lack of proper style. His vocal writing is for the most part singable, yes, truly comfortable for the modern singer, but very frequently his vocal parts, like those of many other composers, are more suitable for instruments and even if his fame continues for a long time he will eventually contribute to the total ruination of both singer and instrumentalist because he is completely indifferent to the way he treats a musical idea. The feeling for music awoke in the hearts of mankind in a beautiful manner and as time went on this feeling became stronger until it was possible for us to understand and claim Gluck as our own and watch the great figure of Mozart rise and grow to perfection before our very eyes. The thoughtful humor of Haydn's instrumental music affected every friend of music, the great works of Handel were studied again and even the dilettanti were charmed by his music, which strives to attain power and might, disdaining every petty device; we witnessed the growth of thriving institutions which were devoted to reviving old church music, the splendid works of the past great masters, it seemed that the taste for honorable and great music would be preserved forever. In the meantime, however, the masses had apparently become familiar with this music, but even though they adopted this noble art and claimed it as their own they could only comprehend it up to a certain point and thus to make it more understandable they found it necessary to change it into something less noble, but more pleasing to them. We had in Germany before only connoisseurs and superficial amateurs, but now, however, a group of dabblers rather than friends of music has come upon the scene who enjoy themselves without thinking. These presumptuous dilettanti with their loud shrieking voices have little by little supplanted the true friends of music, yes, these dabblers pass for what we could call the new enthusiasts, indeed, they often assume the appearance of self-willed, stubborn, unfeeling critics who will not acknowledge the brilliant music of our time because of their envious and ill-humoured dispositions. Rossini has therefore found the most opposition in my native city, Berlin, due to the efforts and splendid zeal of the unforgettable Fasch,[28] the founder of the Berlin *Singakademie,* which our friend, the splendid Zelter, has directed since his death and whose high standards he has continued to maintain. Through the Academy's performances of the old masterpieces and simple noble songs which are more well-known in Berlin than in other cities, the numerous members of the *Singakademie* have become spoiled by only the best music and disdain to perform any work which is ornate and base."

"You will completely fall out of favor with my daughter," said the Baron, "for she believes that it is impossible to have a performance make a lasting impression if the major concern is ostentatious display."

"She is perfectly correct," answered the novice, "but so am I if I maintain that the impression a work of art makes on a person has nothing to do with the value of the art itself. It is just this point around which so much art criticism revolves."

"Therefore, it is fortunate," answered the Baron, "that the genius of art follows a wise path, so to speak, a great composer naturally vehemently opposes any petty disorder and expresses himself with an innate eloquence which is completely lacking in others. I am speaking of Spontini[29] who cannot be praised enough. Let us hope that through his powerful efforts the feeling of the Germans will be elevated again and their addiction to ornate hollow melody will come to an end."

The novice appeared to be worked up to such a passion that he wanted to dominate the entire conversation. "Certainly," he said in a lively manner, "it would be absurd to deny this composer's distinguished talent, however, the pros and cons of his *La Vestale* could be the subject of much debate. It appears quite obvious to me that in Spontini's *Cortez* and his works to follow he went too far, through the uproar of the instruments he portrays a storm, for example, or a wild tumult through the shrieking and shouting of voices. It is difficult to decide in advance just how much the ear can take from instrumental music, even Mozart in this respect has surpassed his predecessors and many a friend of art in his time complained about his great mass of sound, and before Mozart, Handel for many years had employed an extraordinary number of instruments to express his elevated thoughts. But with Handel and Mozart this full sound was still music, their crescendos which roared forth and then evaporated, sinking downward, as it were, into stillness and calm are quite different from this incessant never ending raging of all powers which occurs without preparation, content or importance and which is confusing and more frightening to the listener and exhausts us rather than elevates and stirs our soul. If the well-known modern composer[30] tries once too often to achieve sensational effects, like many actors and dramatists, and if these effects are produced solely by a lot of noise, he may not be Rossini's neighbor, but on the other hand, he does not live that far from him and I would not exactly call them enemies. It is fortunate for us that our highly esteemed Maria von Weber warrants the most beautiful expectations from us, the excellence of his work thus far shows a great deal of promise."

Now the daughter spoke up strongly and her father supported her and tried to drive the novice into a corner because he had attacked her favorite so boldly without really being a member of the musical profession since his violin playing did not count. Amidst much laughing the gathering debated whether *Der Freischütz* was unmusical or not, particularly the scene in which the bullets were cast, some asserted that this part of the opera was the noisiest scene ever written in the annals of the theater and that the music written for it has confused all of Germany and lacks variety, a cheerful element, and also that irony, which made Mozart's impressive set-

117

ting of *Don Giovanni* so unique and lastly that in the case of Mozart one can justify his content and his method because they contrast, but in the case of Weber this contrast has been totally ignored.

The Kapellmeister took the poor novice under his wing who after that dispute did not know what to say and was not allowed to speak further: the Kapellmeister thought that to compare Mozart and Weber the way they did was unfair because when Weber wrote *Der Freischütz* he never intended his work to be placed next to Mozart's magnificent *Don Giovanni*. He furthermore asserted that even if the wolf glen scene goes beyond the limits of music, the overall excellence of the work itself, the nobility of the songs, the originality and ingeniousness, which is so superior and excellent in the best tradition of German art, more than compensates for this one scene, and it is because of these reasons he maintained that one must defend our musical violin playing novice who feels and expresses his thoughts more boldly for the very reason that he is not a member of the musical profession and hence neither tampers with the works of others like a dilettante nor looks at music like a critic. The Kapellmeister said lastly that if no one should be allowed to speak out except musicians then composers would write only for them and that artists would refuse to work only for the members of their craft and be understood and appreciated by this small minority.

"If I could only experience once more the delightful pleasure which was afforded me by Martini's *Lilla*," the novice began once again. "This idyllic, pure, clear music would truly be refreshing after so much noise in our theater. How happy I would also be if I could hear again Paisiello's *Il barbiere di Siviglia* and it grieves me deeply that this opera is not admired like a classic work for that which we regard as classic is complete for all time and no one is allowed to tamper with it. Even if in Rossini there is here and there, perhaps, a brilliant moment, by and large there is no drama in his work and the meaning of the text is lost; nothing, for example, in Rossini could compare to the humor in the role of the old man in Paisiello's opera. I fear also that our modern predilection for numerous instruments will influence the performance of these splendid musical compositions of the past, whose style of orchestration does not warrant further addition or reinforcement, a practice, however, which exists today. I have heard it murmured here and there that this was done, for instance, to Gluck's music. We have already ignored the original orchestration of Mozart's *Figaro* and doubled the number of violins and other instruments, this method of embellishing the score is all the more unsuitable when one considers that the music of this opera is characterized by a wonderful lightness and a cheerful spirit. It is as if they wanted to take flawless diamonds out of their original setting and place them in one of heavy gold in order to make them more decorative. Or to cite another analogy, it is as if two people called witty whimsical remarks to each other through a megaphone."

They finally sang some more songs and the gathering broke up. Upon departing the Baron said to the old Italian, "Goodbye!" But the old man instead of answering shook his head and pointed to heaven with his finger. The novice went home as it was quite late and he did not want to participate in the cold night in an adventure which was contrary to his beliefs. The Count and the Kapellmeister journeyed through the quiet city with the strange Italian and had the gate opened for them in order that they could proceed toward the forest where the old man who was tired of life wanted vehemently to terminate his days on earth, a decision which he had made himself.

As they stood under the dark trees the Count said, "Now old man, have you become reasonable again, and wouldn't you rather go home and go to bed?"

"I will lay myself down upon that mattress of eternity," said the Italian, "and that lovely forgetfulness, that peace, that deep, deep sleep will engulf me like the down of a feather bed. Farewell, Excellency, farewell foolish Kapellmeister, you who will not avail yourself of this beautiful opportunity to rid yourself for all time of all your misery, parts, notes, pauses, music and your singers. Now let me ponder my situation a little longer and then I will call you again; the Kapellmeister will say, 'one, two, three' and with the word, 'three,' pronounced clearly, slowly, loudly and with solemnity, so that the dear echo will benefit from it and take part in my departure, I will shoot myself in the head."

"Certainly you don't want to die in such poor taste like the theater puppet, Hanswurst?"[31]

"So it must be," said the old Italian and laid himself down in a sand trench. The Count and the Kapellmeister walked further into the forest, the night was still, no wind stirred, a soft gentle breeze blew the branches so that the needles of the firs whispered in soft tones, the murmuring continued and then died away like a distant organ as the forest rustled with life.

"The hour is quite solemn," said the Kapellmeister. "A strange feeling has come over me the entire evening," the Count replied in hushed tones, "perhaps, it is I who am closer to death than the old crazy Italian, for never have I felt the emptiness of my existence more, it is as if there is nothing left in the world to fascinate me. I also now believe that the heavenly creature whom I have sought in vain for so long is dead."

"Quiet," exclaimed the Kapellmeister, "don't you hear music?"

"Perhaps, the distant bells."

"No," said the Kapellmeister walking, "I hear it clearly and now I remember the idiotic old man who lived not far from here and from whose house there issued forth the most splendid discant early in the morning at five o'clock upon my arrival."

The Count was deeply moved. "Now come, come," screamed the Italian, "my assassination is supposed to begin now!"

"Shoot or hang yourself," the Count called back to him, "we have something better to do than to listen to your jokes."

They walked further on with the curious Italian following after them. The song could now be heard more distinctly and the Count scratched his face and hands while trying to get out of the thicket in which he had entangled himself deeper and deeper because of his eagerness. Finally he forced his way out of the thicket and found himself standing near the little house whose small windows were lit up. They heard the beautiful Psalm of Marcello, "Qual anelante cervo,"[32] which issued forth from the house with such fullness, such purity, simplicity and nobility that the Kapellmeister was so astonished and overcome that he could scarcely breathe. "It is she! It is she! My only one!" the Count cried out with the most violent emotion and he wanted to come closer to the house but the Kapellmeister held him back firmly, pressed himself to him and then threw himself down upon the Count's feet, which he embraced, and exclaimed, "O most excellent, most fortunate Count! Marry her as you have vowed, but before your marriage grant me that one happiness which I so desire, let her sing the part of the beloved in my ruined opera; then I will gladly die for such a voice appears only once in a lifetime."

The Count struggled to go nearer the house and the Kapellmeister finally had to let go of his impatient leg. As soon as he rushed toward the dwelling and knocked on the small door, the singing stopped.

"Don't make such a fuss," said the old Italian, "whoever is singing is not worth the trouble, it is apparent that you have never heard my wife."

The Kapellmeister, who was now just as beside himself as the Count, knocked on the door with the same enthusiasm as his rival, and as they both competed with each other to see who could knock more powerfully the tempo of their knocking became faster and faster producing in the stillness of the night a most peculiar concert. No sound now could be heard inside the house, but finally the inhabitants lost their patience for a window opened and a soft, hoarse voice said, "What is going on down there? Are you drunk?"

"Let us in," cried the Count.

"We must go in!" screamed the Kapellmeister.

"Where is the singer?" exclaimed the Count.

"I heard her once before the other day early in the morning," said the Kapellmeister, "when you shouted at me, 'it is the devil's grandmother!' "

"But we must be allowed to come in," the Count and the Kapellmeister cried out together.

"Are you mad?" exclaimed the excited voice of the old man and at this exact moment the Italian shouted louder than all of them, "Hortensio! Hortensio! Have we finally caught you? Now I have a reason to live. May he who feels like it kill himself. I do not intend to lose you again, you old hide!"

"I am Count Alten," cried the admirer. "I am the Kapellmeister," exclaimed the companion. "We only want to come in and meet the singer!" "Come down!" said the Italian, "and let us renew our acquaintance."

"Heavens!" moaned the old man, "so late at night? My good gentlemen, if you want something of me, come tomorrow when it is daylight."

"Good," said the Count more calmly, "early in the morning!" The Kapellmeister was also agreeable and as they went away, their peace of mind restored, the Italian said, "I will spend the night here out-of-doors and watch over him. Early in the morning we will all make our visit."

How astonished and alarmed the Count and the Kapellmeister were on the following day when they found the house deserted and empty; an old woman servant said that before daybreak the inhabitants of the house had left and had their belongings removed in the greatest haste. Also the old Italian was nowhere to be found.

A beautiful warm autumn day had dawned, the sun appeared still warm in this late time of year as if it were summer, and this influenced the novice to journey with his daughter into the neighboring mountain valley. Upon their small hired horses they also saw the enthusiast with his clothes fluttering in the wind rushing towards the same region. "Heaven forbid," the novice remarked to his daughter, "that the chatterer is going to visit the valley at the same time we are, if he does he will ruin the day for us with his violent speeches and descriptions."

"We had better be prepared for it," replied the daughter, "for he recently told me how much he likes to visit this valley."

"These people are so bothersome," continued the novice, "who go into rapture over everything even though they feel nothing at all. But they disturb me more in a natural setting than when discussing art because when I am with nature I only want to think quietly, to experience a lovely dream in which enthusiasm and comfort taking turns float by me and immerse my spirit in a contemplative peace in which inertness and creative activity become one and the same; I also feel a touch of overwhelming melancholy mingling with this joy which makes me unable to bear these descriptive babblers when I am observing a landscape."

"They disturb me as much as certain kinds of music," answered the girl, "such as dance music or screeching arias which one often hears near buildings."

When they arrived, the excited enthusiast rushed out of the lodge towards them. "Oh how beautiful," he exclaimed, "that you also took advantage of this splendid day which is probably the last pleasant weather of the season. Let us go immediately to the murmuring brook and then look down from the mountain heights to the valley below. It is a joy to see and feel the vibrations of the hills, the small river, the splendid greenness and the sunlight. Is there any rapture which can come close to or equal that caused by such a vista?"

"I will go with you," replied the novice, "but only on one condition, that you spare me from your descriptions and emotional speeches. How can you show so much enthusiasm? As you yourself recently admitted it is not possible to feel so much."

"With art," replied the enthusiast, "one certainly does one's utmost here and there to please the artist, but in the case of nature—never! It is impossible to express with words the feelings which nature arouses in our souls. I have noted for a long time that you are not a friend of nature, otherwise how could you, as I have often seen you do, creep into the damp theater during the most beautiful spring weather to hear an opera or see a mediocre play which you later criticize."

"Because," answered the novice, "it so happens that on a certain day it is important for me to see a play and I cannot and do not want to combine going to the theater with enjoying nature. Also I must confess that many times I have found myself amidst a beautiful natural setting without truly appreciating it with the trained eye of a hunter if my thoughts are occupied by a cheerful conversation or I find my mind wanders during a lonely walk or if a book happens to capture my attention. Just believe me that when the romantic environment shimmers and plays through your soul instinctively it is all the more enjoyable. If we have to account for ourselves for everything we do then our life would be nothing more than a miserable collecting of facts and the most delicate and spiritual pleasure would vanish."

"Hm! you may be right," said the enthusiast, thoughtfully, "if I had not adopted the mask of the enthusiast and if all my friends had not considered me a zealot, I would try to break the habit. But it is just as bad to pass for a phlegmatic person like you do. But since you do not want to hear anything about the rapture of nature, I will tell you instead about a wonderful scene I witnessed just before you arrived. A young, wondrously beautiful girl stood there on top of the hill looking continuously toward the path which leads toward the city and then began to cry violently. She aroused all my sympathy, I went up to her, but no matter how I tried to force myself on her she would not give me a rational answer regarding her situation. I was uncommonly curious particularly because I had seen this extraordinary charming girl recently at the Baron's home at which time the perplexed melancholy Count devoted his entire attention to her. Look, she is climbing up the hill again to continue her watch."

The form floated up the green knoll with elegance and grace and her full brown locks, her shining eyes, the simplicity of her dress and her bearing had an indescribable effect upon the landscape. The daughter herself felt deeply moved when she saw the beautiful creature crying again, the tears welled up in her own eyes when the mysterious girl wrung her hands with an expression of great pain and then sat down upon the grass miserably.

"Let us climb up to her," said the novice, "the poor creature needs our comfort and support. My daughter should be the one to talk to her; you and I, Herr Kellermann, in the meantime, must remain behind and not alarm the distressed girl in the least with pressing impertinent questions." The daughter climbed up the knoll to her and the mysterious girl confessed that she was waiting for her old father to arrive from the city, but she could not understand why he tarried so long as he had told her to meet him here before they continued their journey further.

"I do not understand why you want to leave our district so soon when you have just recently arrived, from what I hear," the novice said to the girl.

"Oh, gentlemen," answered the beautiful stranger moaning, "my dear father has suffered for a long time from a deep melancholy, from misanthropy and profound world-weariness, for several years he has moved from place to place, becoming more and more impoverished, sicker and sicker, refusing all help, not even allowing me the happiness of helping him, for if it were not for his stubbornness I could assist him with my talent. For me singing and music are the miseries of my life."

"So you do sing after all?" the novice asked in a very lively manner.

"My sorrow, my deep pain," replied the beautiful girl, "is caused because I have broken my vow. I have had to promise my father never to admit that I can sing, also never to sing unless he has given me permission to do so. Therefore, we lived far from the city and avoided all social gatherings, only recently I happened accidentally to be at the home of Baron Fernow where a stranger, a fine proper man, frightened me unduly by constantly asking me if I could sing. Last night when I was practicing a Psalm by Marcello, believing there was no one nearby, a tumult arose in front of the house, my father and I thought the people were robbers or drunkards, the Count finally told us who he was and wanted to come in, a few other people also raved equally loud and my father could only calm them by promising them they could visit us in the morning.

Scarcely had they gone when all our belongings were packed in the greatest haste, a carriage was hired to carry our few possessions here during the night, in the morning I was to travel to this valley and in a few hours, after he fetched our passports, my father promised to meet me here. I have waited for him many hours, certainly he is ill or some misfortune has befallen him and in my anxiety I do not know to whom I can turn for advice or help. Where should I look for him?"

The novice tried to calm her. He suggested they all wait for the old man in the guest house until after dinner, then if he does not arrive, she should go back with him and his daughter to the city for since there is only one path which leads there they should surely meet her father. If, however, this were not the case, then she should stay in his house while he himself would make inquiries. Due to the authoritative manner of the novice and the coaxing caresses of his daughter she became calmer and went with them into the inn. They were even in a good mood during dinner, however, the girl refused the inappropriate request of the enthusiast to sing something for them, because this would be against her sacred vow. Then they discussed the new music which the Kapellmeister had tried to perform in the home of the Baron. She greatly praised the music, but reproached the style of the singers. "I could be totally wrong in this respect," she concluded her criticism, "but according to the principles of my father and his method of singing, which I must practice according to his instructions, this style is just as questionable as it is petty. Yes, if I could just once (but my father would in no way give his consent) sing a role in an opera like that of the Kapellmeister I flatter myself that I would produce a great effect and, perhaps, greater than anyone would expect because my singing style is totally forgotten and its novelty would be all the more striking."

"If you are the one I think you are," replied the novice, "you could, if your disposition were inclined toward it, make a certain enthusiastic person indescribably happy."

The beautiful girl blushed and the enthusiast, Kellermann, as soon as he heard the word, enthusiastic, jumped up from his chair and cried out, "Yes, certainly, adored one! How will my heart be able to stand the magnitude of this joy!"

"Don't trouble yourself for nothing," replied the novice laughing loudly. "I was referring to that unique Count, whom we all know. I hope I can be allowed to predict a happy ending."

The girl did not want to participate in this intimate discussion, but after a pause in the conversation, she praised the young Count as a handsome, sensible man, who, of all the people in the Baron's home that night, had most attracted her attention.

During the journey back they amused themselves with cheerful conversations. The enthusiast who was anxious to show off his horsemanship galloped ahead. When they arrived in the city they saw a great crowd of people in the main street pushing and shouting, the carriage had to stop, a guard cleared the way and the novice was astonished when he noticed the old Italian being led away like a prisoner by the soldiers. "What is going on?" he asked a passer-by. "Well, the brown scoundrel has killed an old man," the spectator answered.

When the crowd had dispersed they were able to continue on down the street, the Count rushed toward them from out of a large house and with an expression of the utmost rapture he helped Julie out of the vehicle. The novice and his daughter followed them hoping to find out what had happened.

In the hall Julie found the old man sitting in an easy chair, pale and shaken, but well and unharmed. They learned that he had been detained by the police while trying to get their passports. When he finally finished his business and was looking for a carriage he met the foolish Italian who immediately attacked him violently in the open street. When he cried for help some passers-by came to his aid, seized the Italian and handed him over to the guard. Julie hugged the old man and tried to calm him with her tenderness. The enthusiast and the Kapellmeister also stood by watching this scene.

"Many thanks," the old man finally said, "I am indebted to you for all your kindness to me, but now we must depart in order to reach our new destination as soon as possible."

He stood up and wanted to leave, Julie remained hesitating and looked embarrassed at those present, the Count, however, walked towards the old man and said with a shaking voice, "Would you want to snatch away from me the happiness of my life for which I have so longed and pursued just as I found it so unexpectedly and so miraculously?"

"What do you mean?" asked the old man.

"I would be profoundly happy," answered the Count, "if your daughter would give me her hand in marriage. I am rich, totally independent, give us your permission to enjoy love, friendship and music as much as it is possible on this earth." The old man, startled, staggered back and had to sit down because he was trembling so much. "Are you serious, Count?" he cried out between violent sobs.

"I promise to prove all this to you and all these friends are my witnesses, but what are Julie's feelings?"

"Now my daughter," said the old man moved, "could you make your father so happy? It is in your power to make amends for all the grief of my life and to make my last days happy ones. Are you sure that it is not a dream? How can it all be possible? Can you decide, my child?"

The daughter was deeply moved. "Heaven!" cried the Count, "I would rather renounce all my hopes than have you force yourself to marry me."

"How could you so misunderstand me?" Julie asked, scarcely audible, "could you not feel how much I was drawn to you? Since the first time we met I have never been able to forget you. But such happiness seemed to me to be so far away that I felt it was an insane dream."

The Count kneeled down before her, the old man, moved, laid their hands in one another and then Julie sank upon the breast of her beloved.

"But now," exclaimed the Count jumping up, "I know that you

are indeed the singer for whom I have searched so long, but in order to completely convince myself that I have found you, sing just one tone for me, one beat."

Julie looked at her father in a questioning manner, but the old man said smiling, "I release you completely from the vow you made me, you have my permission to please your bridegroom."

Then she sang without accompaniment the beginning of Palestrina's *Stabat Mater*, [33] her voice was so strong and full, her tones, increasingly in volume, so controlled and charming that no one could find the words to express his rapture, particularly the Count and the Kapellmeister.

"Yes," said the father when she had finished, "it is the pride of my life to have formed this voice, and I can say without any fatherly delusions that her talent is unique, and now no one will ever hear this performance again."

"What is it that caused you never to allow your daughter to sing in public and to make her deny that she has such talent?" the novice asked.

"Oh, gentlemen," said the old man, "if you knew my story, my years of long misery, how I have been misunderstood and mistreated, you would understand all that I have done. From my earliest youth music was everything that I wanted, but my parents were too poor to obtain a proper musical education for me. I made a meagre living singing in the choir and later by giving lessons. I had to teach myself everything with the greatest difficulty. After I had studied counterpoint and the other skills necessary to compose I believed that I was ready to embark upon the task of writing church music, I thought my compositions were well done, but I found no encouragement, no support, no one showed any interest in me, I lacked refinement and gracious manners. My inclination was to travel to Italy, but the feeble eyes of my parents looked at me so beseechingly that I could not find it in my heart to abandon them. Thus once again I had to give lessons of all kinds in order to earn a small living and the agony of having to teach the violin to a pupil who has no feeling for music, no talent, and to hear the same wrong

notes over and over again is indescribable. Only such a music
teacher experiences what stupid beings there are in the world.
Then I was asked to teach a young man who had supposedly studied
the violin for six years. Oh, I thought at the time, this will be a
consolation, I can teach musically and, perhaps, train a fine musician. He had already studied sonatas, quartets, symphonies and the
most difficult works. And think when I asked him to play something for me, this virtuoso could not even tune his own violin, he
knew nothing about tone production, had no rhythm and was surprised in his innocence to learn that everything in music is related
and is a science. How this strange being who was almost a grown
man rattled together his Pleyel[34] you cannot imagine, every note
was wrong, he played without feeling and cohesiveness, shrieking
and squeaking, all the while making the most unbelievable faces.
Think I had to make him begin all over again with a chorale and
after six or seven years with another teacher, he could not even
perform that."

During this tale the others had looked smilingly at the novice
who cried out, "Is it possible, that I have found again so unexpectedly my esteemed music teacher? Yes, old gentleman, at that time
we both made life miserable for each other."

"Are you that young man whom I taught so many years ago?"
asked the old man in embarrassment, "please forgive me a thousand times, but the whole episode made such a strange impression
on me that I could never forget it. At any rate this is how my youth
passed. My parents died, but during these years I had become old.
Little by little my music began to be performed in small places.
Also here and there a theater attempted to perform my operas, but
never with any success. I met the woman who was to become my
wife, she was a splendid singer and after our marriage I felt that I
needed nothing more from the world. But after the birth of our
daughter, her voice became weaker. Oh, to lose a beautiful voice is
worse than the death of a close friend. But my wife could not accept
her fate, every time she forced herself to sing her voice became
weaker and weaker and utterly exhausted by her violent efforts to

sing she finally sang herself to death. Now my whole heaven was my daughter. The theater which I had directed gave me a small pension which spared me from the most extreme poverty. From this time on I immersed myself more and more in the great church music of the old masters. The present appeared increasingly wretched, all the current styles and techniques were hateful to me. But the most disgusting to me was the new method of singing which was becoming more and more in vogue. A tone if it is correctly produced must rise up like the sun, clear, majestic, becoming brighter and brighter, the listener must feel in it the infinitude of music, yes, the singer must not give the impression that he cannot sustain the tone to the end. Music, correctly executed, moves gently like the sky and looks down upon us from the pure atmosphere and draws our heart heavenward. And what I want to hear purely and simply in a musical sound is the rapture. Flowing out of every musical tone is a tragic and divine enthusiasm which redeems every listener from the limitations of earthly existence. If the female singer is capable of this vision the soul of the composer as well as the meaning of art itself will permeate her entire being so that she herself becomes both creator and poet, and woe to the poor Kapellmeister who wants her to rigidly adhere to the beat and the tempo, for she is the chosen one and like a soaring angel who rises out of the dark pit of human existence and in shining glory flies upward triumphantly to immortality she likewise may transgress the usual and necessary limitations imposed upon her by the printed music."

"That is just what I have recently tried to express," said the novice.

"Most artists," continued the old man, "are only at most intoxicated by their own virtuosity, rarely do we find one who attempts to understand the composer let alone go beyond him. In the latter case by putting into the music what is not there, the composer is glorified and in the first case he is destroyed by virtuosity, but the rapture which results either way is not without some value, because even if the song is performed in a vain manner it will be soulful because the singer is human. My daughter grew up and became all that I had desired. She understood everything I taught her, she developed a voice the like of which I had never heard before. And because of my unshakable faith in her talent I wrote to a great court about her and subsequently she was given the post of chamber singer. Now I thought my days of anguish and poverty were over. The elegant world assembled at the court and she sang a composition by one of the older masters in such a way that tears came to my eyes; my daughter is a proud girl and she was alarmed by the environment of the court, when she finished there was no applause, not one word, no look of approval. The old Kapellmeister came up to me and whispered that it was the opinion of the Prince and the women at court as well as his own that my daughter lacked polish and should seek further instruction from a good singer."

"That is precisely it," the Count exclaimed, "they want polish, method, as they call it, instead of singing. Yes, Julie, that was the time when I stood behind you enraptured by the sound of your voice and could not see your face. Method! The situation is similar to the time when Solimena or Trevisani[35] criticized Raphael because he lacked technique."

"Believe me, father," Julie said, "I can sing better than I did that evening. Yes, in front of friends who understand us and think kindly of our way of thinking, my voice becomes more powerful, my confidence unending. But instinctively I felt a certain fear that night before I sang and I wondered if I should perform for people who know nothing about music. When I sing before friends, the song becomes gold as if it were melted by the heat of their love, but in front of others my courage and my voice fail me and in spite of all my efforts my tone becomes miserable. On this frightening evening I did not look around at the audience, but yet the eyes of the bored court women and the surprised glances of the curious gentlemen made my songs stick in my throat."

"The misfortune of that nonsensical evening made my head spin," the old man began again. "Without notifying anyone, I left the court with my daughter that same cold night. I made her promise never to sing for anyone but me. Even if she found herself amongst people who screeched and twittered enthusiastically around her she had to deny that she knew anything about music. We lived alone and rarely saw other people. I became more and more misanthropic and if it were not for the comfort of my daughter would have died long ago or become insane. And yet there were times when I felt I was losing my mind. I repeatedly changed our place of residence until at last I came to this valley to live alone with nature and near the dark fir trees where my daughter and I could perform our music undisturbed. Recently the Count and the Kapellmeister found me here and wanted to storm my house in the night, their actions, I confess, were totally misunderstood by me for indeed as it turns out their visit resulted in the most unexpected happiness."

The group of friends decided to announce the engagement that night and to invite the Baron and his family to the celebration.

"But wait," cried the Kapellmeister, "Count, you promised me that your beautiful Julie would sing the leading role in my opera before your marriage!"

"So it shall be," said the Count, "if my Julie is agreeable."

They all could tell just by looking at her how much joy it would give her to be able to display her great talent in a brilliant manner.

Before the Count went into the theater, he took the old Italian aside and said to him, "Recently, old fool, you almost caused a terrible disaster, go home now to your native land, I have made preparations for your journey, live there quietly and you will continue to receive your pension from me which will allow you to spend the rest of your life peacefully and undisturbed."

"Excellency," answered the confused old man, "you are generosity itself, on my knees I beg your forgiveness for wanting to thrash your father-in-law, the wicked Hortensio who is the ruination of all music. For a long time I watched his house during the night, but he slipped away from me because I could not keep myself from falling asleep due to my great exhaustion and anger. I searched everywhere for him in all the villages and as I returned weary and exhausted to the city I suddenly saw him running across the street. Count, the desire to attack him was so overpowering that I could not stop myself even if he had been my own father."

The leading role in the Kapellmeister's opera was made just for her and when Julie sang her part her tones were so full, so confident, that the entire audience was enthusiastic. A few friends of the stubborn prima donna whom the Kapellmeister had dismissed wanted to voice their displeasure, but were quickly put to shame. When the great aria was sung there arose such a loud shout of applause, such a rejoicing and a clamour that the opera had to stop. When the audience became calmer one heard a loud excited voice from the first floor shouting, "Worthless! Nothing! Miserable bungling, no technique, only the crazy German soul method of the deranged Hortensio!" It was the old Italian, who once again expressed his opinion, but was requested to leave the theater.

Never had an opera in this city brought such happiness, the Kapellmeister was in rapture, the father, happy, the Count in ecstasy, the novice transplanted back to his youth and the enthusiast without a thing to say which pleased the rest.

Soon thereafter the wedding of the happy pair took place. Then the Count moved to his large estate where in his great salon the music of the past along with the compositions of Hortensio and operas by other composers were performed and the friends who were not present heard through letters about the undiminished joy of these three persons united in such a wondrous manner.

NOTES

1. Tieck uses the term "Kapellmeister" (master of the chapel), in the manner in which it was applied to Baroque and early classic composers in Germany. J. S. Bach, for example, served as Kapellmeister to Prince Ernst of Cöthen.

Like Bach, Tieck's Kapellmeister is a music director, teacher, composer and conductor.

2. Cerberus, the three-headed howling dog who guards the gates of Hades.

3. Notice the similarity of this sentence to the following one by Novalis: "Is it not true that woods and stones are obedient to music and under the spell of music serve man's will like house pets?" (Novalis, *Die Lehrlinge zu Sais. Die Deutschen Romantiker,* Gerhard Stenzel, ed., 2 vols., Stuttgart: Das Bergland-Buch, II, 117).

4. Arioso, a type of vocal composition found in opera and other composite vocal forms in which the words are sung in a style which is both lyrical and declamatory, i.e., halfway between an aria and a recitative; cavatina, a song which is simpler and less elaborate than an aria; finale, concluding section of an act of an opera; adagio, slow; presto, fast.

5. *Bloom Lovely Violet,* a song by Johann Abraham Schulz (1747-1800), based on the poem, "The Boy to a Violet" (1788) by Christian Adolf Overbeck, ED., see facsimile, p. 91.

6. *Here Slumber My Children,* a song by Otto Karl Erdmann Freiherr von Kospoth (d. 1817), based on a poem by Gottlob Wilhelm Burmann (1737-1805), ED.

7. The old name for a grate or strong horizontal bar with long fork-like fingers which was used in early times to close or block off the entrance to a castle.

8. Tieck is referring here to the tremolo, a special effect calling for the bow to move back and forth over the string as fast as possible producing a rapid reiteration of a single note.

9. Passaggio, a flourish or bravura ornament usually employed in vocal music and which is usually improvised.

10. Brocken, a peak in the Harz Mountains upon which witches were supposed to gather on the eve of May Day (April 30).

11. Glass harmonica, see Introduction, p.71, n. 17.

12. Johann Adolpf Hasse (1699-1783), German tenor and composer of operas in the Italian style. Tieck must have been thinking of Hasse when he mentioned the glass harmonica for the composer wrote a well-known composition for voice and this instrument (a setting of a poem by Metatasio) for Marianne Davis, widely acclaimed glass harmonica performer.

13. Nestor, according to legend a wise old man who fought with the Greeks at Troy; Phidias, Praxiteles, Greek sculptors of the 4th and 5th c. B.C.

14. Tieck's discussion of the problem of suicide in the Romantic era is quite timely. When the old Italian says that by taking his own life he will hasten his entry into the afterworld, he is restating the German Romantic justification for suicide as a means of swifter union with God and the beyond, death viewed as a beginning, not an end.

15. Mozart's *Don Juan (Don Giovanni),* composed 1787, première October 29, 1787, Prague National Theater; first Vienna performance, May, 1788; first Berlin production, December, 1790. The greatness of *Don Giovanni* was only

recognized in the early Romantic era. During Mozart's lifetime the opera was thrust into the background by such works as Dittersdorf's *Doktor und Apotheker* (see Arnim's *On Folksongs,* n. 19). In 1788 Dittersdorf's opera was performed twenty-five times in five months, in contrast *Don Giovanni* barely lasted through fifteen performances in Vienna during the same year.

16. The "esteemed musician" is Johann Friedrich Reichardt who originally had a strong aversion to Mozart's music, ED.

17. *Belmont,* i.e., *The Abduction from the Seraglio,* text adopted from an earlier opera, *Belmont and Constanze* by Johann André.

18. Giovanni Paisiello (1740-1816), opera composer best known for his *Il barbiere di Siviglia (The Barber of Seville,* 1782).

19. Vincent Martin y Soler (1754-1806), Spanish composer often referred to by the Italian name, Martini, known particularly for his popular opera, *Una cosa rara* (i.e., *Lilla).*

20. Domenico Cimarosa (1749-1801), opera composer known for his comic operas, the most famous being *The Secret Marriage* (see Introduction, p. 8).

21. The following is a tribute to the Finckenstein family, ED.

22. Feo, Allegri, Bai, Italian Baroque church composers whose music was revived by the Caecilian Movement. Many of the musical compositions mentioned in this paragraph were heard by Tieck during his journey to Rome in 1805. Correggio is one of Tieck's favorite artists and is mentioned in the poet's novella, *Die Gemälde (Paintings).*

23. The poems to which Tieck is referring are discussed in the Introduction, pp. 23-25.

24. Tieck is restating Wackenroder's views on church music, see this author's article, "Wackenroder's Musical Essays in *Phantasien über die Kunst," Journal of Aesthetics and Art Criticism,* Spring, 1972.

25. The singer whom we met at the beginning of the story now suddenly appears at the Baron's home. What has happened to him during the interim is not clear. In order to identify who this singer is I had added the words, "a friend of the Kapellmeister," hoping that the reader will recall the young tenor who also heard the strange voice in the forest as the story opens.

26. Pius Alexander Wolf (1781-1832), dramatist, actor, member of Goethe's circle in Weimar and librettist of Weber's opera, *Preciosa.* Tieck was a close friend of Wolf, ED.

27. Reichardt, the brother-in-law of Tieck's wife, set nearly sixty poems of Goethe to music.

28. Karl Friedrich Christian Fasch (1763-1800) founded the Berlin *Singakademie* in 1790, his successor was Zelter, ED.

29. Gasparo Spontini (1774-1851) was appointed director of music to the Prussian court in Berlin in 1820, a post he retained until the death of Friedrich Wilhelm III in 1841. See Introduction, pp. 47-48.

30. The "well-known modern composer" is Karl Maria von Weber (1786-1826), considered the founder of German Romantic opera. Weber was appointed

director of opera in Dresden in 1816. The immense popularity of *Der Frei-schütz* was brilliantly satirized by Heine in his *Briefe aus Berlin* (*Letters from Berlin,* i.e., the second letter, March, 1822) in which he wrote that "even the dogs in the street were barking the melody of the opera's 'Bridal Wreath Chorus'" (Heine, *Werke,* II, 22).

31. Hanswurst, see Börne's essay on Mozart's Magic Flute, n. 39.

32. Benedetto Marcello (1686-1739), Italian composer. Tieck is referring here to his setting of Psalm 42: "As a doe longs for running streams, so longs my soul for you, my God."

33. Palestrina's famous eight-part setting of the *Stabat Mater* is of course a cappella. In Tieck's day it was not unusual, however, to add an accompaniment to this Motet, hence the sentence, "Julie sang without accompaniment, etc."

34. Ignaz Joseph Pleyel (1757-1831), Austrian composer, violinist, piano maker, pupil of Haydn, ED. A composer of primarily instrumental music, Pleyel wrote a vast number of duets, trios, quartets, etc., for strings.

35. Francesco Solimena (1657-1747), Francesco Trevisani (1656-1764), two late Baroque Italian painters whose works Tieck saw in the Dresden Gallery, ED.

Ludwig Börne
[1786-1837]

HENRIETTE SONTAG IN FRANKFURT [1827]

SINCE THE LOVELY MUSE of song, Henriette Sontag, appeared a year ago in Weimar and the pious German star-priests there honored this constellation of two great persons[1] in a strange manner, amidst the sounds of zither and cymbals and an atmosphere of semi-darkness, scented hyacinths and Moorish-Spanish customs, and these star-priests have sung: "The King of poets has nourished this wonder-child with food and drink," instead of simply saying: "Fraulein Sontag has dined this evening with Goethe"—since that time I have become quite enraged about foolish people who switch sides overnight and who, accustomed as they were to only cooking their potatoes near the flame of Prometheus and hiding their moderate ability for enjoying life amidst the hard bitter peelings,[2] suddenly swallowed fire and became sweet and started to wobble, wiggle and ogle like jelly.[3] I had in mind the most annoying things which I wanted to print, but it was to my advantage that I reflected about my thoughts and did not write them down. How they would have ridiculed the stubborn Rhadamanthus,[4] who in the end became the champion of a beautiful maiden and defended her. Truly since I heard and saw the sorceress she has bewitched me like the

138

others and I no longer know what I am saying. Only in the twi-light, as in dreams, do I remember that during that time I thought my soul was being reincarnated: I also thought then that it does not seem right that we Germans, who are so difficult to inspire, only start drinking after others have become intoxicated and are suffer-ing from headaches, and that by the same token we, with our young innocent hearts, are captivated by the first enticing female we see, regardless of the fact that a beautiful woman is not exempt from aging nor committed to being charitable because she is plea-sant. But now I think differently and say: it is beautiful to enjoy the moment, why save for our grandchildren. Who knows how long it will be until we are allowed once again to proclaim our admiration with a loud voice, to pay homage to a deity whom we selected ourselves, who was not pushed upon us. Now I would like to praise this sorceress who has transformed a nation, but where can I find the words? Even the enormous mass of words put on paper here in Frankfurt since we lost our heads over her is exhausted. If one could offer a prize of one hundred ducats for the invention of a new adjec-tive which has not been used for Henriette Sontag, no one would win the prize. They have called her: the nameless one, the heavenly one, the highly praised one, the unrivaled one, the most celebrated one, the divine maiden, the delicate pearl, the maidenly singer, dear Henriette, lovely maid, charming maiden, the heroine of song, the favorite of the gods, the treasure of singing, German maiden, the pearl of German opera. I say to all of these adjectives, yes, from the bottom of my heart. Even sober critics have expressed the following opinion about her: even if her charming appearance, her acting ability and her singing could be appraised individually, there is no one singer who possesses and unifies these gifts of art and nature, only she is capable of this. I agree with this opinion, al-though I admit the rarity of this combination of talents could not prejudice me; no matter how much I tried I could not see or hear all of these talents at one time and I had to add up each of her singular merits in order to arrive at a picture of her total worth. This I have to take into consideration: whatever could cause such excitement every day of the week in a German city without being ordered by the police or by the calendar must be worthy, must be something beautiful. As a way of praising our singer I want to speak about the tumult she caused here, for it can be said that although such a universal intoxication does not praise the drinker, it does praise the wine.

Henriette Sontag could say like Caesar, with a small change: I came, they saw, I conquered. Her battle was only a game, she had won before she had arrived here. The first honor bestowed upon her by the awed Frankfurters, an honor that was also the most important because it demonstrated that she represented the very best German taste and culture, was presented to her by the local *Fremdenblättchen*[5] which saluted her with the words: "Fraulein Sontag, Royal Prussian Chamber Singer with Attendants and Servants." That is to say our daily *Fremdenblättchen* described the worth and dignity of the travellers in a highly witty, proper and legal manner. If a stranger is rich, then he has one attendant; if he is very rich he has attendants; if, at the same time, he is rich and a person of noble rank, he has servants; and if he is very distinguished he has a retinue and attendants. Instead of the word, retinue, one, incidentally, sometimes uses the word, suite; however, even the teachers of feudal law in Frankfurt cannot agree as to the exact distinction between these two rather delicate feudal terms. People of nobility it is assumed travel with an esteemed retinue and servants. Thus while they acknowledged the attendants and servants of Fraulein Sontag they led her to the steps of the throne and if they had given her any further honors, it would have caused a rebellion. As we have spoken of the first honor given her, it might be well to mention the last, namely, that when she departed the landlord of the inn, in which Fraulein Sontag spent fourteen days, refused to let her pay for her accommodations. And through this act he ennobled and rejuvenated the old inn, *Romanischen Kaiser,* and turned it into a Prytaneum[6] in which famous Germans are entertained in the name of the fatherland. The news of the battle of Navario and the war-like defiance of the Infidel had reached here shortly before she arrived and yet the singer still captured the attention of the public and did so even though the smallest bit of discord between the powers caused an immediate heated reaction among the Frankfurt government officials.[7] It was wonderful to hear the sweet tones of the nightingale piercing through the wild Turkish music. The Sultan and Sontag, Codrington and Othello, the Divan and the Barber, everything merged together.[8] Even the Jews became slightly dizzy and if one heard them speaking about the eighth and the quarter at the stock-exchange, one did not know whether they meant percentages or musical notes. The entrance prices to the theater were doubled and that says a great deal because we Frank-furters who are so wealthy cannot tolerate any unusual expense. The spectators come in great flocks and not only from Frankfurt and nearby cities, but strangers came from distant locations such as Cologne and Hanover. It was like the Olympics. An Englishman who could not obtain a private box wanted to rent the entire first floor for himself and when he was told that this was out of the question he became quite surprised by our strange continental prudishness. A young man journeyed from Wiesbaden on foot, arrived here as the theater was opening, elbowed his way in and obtained a seat, which he, however, very generously relinquished to a weak lady. He stood up, but then fainted before the perfor-mance began and because there was no room for him to fall, he was shoved upright and passed lifeless from hand to hand towards the door and out to the street, whereupon he recovered himself just as the curtain had fallen and went back to Wiesbaden that same night. One local resident was so exhausted because of the lack of room and the stuffiness of the theater that he had to go home and that same evening died. People also talked about certain illnesses and injuries which occurred that night and about some persons who had to stay in bed for several days. In those days the *Intelligenz-Blatt*[9] was filled with advertisements for lost necklaces, rings, armbands, clocks, veils and other things which women can lose in the crowd. When I came to the optician's shop on the day of Son-tag's first appearance to fetch my opera glasses which I had left to be repaired, the proprietor had to search for them among fifty other pairs which had been left there for the same reason. It was a universal eye-mobilization of every person in Frankfurt who was capable of bearing arms and the many hundred pairs of opera glasses shimmering in the splendor of the new chandeliers which were all directed at this weak young lady presented a frightful appearance. But never had an artillery been employed more poorly, for the enemy was not hurt at all, only the incompetent artillery members suffered injuries.

The theater was opened two hours earlier than was customary and a long time before that the great square was already covered with people. Half of the crowd had come to push their way into the opera house, the other half to watch the battle from behind the front lines. A local theater critic had described the crowd quite aptly with these words: "One would have believed that a pair of golden boots would be given to the first person who got his foot in the door." Now one should not think that to take the local theater by storm is a simple feat or merely an enjoyable fight. The theater is not at all constructed to facilitate entering, on the contrary, it is quite difficult to get in, it is built like a fortress, Vauban[10] would not have to be ashamed of this edifice. A narrow, steep staircase of approximately twelve steps leads directly upwards from the street to the theater, this staircase is divided by the narrow entrance into two halves, without a landing either in front or behind the door. This little door opens to the outside in a dramatic fashion, like a *coup de théâtre,* suddenly it is pushed open, quickly and unexpectedly, so that the crowd standing on the staircase can be easily thrown down the stairs. If one wonders why the Frankfurters during these times did not break their necks, it is due to their splendid gymnastic training and in particular to the practice they gained since childhood of storming this dangerous staircase. If a person is able to pass by the first door and climbs up the second half of the staircase he will eventually reach another half-opened door. However, behind this door stands a giant with broad chest and outstretched arms restraining the anxious theater-goers. Whoever is rather small can slip through under the arms of this giant, but larger persons must wait until the turnpike opens.

I had not thought it was possible to satisfy the tense expectations of this mob until I saw it happen myself. Every spectator admitted that Fraulein Sontag went beyond all expectations. Every movement she makes is accompanied by a charming, indescribable gracefulness, and because in her case it is almost impossible to separate appearance from reality, we are at a loss to know what it is about her that could so have enticed us and blinded us. Her manners, conduct and dress are never at variance with propriety even in playful roles which can so easily be offensive in the theater, and whenever she performs a serious part she does so with the utmost nobility, a nobility which is at the same time both touching and authoritative. Madame Catalani[11] is said to have formed the following opinion about her: she is unique in her genre, but her genre is small; however, whoever has heard Sontag as Desdemona in Rossini's *Otello* will find this opinion quite unjust. Her simple songs, which speak to the heart, are just as admirable as her ornate ones, which only play with our ears. One saw old men crying when she sang, mere affectation no matter how incomparable or unique it is, could never create an effect like this. Her quiet tones, her wonderful intricate trills, runs and cadenzas resemble the charming childlike ornaments on a Gothic building, which serve to ease the stern, severe quality of the lofty arches and columns and which unite the pleasure of the sky with the pleasure of earth, yet these ornaments do not degrade or detract from its serious quality. The enthusiasm which Henriette Sontag as Desdemona kindled here was equal to a Greek fire which could not be extinguished and—But now I must cling to the rock of reason which is my only salvation. Perhaps, I was swept away, perhaps, it was not merely a figure of speech when I said earlier: "I no longer know what I am saying." If something like that happened to me, something human, then I do not want to let myself be exposed to ridicule and rather than express myself further I will mingle among my fellow-sufferers and relate some of the remarks which certain theater-critics here and in Darmstadt

143

have said, sung and vehemently exclaimed about Sontag. Thus united we mock the mockers!

My head swims! I have seen drunk Germans, but intoxicated not from wine, but from enthusiasm. It is a time of giving birth, the century will become a father and great things will happen. What has been written, what stories have been told! It was like a mobilization in Olympia; even the women, children, old men and veterans of mythology had to take up arms. Serious, stern philologists have written simple little poems and flirting Anacreons[12] have spoken with the beautiful maiden about death and immortality, about the misery of the earth and the blessedness of heaven and they have asked her to preserve her naturalness which she has until now never lost. A hermit sang: "Darling! come raise my veil! Come, decipher my lofty thoughts." But, oh, the darling has gone to Paris and has not solved the riddle of this veiled hermit's elevated thoughts! The voice of a spirit calling to Henriette Sontag was heard, but this voice did not sound like a gloomy tone rising out of a dark tomb, rather it sounded like the whispering of sweet strings in a Spanish night and the spirit-voice was full of life. The century of Volta[13] was already extremely happy when it electrified joy once, but that was not enough any more, for our singer jolted her critical frogs with another bolt of electricity, more electric joy. A stargazer spoke about the Milky Way which reveals new worlds to the eye of the lucky observer.[14] There were no arguments, no opinions, the palm of contentment[15] stirred every soul and each discord vanished. Ah, why don't they send the singer to Constantinople so that she could soothe the Divan? Despite the cold weather of the German November days, the singer was surrounded by the warm pleasant air of the south.[16] Another said that one day he could tell his grandchildren proudly: "I also lived in the great age." A poet sang prophetically and sincerely: "When I find that I am near you, I lose breath, movement, spirit and life." And another:

> How it was only a small word
> Which she said to me!
> How it was just a silver glance

Which I was to see.
And I lived for a long time with joy,
Just from one word, just from one glance.

If this poet can live on so little, then he will by all means reach the ripe old age of Cornaro.[17] A critic longed to be Argus-eyed so that he could absorb every single charm of her lovely appearance and without wanting to suddenly found himself writing poetry. Another prose writer had very picturesque and physical thought-flakes because the winter days had changed water into snow. Another described the singer with these words: "O delicate pearl beaming in the light of my tender glance. You roll over the youthful cheek so that one more angel may be allowed to protect the souls of all virtuous beings for an eon." An aged poet looking back over his experiences sang: "Vigor penetrates all of our limbs." And the welcome conclusion of a sonnet by another poet reads as follows:

To honor and to praise the eternal ray
Perhaps, the harmony of the spheres sounded
On the first Sunday as God said: "It is done!"
To grant us the wondrous sound of that Sunday
God now to the earth a Sontag presented
And gave us ears to hear the splendid one.

This theological sonnet-writer asserts without hesitation that humanity received ears when it was six thousand years old.[18] Ah, he may be right. For six thousand years history has spoken to us, but we did not listen. The creator, however, will not look down upon us with disfavor if, in the future, whenever Sontag does not sing, we use our ears for something else.

Henriette Sontag has inspired, given pleasure and brought sorrow to the people living by the Main and the Rhine and to inanimate nature as well. We have read: "Nature has celebrated the arrival of Sontag in Frankfurt by a special sign; for the moment she came within our city walls, a shining meteor became visible on the horizon and fell to earth with a cannon-roar." I have to admit that another person disputed this statement claiming that the meteor had appeared thirty hours after Sontag's arrival and in order to substantiate his opinion he had consulted the report of the local physics society. But what an unbelieving Gibbon[19] says deserves no consideration and we should not let him rob us of our happiness. We have read further: "No sooner had the heroine of song left our city walls than heaven itself began to cry." I can affirm this wonder; for I have seen with my own eyes that it began to rain as soon as the heroine of song had left the gates of the city behind her.

In all justice to our snow-blind Pindars[20] we have to admit that in their high-flown[21] tributes to Sontag they knew how to avoid every possible restraint and nowhere did they allow themselves to be bound by any present law. In their Dithyrambs[22] every word which these authors wanted to emphasize had to be funny, dark, shimmering black and ready to soar into the air. They could not free themselves, however, from the common thought that the name of the singer at the same time is the name of a day of the week. They made the most unbelievable efforts to avoid this imagery, but even if they could have become the devil himself, it was no use. Therefore a never-ending stream of comparisons between her name and the day of the week resulted and similarly countless phrases praising the sun and the day. I do not know what price I would have paid to see the public's reaction if her name had been Freitag instead of Sontag.[23] Then some German newspaper writer would have undoubtedly sung about freedom and one would see another type of emphasis on the word, *Freiheit;* the censor would have been intoxicated with all the references to liberty. I could still tell a lot about what this enormous mass of Dithyrambs said, I could talk about the tribe of ingratiating people and I could further relate to you about the "Brekeke Koax Koax"[24] which the populace of the swamp sang again and again under the rising foam; but this is enough. I must stop here before somebody says to me: "Not all who ridicule their chains are free!"[25]

THE ABDUCTION FROM THE SERAGLIO,
OPERA BY MOZART[26]

Is there a realm above this earth where one expresses himself only in musical tones—the masters of the art of music lead you there while they raise your spirit upward: only Mozart alone brings this heavenly realm down into our mortal hearts, whereas other composers make us climb up to it. Only he is capable of accomplishing this task, and it is this ability which makes Mozart the greatest of all composers. We do not have to glorify Mozart's music nor strain our minds to enjoy it, like a mirror it reflects the emotion each person feels at the moment in noble outlines; each person perceives in his music the poetry of his existence. His music is so elevating and yet so condescending, so proud and yet so accessible to everyone, so profound and at the same time so clear, so revered and childlike, strong and mild and yet so full of life in its peacefulness. The primary function of music is to express love and religion and when used in this manner, as it is to such an extent in Mozart, achieves an indescribable heavenliness. But even more admirable than the poet's ability to impart a majesty and loftiness to words is Mozart's ability to elevate the common impulse, to see poetry in common speech, molten color in dirt and harmony in noise. The arias of Constanza, of Donna Anna and the frightful entrance of the stone guest[27] are not easily imitated just as one cannot duplicate the songs of Asian.[28] Such a splendid character, such a transfigured grumbler and cringing woman watcher, how he tortures himself angrily at the bolted grating, through which he daily sees the honey which he is not permitted to taste, such an angry chap who hates the world because he cannot love, it will be a long time before he will be portrayed in this manner again.

LA VESTALE, OPERA BY SPONTINI

How appropriately this music represents the splendor of Rome! Nobility, power, glitter and opulence. If only the excessive amount of beautiful things which are piled up, one next to the other, were less disturbing. Such a broad stream of tones which cannot be grasped by our ears cannot help but lose its tranquility and clarity, for this stream of tones is like a large body of water forcing its way through a narrow gorge, foaming, raging and tumbling wildly. For this reason Spontini's music is accused of being confused and impure. The instrumentation is truly republican, so many talk all at once that no one ever knows who is right or who has the power. Even if the opinion held by discerning people is true, namely, that the errors in Spontini's opera only become obvious after the dazzle and richness of the music has worn off through repeated listenings, there are still, nevertheless, some details which cannot be criticized. How satisfying to the ear, for example, are the sung recitatives and how happy one is to get away at least from the terrible impressions of spoken dialogue which cuts the dramatic unity into a hundred pieces and transfers the listener to the concert hall. The "Hymn to the Vestal Virgins," with which the second scene of the first act begins, however, prompts one to ask the following question: should a song written for a religious ceremony of the Romans, who when facing the empty blue sky, express their attitude toward nature and their religious feelings not with a sense of fear or foreboding, but with great joy, be allowed to be composed in the style of Christian church music as it is done here? I approached a scholar for his expert opinion of this opera and he refused to say anything in public about it because his judgement would upset many people. What a beautiful tribute to the belief in freedom above rules, nature above doctrine!

The dances and battle scenes which are interwoven throughout this opera provide the listener, in a casual manner, with a strange artistic treat, for they excite the curiousity without satisfying it.

One should not occupy himself at all with such things on our stage.
To be sure it is not quite respectable for a single girl to frisk about
among sixteen warriors, this young lady is also not capable of show-
ing the audiences that there is a distinction between beauty and
strength of character. In general the outward appearance of this
opera, the staging and the scenery, is characterized by a greatly
disturbing feeling of poverty. Cato[29] would have to laugh if he saw
the victory-box in which Lucinius is pushed onto the stage. What
flimsy troops, what a rambling bundle of rubbish, what scenery,
what a shabby bookbound work! It is astonishing how one can
become accustomed to anything.

THE LANDSLIDE, OPERA BY WEIGL

Parturiunt montes, nascetur ridiculus mus[30]

It is always the same: nothing is forbidden in a *Singspiel,* the art of
the drama has no requirements here, everything which roars in the
world is brought into its music. Beautiful principles! To allow the
human heart with its small joys to be crushed by a landslide, what
an offensive play of life! How ridiculous for grown-up children to
watch a Nuremberg earthquake. Do they want to make a fool of us?
The frail body battling against all-powerful nature, how distasteful! In a battle with such uneven odds there is no nobility for either
the victor or the defeated. The music of this opera is tolerable or
less than that. We look in vain for some trace of the composer of *The
Swiss Family,*[31] whose melodies in this earlier work flashed through
all the fibers of our being. In *The Landslide* he comes close several
times, but soon strays far from the path again.

LUDWIG BÖRNE

THE SWISS FAMILY, OPERA BY WEIGL

The leaders of Sparta would have tolerated this music, even cherished it, although they would have condemned similarly oriented musical compositions which absorb like a loose sponge the very essence of bravery. The music of this opera follows the inclinations of one's heart, but it is the course of nature, simple, honorable and powerful, which it pursues. The composer has succeeded in a masterful fashion in describing the various nuances of one single emotion with all its minute peculiarities. Love, with all its various manifestations permeates the entire work, the passionate yearning for the homeland, the anxiety of the parents, the submission of the child, the love between a man and a woman, sadness and happiness, and at last, gratitude; how well these various types of love are kept separate and yet at the same time are related to each other. Let us compare the loud outcries of thirty noisy operas with *The Swiss Family*—in the former the desperate characters whine, the sweet arias which express the tempo of a waltz or hops as if it were dancing an *écossaise*,[32] even these sound like a complaint. Now let us ask the scholars after comparing the songs of *The Swiss Family* with those just mentioned whether they still would like to claim in the usual manner that Weigl's music has no intellectual appeal because everyone can understand the simplicity of his music.

THE MAGIC FLUTE, OPERA BY MOZART

Did it have holes and keys? If it did I did not see them, anyway the flute was very ugly. A magic flute should actually be more beautiful than a real one. And how did you like the Glockenspiel? The fairies who are otherwise usually so generous have suddenly it seemed become stingy. At this moment, so that we do not forget, I want to admonish Herr Obermayer who played Papageno for in my opinion he jokes at the wrong time such as when he bangs so hard upon an old drum with his drumsticks so that one hears the wood being struck. Papageno after all is supposed to pretend to be playing his bells, which are actually behind the scene, yet, why then is he allowed to make noise with his drum at this time? This rogue we have been talking about also did a rather poor job of carrying his Papagena away in his arms—we still do not have a *Kreuzerkomödie*.[33] There was not an ounce of magic this evening. The system of gravity, the whole handbook of physics, nothing worked. During the transformation of the old woman into the young feathered maiden,[34] the cowl remained lying on the ground and would not disappear. Pamina's dagger likewise did the same thing, there it remained lying on the stage. The Queen of the Night at one time seemed to faint, but the shining gods were too well-inclined towards Mademoiselle Friedel to surrender her to the power of the underworld. Then she took a side road.[35] All of our operas are comic operas, whether it says so on the poster or not. Herr Meggenhof played Sarastro. He did quite well in this his first operatic attempt and I can speak favorably about him. Even if one considers how much his shyness hampered his singing, one can still expect that in the future, given more confidence, the young artist will develop a strong, penetrating pure voice. The demands of the bass selections follow certain standards and are therefore more difficult to perform than the tenor and soprano parts. The latter get along well with the instruments, for one thing they are accompanied by many more members of the orchestra and are supported by the instruments which share their same melodic lines, this, however, is not true of the bass voice which stands alone. Also the bass singer with his more serious manner is not permitted to hide his mistakes amidst embellishments and flirtations.

Since the creation of our theater, Mozart's *Magic Flute*[36] has become the most frequently performed of all *Singspiel*.[37] In the year

1793 when it appeared for the first time it was given seventeen times, in the following year, twenty-six times, in 1795, twelve times, in 1796, ten times, in 1797, eight times, later more seldom, but at least once a year with the sole exception of 1812.[38] Until now (the present year not included) the opera has been performed one hundred and thirty-seven times. This music is like a church hymn to us, like a prayer, it is in all of our ears, in all of our hearts, it is a part of our lives. Our excellent orchestra could probably play it by heart. If a musical composition maintains its power for such a long time and captures our love time and time again, this proves not merely its worth, but it also proves that we recognize its worth. As Germans we cannot pay enough homage to Mozart. We should pay homage to him, however, not only because he is a German, but because we can bask in our pride, we can boast to all the peoples of Europe that this greatest of masters is a German. Germany has the greatest number of distinguished men in the sciences and the arts, a number which is quite large compared to other countries. But even though we have this great number, we do not possess the most outstanding, the greatest scientists and artists. However, an exception to this occurs in philosophy and music. Music is a metaphysical art, a transcendental art to Germans. If one considers how often *The Magic Flute* excites and delights the admiration of the experts, how often the crowd is so pleased and how much money is brought into the theater cash register, one would be allowed to assert and rightly so that this opera which is performed on our stage in the plainest and most simple fashion in some magic way comes before our eyes bedecked in brilliance and polish, the dazzling spectacle is in our minds, not on the stage. May you always see the divine Mozart only as a servant of your cash register, but even a servant gets a new outfit from time to time. Faded, old obsolete decorations: the very ones which were used twenty-seven years ago. In such a period of time even the most massive edifice, not to mention a painted one, becomes damaged and needs to be repaired. An old soldier's whistle, an old ribbon box pounded upon by two wooden sticks, out of this the sound of the Glockenspiel is supposed to emerge. Presents do not cost the fairies a penny: therefore they are always beautiful to look at; their splendor can be imitated with just some color, paper and glass. For all that, may the old snake scare Tamino another thousand years and may it be stabbed to death another million times, such a snake never gives up, but Papageno's coat is worthless. The poor bird catcher looks like a Hanswurst[39] in it even if his costume may have many colored feathers, colorful like a hummingbird, a parrot, a peacock; but what bird has such clearly defined symmetrical areas of color on its body. Earlier his costume was decorated with natural feathers, but they fell off because of old age. When the deceased singer, Lux, who so far had not been replaced, played Papageno he caught mice during the performance (may our *Fiat Lux* be replaced)[40] and he was ridiculed on the spot, but this helped because now they had to provide a new costume for him; this new one, however, was not made of real feathers, but imitation ones, made of silk and wool: the whole effect of his costume was ruined. Also it would be too much to wish that some more fowl be placed in the large bird cage, there are now only two skinny hens in it. If these improvements were made, then there would be nothing further to wish for since the cowls of the priests were washed two years ago. Great men who have made contributions to humanity are never appreciated by their contemporaries, but future generations will admire and appreciate the fact that I was the person who through a reprimand in *Die Wage*[41] had brought about the cleaning of the priests' cowls. Herr Dobler from Linz appeared as Sarastro and was applauded. It is said that we will keep this good singer with us in Frankfurt.

TANCRED, GRAND HEROIC OPERA BY ROSSINI

It is grand, if by this term we mean that the opera is long, but there is absolutely nothing heroic in it. One could adapt the music of this opera to the most beloved novel of August Lafontaine[42] and not have one criticism directed against this procedure. It is inconceivable how a composer with some intelligence could have composed music which is so inappropriate to the dramatic action. How could it be that *Tancred* has received such praise? Already when I heard this opera for the first time, my ear ached like the stomach does when it is given nothing during an entire meal, but candy. Children and women may be attracted to such music, but men can only take it in small doses, like dessert. The whole opera, how it lacks character, how it drags, how sentimental it is, how crammed it is with stereotyped musical phrases and platitudes. If the singer had sung only three notes, one would already know how the rest of the melody would sound. What lack of depth, what an offensive manner the insipid lovesickness of the characters has! The music does not even abandon its childish, frivolous character in the battle-marches. You see a butterfly winging its way over the battlefield.

Arsis appears with a bare head, even outside.[43] The choir of warriors sings right at the beginning with all the sentimentality of Rossini's music: "Only in the arms of true love blossoms the happiness of life." Wouldn't it be great if the soldiers of every prince were no more dangerous than these minnesingers? Mademoiselle Friedel as Tancred not only earned the approval of everyone, but she had a pleasing little moustache as well. She was called to take a bow and thanked the audience with the following words: "Not only in *Tancred,* but also with every step of my life I will try to make myself worthy of your applause. Good night!" I don't know why the people laughed. Such a polite thank you should have probably deserved a friendly response. The tuning-hammers[44] in the orchestra pit, perhaps, were not quite satisfied with the promise she made concerning her conduct in the future

FANCHON, OPERA BY HIMMEL

It is easy to learn how to observe singers in a lenient, humorous manner, all one has to do is observe how well-qualified musicians are turned into awkward, clumsy, provincial beings when they are placed among the circle of Fanchon's friends. The highest refinement of a German critic is silence. However, Herr Hill as Saintval and Herr Krönner as the Abbot were not lacking in cleverness. Herr Kellner from Hanover as guest performer played the paper-hanger without humor or feeling. One must take into consideration the fact that the performance was at its best and the theater was empty. Herr Schmidt as Fanchon's brother showed some personality, especially in the scene where he threw the paper-hanger upon the sofa and thrashed him. Herr Leissring played the grocer in an amusing manner. Herr Haas, Fanchon's head house steward, believed he had to walk as quietly as possible, pitter-patter, every time he came in or went out. I don't know whether this was to signify senility or something else.

Since I just mentioned Herr Kellner, I will tell my readers that this singer came to visit me twice before he left our city, but missed me both times. The opinions are divided. Some maintain he had only come to see me in order to beg me to write more considerately about his wife than I did in *Maria Stuart*.[45] Whatever his intentions may have been, I would have known how to deal with his threats and resist his sugary words. I am speaking publicly about this situation because, perhaps, by this means I will be successful in preventing future strange performers from trying to seek me out in order to influence my judgement concerning their abilities.

Such persons might benefit from the example set by the local artists. The latter, although living near me, have never attempted to influence my opinion by conversing with me, by their discreet and considerate behavior they spare me the sad choice of either deceiving my readers with distasteful tenderness or deceiving them with hypocritical promises which I don't intend to fulfill.

CAMILLA, OPERA BY PAER

Because of the impeccable reputation Paer's *Camilla* has, the singers were not able to malign this opera, no matter how subtly they tried to destroy it. Herr Kaintz, member of the Royal City Theatre of Prague, represented the Duke. If the Bohemian citizens have no better governmental representatives than singers like this, it is unfortunate for them. Madame Urspruch sang Camilla. What horrible amusement, she shrieked and ran after musical sounds like a hunting hound! The poor wild beasts! Camilla, who should appear like a penitent, was dressed wrongly for the part. Is this according to the rules? Mademoiselle Wagner as the gardener's bride, Ghitta, was quite frivolous, saucy, full of love, very full of love. Her bridegroom is called Antonio.[47]

SARGIN, OPERA BY PAER

Madame Seidler-Wranitzky[48] of Berlin appeared as Sophie. It has been said without exaggeration that she is a singer with unusual gifts. She possesses voice, acting ability and physical charm and makes an exciting and agreeable impression at all times. No valiant song is made to sound ridiculous by some delicate thin figure, nor is a cooing love song made to sound comical by being sung by some aged and corpulent little dove; everything is harmonious here. Madame Seidler has a very lovely voice, a modest genuine feminine type of elocution and acting ability of the utmost grace.

LILLA, OPERA BY MARTIN[49]

Because we are not acquainted enough with this music from the good old days, we cannot become emotional about it. How pleasant it is! The feeling that arises from this music is a happy one, and like a stream this happy feeling flows through blossoming meadows, it touches us just enough to carry our hearts away, our souls are not cast downward, for there is very little that is stormy in this score. What simple nourishment! But yet on the other hand it is refreshing enough for a healthy appetite. What a sweet still life! What serenity there is in its pleasure and sadness, what friendly soothing melodies. Rustic passion, rustic love, rustic hate, rustic scorn, rustic mockery! A mild spring breeze blows over the entire opera, arousing our feelings, there is no need here for a stormy summer or a blood-curdling winter! But we poor people who have to listen to the revolutionary operas, how our heart and ear are hurled hither and thither between incredible pain and natural joys, between the roaring of the lioness and the cooing of the slaughtered pigeon. At one point a proud Semiramis[50] sings like the most languishing Louise,[51] at another point a love-sick peasant maiden with plump red cheeks tries to be magnificent like Cleopatra who puts the snake to her bosom in order to heal through deadly poison the more deadly poison in her heart. There is a peace and cheerfulness in the music of *Lilla* which we are not familiar with anymore, neither in the world of music nor in the outside world. One would almost like to be a simpleton and wish back those innocent times when we were still uncomplicated beings, when we lived patiently like pious shepherds in secluded valleys and revered piously and childishly the more mighty ones living on the side of the mountains, believing them to be superior beings.

DER FREISCHÜTZ, [1822][52], OPERA BY WEBER

Have you been to a performance of *Der Freischütz?* It seems to me I heard or read somewhere that you were acquainted with this opera. *Der Freischütz* has been performed three times here in the last two weeks. Our good people were delighted by it, but this gives me some concern; what I mean to say is that I feel like one who hesitates to take a glass of wine even if it is for a bit of moderate pleasure because he is aware of the intoxicating effect of this drink. But I did take the glass of wine after all and found it is a genuine German wine, which only our father Rhine can produce; that is—I can't finish what I wanted to say because I can't stop laughing; when I have pulled myself together I'll say more about the opera—if one wants to believe that only music can express the character of a people, that is acceptable, but to say that we have no German music is like saying that the German people have no character. But that is the way it stands. Weber gave us the first German opera and because it is considered as such it has become more than just an opera, it has become a beautiful token of a more beautiful object. I am really no music scholar, I can't substantiate my feelings, but I know you trust me. Imagine a German Don Juan, but not one who drinks champagne and loves the ladies, but one who loves country wine and country girls, this is *Der Freischütz*. The Overture is written in a very noble style, and the lighter parts of it, as in all the parts of the opera, are executed with the most elegant grace. The villain's song,[53] which the evil huntsman sings, will please you; also the way the piccolo[54] cries out so insolently is a very good device. Ah, and the Chorus of the Bridesmaids! One would like to melt from pleasure. Our young ladies have been coughing for two weeks because they cannot stop singing this sweet melody, "We wind the bridal wreath for you with violet blue silk."[55] What magic there is in this violet blue silk, one could tie Samson with it![56] Everyone, whether of noble or humble origin, is delighted by the hunting song in the third act.[57] The previously mentioned music selections are, perhaps, not the best parts of the opera, but they are the most charming and seem to have gained greater prominence because of their popular appeal. The Chorus of the Spirits which precedes the wild hunt and the frightful song which accompanies it are quite effective;[58] but in truth I do not really understand this part of the opera, my attention wanders during this scene in which the wild hordes appear, the music numbs my ear. Dear friend, what an uproar, what a horror, what a frightful scene! A poor man in Cassel became insane because of this spectacle and had to be put in chains and taken to the madhouse, but here nothing like that has happened yet:

> The knights looked courageously
> And the beautiful women cast down their eyes.[59]

However, not all the women looked down, several beautiful ones did turn their heads away, but others stared rigidly at the frightful scene with the greatest fear and despair. Some friends of music maintain that not all of Weber's material was his own,[60] but, perhaps, they are mistaken. In each work in which the German spirit is represented that which is familiar to the Germans has to be present and recognized, for that is the way we Germans are, they want to unify the colors of art and science which in the prism of the people is refracted in order to produce the pure light of knowledge. Nevertheless, this does not justify that one should turn to something improper: colors are the daughters of light. You are like one of those inquisitive children who cannot fall asleep at night if they do not discover something new every day and you are probably becoming bored with my prism and would rather I tell you how all the Madame Müllers[61] in the whole of Germany have sung each evening and whether or not the audiences were pleased. The opera was performed excellently. The stage manager who was responsible for the direction of the entire production, the Kapellmeister who rehearsed and conducted the opera, and all the singers deserve great praise because of their accomplishments; the singer who performed the role of Agathe was especially good. Also the prop man who could have made a fool of himself during the performance came out of this devilish confusion with honor. To be a little critical, it appears to me that those who were supposed to laugh in the opera overdid it,[62] especially the women in the choir. Max to be sure already has a fiancée, but he still continues to be a handsome fellow and later it becomes obvious that the whole world loves him. Why, however, was he teased so venomously during the scene where he becomes justifiably annoyed?[63] Furthermore, I believe that the tempo of the hunting song was too fast. But don't ask me what I think of the libretto. I want to enjoy my freedom and make things as comfortable as possible for myself. Why did I laugh so much previously? How could I help myself? I have been caught up in German affairs just like everyone else, but with me it is a fever which will pass, with the others it is a lingering sickness. These good people are to be pitied and not criticized. Voltaire once said, "If there is no God, invent one!" Thus one could say, "Whoever has no fatherland, invent one!" The Germans have tried it in all kinds of ways, with German coats,[64] with the *Nibelingenlied,* with the German school of painters and since *Der Freischütz* they are trying it with music. They wish they had a hat under which they could bring all German heads. Let us allow them their folly, let us allow them to indulge themselves in their fatherland substitutes. Only they should not forget that it is not virtues but character weaknesses which impart to a nation those peculiarities which separate it from other peoples. Virtue is the common good of all. They should not speak of German faithfulness, of German perseverance, of German diligence, that is ridiculous and irrelevant. What an ear-splitting cry of jubilation *Der Freischütz* has caused just because it is a German work. Is it flattering to Weber to receive such great

Scene from *Der Freischütz* (Max and Caspar in the Wolf's Glen), Drawing by Moritz von Schwind, c. 1850. Courtesy, Staatliche Graphische Sammlung, Munich.

praise just because of his geographical background? Some have written: "How we long to see Weber in person, the man whose splendid talent promises that a new sun will rise over our music which is veiled in darkness." Another person said the following: "At last a German has succeeded in bringing honor to Germany, uniting its various factions which have been at odds with one another for so long under one modest, truthful banner." A third wrote: "The nation looks upon him with pride and joy." Persons in Vienna[65] report that "the enthusiasm *Der Freischütz* has caused grows larger and larger with each performance like an avalanche rolling down into the valley." (That would be like frozen fire.) But the small *Abendblättern*[66] which as usual hatches its praise like the Egyptians bake bread, impetuously and without thinking, cried the loudest. Amongst other things this paper contained the following sonnet dedicated to Weber:

> The free marksman has hit the target,
> It was his restless eager striving
> And courage of thought which gave him his goal,
> A god has cast his arrow with might.
>
> He penetrated through the veil of clouds, without tiring,
> A magic stroke—he awoke new life,
> Elevating the chaos of sound to something meaningful,
> Breaking the yoke of his fellow German artists.

Because of *Der Freischütz* it is said that the Germans are waging a musical war against Rossini. Let's hope they do not fare as well as Napoleon—"the wicked one is gone, the wicked ones remain." The sonnet continues:

> How lucky we are that we are permitted to praise a master,
> To view a German work of art with pride,
> And to praise the mother of Weber because of her noble son.
>
> But is it German to elevate the noble one
> And to almost silently ignore the father?
> A child has elevated you, Maria.[67]

We Germans never lack the firewood, only the fire. Now since the fire burns the lovely people will all come running to it and throw in their sacks of twigs.[68] Heaven be merciful! But enough of *Der Freischütz*. Allow me to say only that Weber is currently working on two new operas, the first, *Euryanthe*, is a serious opera, its libretto is by Helmina von Chézy and it has already passed the Viennese censor which is very flattering for the poetess as well as for the whole German nation; the second, *Die drei Pintos*,[70] is a comic opera, its libretto is by Theodor Hell.

LETTER FROM FRANKFURT [January 4, 1821]

Three years ago a group of men and women formed here a society called the *Cäcilienverein* whose purpose it was to study and perform vocal music, the method and manner of this society deserves our utmost encouragement, at the same time, however, its stature is such that it actually can do very well without our help. Singing is the original speech of the heart, instrumental music is but a translation of this speech, women intuitively pay homage to the muse of song for it is part of their nature to express themselves naturally by singing. The fact that this society truly understood its purpose and its goal and so quickly obtained it is due to the leadership of Herr Schelbe, former singer of our theater, a man who unites feeling and love of music with the skill of a public performer, which many an accomplished person cannot do. The *Cäcilienverein,* thinking that it would lose something of its dignity if it were accessible to everyone, restricts the number of its performers to only those who belong to the society, nevertheless, its membership continues to grow and the number of practice sessions has increased, the music enjoyed more and more. The organization seldom performs for the outside world, thus the public rarely hears how well this group is trained or witnesses the high degree of perfection it has attained.

But an occasion presented itself when the *Cäcilienverein* demonstrated its skillful musicianship: this occurred on December fifth when they were asked to perform for a most praiseworthy event, the anniversary of the death of a great man, a man who would have created music if heaven itself had not already done so—Mozart. The organizers of this memorial concert wanted to express their sorrow over his death and at the same time to ease the grief associated with the loss of this great artist by a performance of the composer's *Requiem,*[71] this most beautiful transfiguration of death. The hall was draped in black and everything else connected with the concert was designed to express a unified spirit of grief. The audience appeared in mourning clothes and never was such unity of emotion so visible to the outside world. The musical performance achieved that high degree of excellence which can only be obtained when people who are acquainted with art are also at the same time lovers of art. By chance, the instrumentalists were not available on that day, but even if something was lost by the lack of instrumental accompaniment, this loss was, nevertheless, compensated by the fact that the vocal parts which are normally suppressed by the dominating instruments could be heard much more clearly and enjoyed for their own sake. The importance of the concert was heightened in still another way: Mozart's son,[72] an artist in his own right, was present and allowed to enjoy the respect given his father and music. A short time thereafter he himself gave a concert which was attended by an audience whose size is seldom seen. The *Cäcilienverein* also showed the young Mozart how much they respected him by performing one of his own cantatas. The achievements of young Mozart, his musical compositions as well as his playing, greatly pleased everyone and those present that day were surprised to find still so much strength in the son, accustomed as we are to seeing nature exhausted after the creation of such a father. During the last two months, two other concerts were given here, one in the autumn, one in the winter. One featured Herr de Groot, a member of the local orchestra and a talented and pleasant clarinet player, the other was given by the whole orchestra for the benefit of the theater pension fund. Concerning the latter, the thoughtless selection of musical compositions was criticized. The organizers of this event should have taken advantage of the fact that this was a benefit concert and provided us with some new music, it was not necessary at this time to sacrifice the dignity of art to monetary considerations. There is still a lot of splendid modern music which we have not heard. Of course, the honorable, but decidedly worn out musical fare which they doled out to us brought the deserving actors small profit or recognition.

NOTES

1. Goethe and Henriette Sontag dined together on September 4, 1826. This long first sentence, incidentally, is a good example of a conspicuous trait of Börne's literary style, i.e., the tendency to delay the clarification of his ideas to some further point in his paragraph structure. The way in which he proceeds from an ambiguous image to a later clarification of this image tends more to resemble poetry than prose. Through this method, however, his main ideas achieve a striking emphasis.
2. As of fruits and vegetables.
3. It is difficult to understand exactly what Börne's imagery implies here. Perhaps, he is inferring that by basking in the light of Goethe's genius (Prometheus being Goethe) the "foolish people" assume that some of Goethe's greatness (the fire) will rub off on them.
4. Rhadamanthus, a highly esteemed judge in Greek mythology and the son of Zeus.
5. *Newspaper for Foreign Events*. Sontag was a Prussian and probably considered foreign to some extent, hence the notice about her in this newspaper. The fact that this paper considered her to be the paragon of German taste and culture was indeed a great tribute.
6. Prytane, a member of the city council in ancient Greece. Prytaneum, a place where the city council met, much like a city hall.
7. Börne is referring here to the Greek revolt (1821-1829) against Turkey. The Greeks fought the Turkish-Egyptian forces unaided until 1827. On October 20, 1827 when the Turks refused to agree to an armistice a combined Russian, French and British fleet defeated the Egyptians at Navario.
8. Sultan, i.e., Mahmud II, ruler of Turkey; Codrington, Sir Edward Codrington (1770-1851), British Admiral and commander of the allied fleet at Nava-

rio. The reference to *Othello* is quite appropriate here as Shakespeare's drama is laid against the background of the Turkish invasion of Cyprus (1570); Divan, the Turkish Council of State; Barber, i.e., Figaro, a character in Rossini's popular opera, *The Barber of Seville* (1816).

9. *Intelligenz-Blatt,* literally, *The Advertiser,* a local Frankfurt newspaper.

10. Marquis de Vauban (1633-1707), French soldier and military engineer; marshall of France.

11. Angelica Catalani (1780-1849), famous Italian opera singer well-known in her day for her extravagant demands, jealousy of other singers and love of excessively ornate arias. She appeared in Germany in 1816 and 1827.

12. Anacreon (572-488? B.C.), Greek lyric poet.

13. Alessandro Volta (1745-1825) first devised an apparatus for chemically producing electric currents. This sentence thus contains a play on the word "electric;" the century experienced two electric jolts, one produced chemically by Volta, the other by Sontag's singing.

14. The Milky Way here is Sontag: like the stars, the more you watch her, the more she reveals to you.

15. The palm tree, a symbol of peace and safety, again refers to Sontag.

16. Börne uses the term "hesperischen Lüften" here which I have translated as meaning the sunny warm climate of Italy; Hesperia is the ancient Greek name for Italy.

17. Luigi Cornaro, Italian writer born in 1467 and who wrote his most important work, *Discorsi della vita sobria* in 1558.

18. Reference to the time when God gave the Commandments to the Jews.

19. Edward Gibbon (1734-1794), English historian, author of *Decline and Fall of the Roman Empire.*

20. Pindar, a Greek lyric poet (522?-433 B.C.).

21. I have translated Börne's extremely long compound, "Lufteinlufthindurchaufschwimmenden," here as "high-flown," a more literal translation, perhaps, might be, "swimming and floating up and down in the air."

22. Dithyramb, the name of an ancient form of Greek poetry (hymns to Dionysus) characterized by a wild emotional quality.

23. Sontag from: *die Sonne* (the sun), *der Tag* (the day); *Sontag,* Sunday. *Der Freitag* (Friday); *die Freiheit* (freedom, liberty).

24. Possibly the sound of frogs. Börne had mentioned earlier how Sontag had charmed her "critical frogs." It is also possible he is referring to the chorus of frogs in Aristophanes' comedy, *Batrachoi (The Frogs,* 405 B.C.).

25. Börne is quoting from Lessing's *Nathan der Weise* (IV, 4, line 2758).

26. This opera review and those that follow appeared in Börne's journal, *Die Wage,* between the years 1818-1821.

27. This review seems to discuss *Don Giovanni* more than *The Abduction:* Constanza, Belmonte's beloved in *The Abduction;* Donna Anna, leading role in *Don Giovanni,* the stone guest, the statue of Donna Anna's father, "the splendid character," Don Giovanni.

28. Osmin-Osian? Börne might also be referring here to Le Sueur's opera, *Ossian, ou les Bardes,* 1804.
29. Cato, Roman Consul (234-149 B.C.).
30. "The mountains labor [as in childbirth] and a funny little mouse is born" (Horace, *Poetics*). Horace (and hence Börne) is criticizing poets who start their poems on a large scale with grandiose ideas, but whose products are "ridiculous." It is thus better to begin modestly and work up to something worthwhile.
31. *The Swiss Family* was considered in the Romantic era to be Weigl's best opera.
32. *Ecossaise,* a French dance based upon Scottish rhythms and similar to the *Shottisch*.
33. Kreuzer, a minor coin worth about a half cent. Perhaps Börne is implying here that we still don't have a comedy worth very much.
34. *Magic Flute:* Act II, scene 5.
35. *Magic Flute:* Act II, scene 9. In this scene a burst of lightning and a crash of thunder herald the downfall of the Queen of the Night; her three attendants and Monostatos as well as the Queen are supposed to descend into the underworld. What might have happened during the performance which Börne is describing is that the Queen of the Night instead of disappearing just walked off the stage (i.e., "took a side road").
36. The following is a translation of a second critique of Mozart's *Magic Flute* which Börne wrote for *Die Wage* in June, 1819; the preceding appeared in this journal in October, 1818.
37. Börne is correct in calling Mozart's *Magic Flute* a Singspiel for the opera was originally designed to provide the Viennese public with another German comic opera with its customary dialogue. However, the music of *The Magic Flute* far transcends that usually associated with the Singspiel.
38. The year of the invasion of Russia by Napoleon's troops.
39. Hanswurst, the German name for the puppet or comic character, Punch, who was originally a member of the Italian *Commedia dell'Arte* or earlier French or Italian comedy groups. The reference here is to the earlier Punch who was depicted as a large, bulky stupid figure dressed in a loose white shirt and very full trousers and not the later humpbacked wife-beating figure. Punch was introduced to German audiences probably by English comedians early in the seventeenth century.
40. *Fiat Lux,* Latin for "Let there be light." Obviously there is a play on the word *Lux* which is the name of the singer.
41. The complete title of Börne's journal originally was: *Die Wage, Eine Zeitschrift für Bürgerleben, Wissenschaft und Kunst (The Balance. A Newspaper for City Life, Scholarship and Art).*
42. August Lafontaine (1758-1831), German writer of French ancestry. Lafontaine was the author of many popular sentimental and trivial novels and romances which appealed to the German bourgeoisie.
43. The following is a translation of Börne's critique of *Tancred* which appeared

in *Die Wage* (November, 1818); the preceeding essay on the same opera was taken from Börne's *Collected Works* (see Editions).

44. Tuning hammers, perhaps a reference to the string players in the orchestra who often tune their instruments with a tuning fork or tuning hammer.

45. *Maria Stuart,* drama by Schiller reviewed in *Die Wage* in 1818.

46. Rossini played the child's part in Paer's *Camilla* at the age of seven.

47. This character in the opera is usually called Gennaro.

48. Caroline Wranitzky-Seidler (1794-1872), eminent singer of the Romantic age, daughter of the Austrian composer and violinist, Anton Wranitzky. She was also the first Agathe of Weber's *Der Freischütz.*

49. See *Musical Sorrows and Joys,* n. 19.

50. The story of Semiramis, legendary queen of Assyria, was set by several composers: Gluck (in 1748), Hasse (in 1774), Borghi (in 1791), Catel (in 1802), Meyerbeer (in 1818), Rossini (in 1823). As Börne's review was written in 1819 it is likely he is referring to Meyerbeer's opera.

51. Possibly the heroine of F. L. Benda's opera, *Louise* (1791), which was revived in Königsberg in 1820.

52. This selection was taken from one of Börne's confidential letters. The letter is addressed to a woman, probably Jeanette Wohl, lifelong intimate friend of Börne from 1816 until his death in 1837.

53. Caspar's song in Act I (no. 4), "Hier im ird'schen Jammerthal" ("Here in This Earthly Vale").

54. Börne used the term "Pickelpfeifen" here which I translated as piccolo. It would appear that he is referring to Caspar's aria, "Schweig, Schweig!" ("Be Silent, Be Silent!"), in the first act (no. 5). At the word "Ketten" (victim) in this aria one shrill piccolo plays part of the melody associated with the Wolf's Glen scene; through this device Weber symbolizes the evil nature of Max's enemy.

55. Chorus of the Bridesmaids, i.e., "Wir winden dir den Jungfernkranz" ("We Bind the Bridal Wreath for You," Act III, no. 14).

56. Heine's well-known critique of *Der Freischütz* (see *Musical Sorrows and Joys,* n. 30) was written approximately at the same time as Börne's letter; both essays share many similarities.

57. Huntsmen's Chorus, i.e., "Was gleicht wohl auf Erden dem Jäger" ("The Joy of the Hunter on Earth," Act III, no. 15).

58. Chorus of the Spirits, etc., reference to the Finale of Act II, the famous Wolf's Glen scene.

59. Börne appears in this quote, perhaps, to be paraphrasing the words of the shocked characters in Act III (scene 3) who have just heard Agathe cry out to Max not to shoot the dove.

60. For a good discussion of Weber's use of other sources in *Der Freischütz* see Warrack's *Weber* (p. 20, n. 52).

61. Louise Müller, German singer who performed the part of Marcellina in the first performance of *Fidelio* (1805); Kleist mentions her in "Theater News"

(review published in his *Berliner Abendblättern,* i.e., *Berlin Evening News*).

62. Chorus of laughing peasants who in the first act tease and deride Max, a young forester of noble character, after he has been defeated in a shooting match by a coarse commoner, Kilian.

63. Börne is referring to the same scene described in n. 62.

64. The custom of wearing old German costumes which was quite common in this period is depicted by Friedrich in his painting, "Landscape with Rainbow," and described by Eichendorff in his *Taugenichts* (i.e., *Memoirs of a Good-for-Nothing,* New York: Frederick Ungar, 1955, p. 41).

65. *Der Freischütz* was performed in Vienna (*Kärntnertor* Theater) on November 3, 1821; the first Berlin production took place in the *Schauspielhaus,* June 18, 1821.

66. I.e., *Evening News.*

67. The last line of this sonnet reads, "Ein Kind hat dich, Maria, hoch erhoben." I believe Börne means by "Kind" not child, but Friedrich Kind, the librettist of *Der Freischütz,* but because of the uncertainty of his imagery I retained the word child. Maria refers probably to the composer or possibly his son, Max Maria (born April 25, 1822), who was named after the hero of this opera. At any rate this sentence could be interpreted in many ways.

68. Literally, everybody jumped on the bandwagon and wrote German operas.

69. Helmina von Chézy (née Wilhelmine von Klencke, 1783-1856). The original source of the libretto was the French medieval romance, *Roman de la violette,* which Helmina translated into German for Friedrich Schlegel's collection of medieval poems.

70. The name Pinto refers to a character in the opera, Don Pinto de Fonseca. The three Pintos are Don Pinto, his son and Don Gaston who disguises himself as a member of the Pinto family. The opera was never completed; Mahler finished the score and performed the work in 1888.

71. Mozart died before he finished the *Requiem;* supposedly it was completed by his pupil Süssmayr. The *Requiem* was possibly commissioned by Count Walsegg in the summer of 1791.

72. Börne is referring here to the younger of Mozart's two surviving sons, Franz Xaver Wolfgang Amadeus Mozart (1791-1844). A pupil of Salieri and Hummel, among others, he gave his first public concert in 1805 at the age of fourteen at the Theater an der Wien at which time a Cantata he had composed for Haydn's 73rd birthday was performed. Mozart's son was a gifted pianist and composer, but after his death his works fell into oblivion.

Achim von Arnim

[1781-1831]

PRINCE GANZGOTT AND THE SINGER HALBGOTT[1]

A Conversation at the Spa[2] [1818]

THE EVENING SUN shone burning red through the dust and the only moisture falling upon the parched man-made road came from the forehead of the overheated singer. "Oh, you accursed roads," moaned the tired singer, "if I look down your infinite lines I feel as if I will reach the sun rather than Carlsbad and nothing refreshes me so much as the thought that at this moment my ungrateful public squeezes itself with much annoyance into the narrow theater seats and stretches in boredom waiting for the spoiled opera to begin, the dear people will regret how they treated me, I will regain my voice, but I will not come back!" — With these words Halbgott attempted the most difficult arpeggios and this diversion hastened the course of his journey; before he was aware of it he had reached the beginning of the powerfully built main road from which he could see for the first time the mysterious deep valley of Carlsbad. He saw the promised land spreading out before him and exclaimed: "Here I will find my true public! the Kaiser, Kings, Princes, you are qualified to judge me, you descend from God's grace like myself! You will not deny me the right to use my low register, you will not force me to sing higher than I am capable of if my uvula has become swollen because of a cold. Here at the spa I will recover my high tones; I can defy the misty forms which the biting evening wind is blowing at me; they are the evil spirits of my public!" — But he was sorry that in his annoyance he had forgotten his overcoat for he noticed now for the first time that he was still strolling along in the tight-fitting costume with the star which he had worn during the last performance. That is the reason, he thought smiling, why the people he met along the way greeted him in such a humiliating manner, indeed now why should he be ashamed about something which was unintentional on his part, no prince would be humiliated by it. "Anyway," he thought, "the star is the last silver I have and it is lucky that it is not embroidered, but made from real silver. Today everything used in costumes is genuine, a true advance in theatrical art!" — Amidst such thoughts he entered the narrow lanes in which could be heard the merry melodies of farewell serenades. "The young pedestrians would like to treat us artists the way they do these wretched beer-hall fiddlers so that we have to toil hours for a few coins hoping to catch their attention for just a few minutes!" — He hurried on further and soon the temple halls of the hot spring, which he thought was some kind of a laundry, stood steaming before him: he saw a white figure in one of the halls which bowed up and down: the singer thanked it politely—but it was the spring itself! "Brother Titan,"[3] he called, "you and I have experienced the same things, you are still raging, humiliated son of the gods, you cannot lift up the rock which weighs you down! Stop," he interrupted himself, "What are you carrying? A dead body? Someone who has been murdered? Account for yourself!" — "Your excellency," a man answered, "if it pleases your majesty we wanted to boil a pig here in the hot spring." — "Oh, if only a piece of rib already cooked was destined for me!" moaned the singer to himself, and then left it up to chance that he would find an inn. "The best inn gives the most credit!" — With these words he suddenly found himself standing

before an imposing house and asked a passer-by: "Is this an Inn?"
— The man greeted him with respect and answered: "This is your
majesty's hotel; it often happens that many a stranger loses his way
at night." — "My dwelling!" thought Halbgott, "it will do for
me; I do not want to reject the kindness of fate, just as I never
avoided her persecution; in the end the world is fair to everyone."
— He walked into the house, immediately a few voices called:
"His majesty!" — Two waiters suddenly appeared before him with
silver candelabras and lighted up the staircase in front of him. "It is
not bad to be treated with such attention as if I was an ambassador
even if they have mistaken me for someone else," he said to himself. The singer cheerfully followed the lighted candles and soon
found himself in a room which although well-furnished did not
really have the appearance of belonging to nobility, inside the
room the tables were covered with minerals. The waiter expressed
his regrets that none of his majesty's people had come home yet and
asked whether he should bring in the soup. The singer nodded
while he gathered together the minerals from one of the tables and
threw them into a corner in order to make room for his script which
he had in his pocket and which he wanted to go over again. He
rejoiced over the fact that his coarse falsetto had come back again,
but he was even more pleased over the prospect of having supper.
Then the waiter came in with a little bowl of soup which he placed
upon a table which had been set. Halbgott tasted it. "Pfui, what is
this?" — "Soup from the spring which your majesty orders every
evening!" — "Not today," cried the singer, "take the spring water
away! Bring me pheasants, trout, champagne! My appetite has
returned today, thank God." — "That usually happens after a period of time," said the waiter, "your majesty looks much better
today." He hurried away, he came back; large trout, partridges and
good wine soon decorated the table. The waiter humbly apologized
for not having been able to procure a pheasant. The singer pardoned him and what is more amidst his great pleasure he forgave
everyone who had persecuted him. "I embrace all you million people out there," he exclaimed. "Here is a kiss for the best of worlds!"

— The waiter had to write down for him the address of the shop which had supplied the champagne, then Halbgott dismissed him so that he could retire for the evening. He saw a bed winking at him from the next room. "That is a bed after my own heart," he said, "Mattress, eiderdown quilt, a pair of elegantly embroidered slippers. Each of the slippers has a coat of arms embroidered upon them, what do they represent? From now on I must wear those instead of my own insignia which depicts the head of Apollo.[4] If only I were a diplomat! One of the coats of arms is also upon the shoe tree, it could, perhaps, tell me something about my own origin. By God! Once I saw that insignia at my mother's house!" — But before he had finished thinking about the coat of arms he had already taken off his clothes and his reflections were soon hushed under the bed covers. He had hardly slept happily but an hour when he was awakened by a shove and someone screaming frightfully for help. He opened his eyes and saw in the reflection of the nightlight his double standing in front of his bed, and this double with his nightgown fluttering drew a sword and assumed the position to attack. Now other people entered the room who stared at the bed with equal astonishment. "The strawberries have poisoned me!" moaned the man with the sword, "I see myself in my own bed." — The singer was the first one to regain his composure and he jumped out of bed, clasped the hand of the shocked double and said: "We look like brothers, perhaps, it so happens that we are, it is late, we both are tired, the bed is large. Dear brother, don't catch cold, bathing in the spa could have opened your pores and your soul could be exposed as through an opening in a grating, bathing could be injurious to your health, your soul could escape right through you; I also do not want to catch cold, therefore take half of the bed, I have nothing against it and am free from all pestilence, I hope you are also!" — The Prince who was already trembling from the night air and who could not help feeling a certain pleasure from the strange manner of his double agreed to the temporary conditions and jumped into the bed from where he continued his conversation. "Who are you?" he asked with author-

173

ity. "Who gave you the right to use my bed?" — "Let us talk about it in the morning," answered his bedfellow yawning. "If you had walked eight long miles in twenty-four hours you would not question the right to a good night's sleep especially if it was forced upon you by obliging servants; unfortunate circumstances and corns on my feet have plagued me, champagne has consoled me, moreover, I am trustworthy; I possess a star, which is my only wealth, a hunting uniform, a type of watch in my trousers, everything I own is in your hands. Good night!" — The chamberlain of the Prince reported the mistake of the waiter, showed his master the sleeping stranger's star which according to the whims of the theater director had been made to look like a spider in its web in order to prevent people from thinking it was a star made out of silver. The chamberlain was even more surprised by the watch whose chain was sewed with several stitches to Halbgott's trousers so that the singer could put both on at the same time. The cheerful Prince could not conceal from the chamberlain that finally he had come across an amusing adventure. He said, moreover, that it was the first evening he felt well and that the bed was wide and could very well accommodate both of them. — The chamberlain was happy that this peculiar event had turned out well, but secretly he had his bed brought into the adjoining room in order to make sure that the stranger could not inflict any harm upon his master.

The Prince awoke first and proceeded to dress and groom himself as he had been taught since a youth, giving equal attention to those preparations which are necessary as well as unnecessary. The singer had also gradually woken up and watched the morning activity smiling with astonishment, the countless brushes, dental powders, tinctures, the many servants on the left and right helping the Prince with his preparations. Finally he could no longer contain himself and exclaimed, "Brother, you act like my old mother, who was beautiful in her time and believes that with a few tricks she can continue to stay the same!" — With these words he sprang out of bed and stood in a few minutes washed, combed and dressed in the clothing of the Prince which had been put out for him instead of his own. Before the fussy gentleman he stood and then reached for his music while the Prince had the minerals carefully picked up which the singer had previously thrown on the floor. The singer sang now so splendidly that the Prince who was a passionate admirer of music embraced him so delighted was he by the first tones and thereupon swore, even if the singer is not secretly also a Prince, he would still have to remain with him for the rest of his life. Then the Prince tried a song himself, and Halbgott assured him he could become a great musician only he would have to promise never to touch the fatal minerals while he was singing because they made noise. "Out of the window with them," said the Prince, "if they bother you; I have always been told what to do and the only activity I have which brings me joy is singing." — "Have you forgotten the hot spring?" the chamberlain asked the Prince seriously and offered him an extremely long porcelain goblet and a bundle of sage leaves. The Prince put his left thumb through the handle on the goblet and the bundle of sage leaves into his buttonhole like a medal, ordered that the singer be given the same things and then hurried ahead with a concerned expression as he said, "Yes, it is high time to go to the spa!" — Then he seized the singer by the arm, made a solemn face and said: "It pleases me to introduce you to the secret wonder of healing mother nature! — The water tastes terrible!" said the Prince as they stood by the spring. — "Ugh!" exclaimed the singer, "what person wants to drink warm water; if you add rum, lemon and sugar to it, it will be worth something. And do you see the people, dear Prince, who count the moments in order to prolong drinking this offensive water as much as possible; what yellow faces, what swollen stomachs. Look how the servants run about with keys! Here are genuine chamberlains, my good servants of the Prince. Your majesty, there is danger here, over there someone is already fainting and there another walks around as if dazed by a funeral sermon and how they speak with one another as if they were half mad because of the effects of the mineral water! For God's sake, your majesty, don't mix with this insane water society, you are young, the only thing you lack is mental exercise; I will cure you, trust the goblet to me, I will place it next to mine; give me your hand, we want to cure our minds, and let old Hebe[5] take the cups and put them along with the sage leaves into the subterranean stone caverns so that the cursed stuff may stand as a warning to everyone and show that what the people so greedily swallow here in their ignorance is fraught with danger. Your hand, Prince, I will make you well, only heed my advice, this water is no friend of man!" — "You are my benefactor," exclaimed the Prince, "you have released me from the power which this fatal water has over me, take my goblet and my hand, I will drink no more from this subterranean sewer. I want to trust you, I want to tell you about the distress which my wife has caused me; you have lived in the world, but I have only observed it from a safe distance, here, we seal our bond!" — With these words the Prince seized the arm of the singer, ordered the chamberlain to remain behind, and ceased to listen to the spa doctor who prescribed for him on this day to drink a half cup of water from the spa of *Neubrunnen,* a half cup of water from the spa, *Mühlbad,* and the same amount from the spa, *Theresienbrunnen.* "Not one more drop!" he exclaimed, "no Prince from the House of Ganzgott has drunk so much water as I." And as they shook hands a crash was heard in the depth of the river, Töpel. "The spa basin has burst!" cried out many people who hurried down into the deep recesses of nature in order to see what had happened. — "A good omen for us," exclaimed Halbgott, "it is a sign that we should drink good coffee instead of water!" — "The city is lost!" many cried out. — "No," replied those who were better informed, "nature has only rid herself of the cork which choked her; we will put it back in again and the hot spring will come back." — "Not for all the world will I wait for it!" thought Halbgott and took Ganzgott by the arm and led him instinctively drawn by the aroma of the coffee to the Bohemian cafe in Puppschen Alley. — "Such enormous trees do not grow near the hot spring, only near coffee!" — Some time was required before the coffee, chocolate and zwieback was made for them for no one ate breakfast so early. While they passed away the time now at the copper engraving booth, both noticed that many passers-by were looking at them with curiosity; they heard many call the singer the Prince's brother. The Prince said with some anxiety: "At last I may ask my guest and friend his name and origin, just now many passers-by thought we were brothers and my heart is sympathetic to this idea." — "Certainly," the singer replied, "would your majesty like to know whether his noble father was in the vicinity of my birthplace? If so, I would answer as that Greek[6] answered Augustus, my father, on the contrary, had been in the residence of his majesty's mother, for he has often told me of the splendid gardens, the castle and the boating excursions. However, these are trifles concerning which I am not that well acquainted; my father died young and my mother pretended innocence; I was not permitted to ask her about my parentage. Enough, something strange may be the undercurrent of my existence. In spite of everything somehow we belong together like two strings of an instrument; I will call myself Halbgott after my alleged father and you will be Ganzgott, and yet so much of the happiness which I have experienced you have never had!" — "To be sure," moaned the Prince, "everything remains out of my reach. If you had not crept uninvited into my bed, I would never have met you! I am given a detailed report about every stranger who comes to my lodging, I am notified in advance about his whole life. Every transaction is so thoroughly completed before it reaches me that even my pen is brought to me already dipped in ink. I enjoy music and acting, but everyone warns me against these arts; I am not allowed to sing to anyone for fear I will compromise my dignity; how happy I would be if only I could do as I like for just a few days, to be like you!" — "Try it, your majesty," exclaimed the singer, "how happy I could make your country in only a few days and myself in the bargain! But your majesty must know about my situation about everything horrible which has plagued me; I am alienated from my mother and from the entire public. While the critics make the highest demands on us, the crowd treats us with disdain; I have shook the dust off my feet, I don't want to see my homeland again. The world is cruel, don't think that we all don't have to live with our own grief." — "And what sorrows have you experienced?" asked the Prince. — "Those damned prophetic mice," exclaimed the singer, "have not allowed my mother to peacefully pursue her fortune-telling, which after all, is her main talent. I reproached her kindly for taming so many mice who would follow her around the house like a troop of her own children. In desperation she wanted to kill herself. I beat them and stepped on the small restless animals, but like a troop of flies in the sunshine, I saw them always there, where my authority did not reach. Once in the night, when they almost chewed the nails off my fingers, I came across the lucky idea to meow like a cat." — "Oh, I can do that too," the Prince said softly, "but I am ashamed to meow in front of my people, every once in a while I have tricked the cats in the castle garden at night with my meowing." — "I was not ashamed of this skill, said the singer, "I meowed; the mice squealed from fear and fled, but my mother believed that I was doing it in my sleep. Now there was in her medicine cabinet no better remedy than sprinkling cold water over a person; so a glass of ice cold water ran down my warm chest; I screamed, a second glass followed. I had to be silent, otherwise she would have drowned me; but the sad result of this treatment made itself felt immediately. In the morning my throat was raw, my uvula was swollen and my falsetto, my high tones, which knew how to creep into everyone's heart like a snake, was gone. I ran to the director, I swore that I could not sing, but he showed me the order from the ruling Duke who had requested the opera for important guests. I had to submit to the demands and tried everything to restore my voice. My mother cooked up all the salves which she had used in vain for her own voice; someone brought me fresh eggs, another, the insides of a herring; one doctor advised me to fast, another to take a magnetic cure. The esteemed public gave me the worst cure and made things uncomfortable for me; the audience was annoyed that I performed the arpeggios in my low register which normally I sang falsetto; they screamed: "higher, higher!" I shrugged my shoulders and sang lower. They pounded and squealed with disapproval, I pounded and squealed back with disapproval. They threw apples at me; fortunately the scene in which I was singing was a domestic one and a basket of potatoes was near me: I nimbly tossed them at the audience and each toss was a hit. The people came to get me; a friend, posted near the trap-door, opened the lid for me, I escaped into the underworld of the theater and from there through a sewer vault. I found myself standing outside upon the main street and scarcely knew how it all happened, but I thanked God and decided to avoid the city forever and to travel here where the nobility gathered in the hopes that they would treat me fairly." — "Delightful, delightful!" exclaimed the Prince, "too bad I can't experience something like that, nothing ever happens to me, I am hemmed in by a thousand considerations! When I die, I will not have lived at all. If we could take each other's place for some time, how I could pacify your mother and appease the public. My relations with people have always been a concern to me so much so that I can't even sever myself from the most annoying servants; I would soon set everything right." — "Your majesty, do that service for me," said the singer, "for just between us, if I disregard the irritations, I have to admit that I lived quite well in our city and had many friends there!" — "But dear Halbgott," continued the Prince, meditating, "as payment for my efforts, could you also put my affairs in order? I live most uncomfortably, the behavior of my boring court takes every pleasure away from me, even the Princess. Every little event in my daily life is thought out, down to the last detail, by these brazen people, whether it is appropriate at the larger courts or not, and what have I to expect from these grand courts? Bothersome interferences, expenditures, nothing else; it was a mistake on my father's part to make me marry the daughter of a great powerful nobleman; to be sure her love could compensate me for all I have to endure, but the court interferes and separates her from me to insure their own interests; everyone whom I thought was my friend has betrayed me." — "Leave everything to me, your majesty," exclaimed the singer with enthusiasm, "I will rid the court of these people who bother you and at the same time the restraints of court life will be good for me; just give me one day to rule your castle, and I will put everything in order!" — "You will not overcome the coldness of the Princess!" exclaimed the Prince. — Amidst such plans the coffee was drunk; enthused by the way their plans had developed, the two unhappy ones walked toward the village, Hammer. It was splendid weather, the fresh green of the meadow sparkled in the dew, lovely children played around them, and the charming flower-boxes of the many cabinet makers, who lived in the village, gleamed in front of the windows. "What beautiful work is done in those dark wooden cottages!" — "If those were only my children," the Prince remarked, "but unfortunately, I have yet to experience the joy of fatherhood; after my death my happy unified country will be split into three kingdoms each ruled by one of my relatives." — The singer vehemently asked the Prince in this case to adopt him; he would marry, let the state pay for the festivities, and he would bring heirs into the world. — The Prince regretted that it would not be possible. So they came amidst much joking to Aicha and to the uniquely formed rock of Hans Heiling. Here they rested; an old fogey, who was their guide, related to them in a most boring manner, the legend of Hans Heiling, who with his whole wedding party was turned into stone. Halbgott asserted: it had been Hans Boring who so bored his betrothed and all the company along the way that they fell asleep and were thus turned into stone. — "That is my fate," exclaimed the Prince, "I bore myself and others by the restraints of court life; my wife and my whole court are already turned into stone; only a quick decision can rescue us from ruin. Here I swear it: we will take each other's place, what was said in jest will now become a reality, otherwise I will never break the stone shell. Who knows, perhaps, my people have considered me for a long time to be just a Hans Boring?" — Halbgott seized the hand of the Prince with enthusiasm; here amidst the rustling of the clear streams, amidst the strange stone forms, the bond, which they had formed early in the morning near the bubbling hot stream of hell surrounded by jaundiced wanderers, was strengthened. How they both were transformed; the sing-

er gestured and spoke like the Prince, the Prince tried to imitate
the easy-going manner of the singer and addressed an inhabitant
of Aicha with familiarity: "My dear man, how can you be eating
already, it is only noon?" The Prince also asked him whether he had
a strong cup of coffee after his meal. The Prince asked the village
blacksmith why he did not use a steam engine to work his bellows.
He then admonished a woman, whose hair had fallen into disarray
around her face from hard work, why she had not properly groomed
herself in the morning. He advised placing the cheese under a glass
cover. In the kitchen he warned against using a copper kettle which
was dangerous and advised replacing it with one made of silver. He
suggested feeding the cows in the barn which had just been driven
up the mountain to pasture; in short: he believed to have given
much good advice, and yet everyone laughed at him. He was surprised by the attitude of the people, but the singer showed him
how estranged he had become from the ways of the world and the
Prince was happy that he finally was becoming acquainted with his
people. In the evening the singer sat in the royal carriage dressed in
the uniform of the Prince with the chamberlain, who was the only
one who knew about their secret. The servants had to remain behind, their gossiping was not to be trusted. The chamberlain because of his rare, cautious nature was completely worthy of the
highest confidence; but only at the end of the two-day journey and
after all the necessities were already agreed upon, did the chamberlain develop such a liking for the singer that he felt he should
inform him of the danger of the situation. "You trust the Prince
because he has agreed to the change of identities in such a solemn
manner," he said. "Do you hope that the Prince will extricate you
from all the unpleasantness which your encounter with the Princess
and the court could bring about? You are mistaken; for when it
comes to plans, intentions, friendships, no one is more unreliable
than our esteemed Prince. If something goes wrong or gives offense
then he tries to put the blame upon someone else and he also has a
talent for getting himself out of difficult situations by making the
other person look guilty. Even if I still cared a lot about his favor, I

would not have accepted this assignment for anything, it is a trap. Through an inheritance left to me by a relative I have become independent for some time; the court has bored me more than I can stand and this joke of yours at least, perhaps, will enable me to leave his majesty's service laughing." — After the chamberlain assured him that it would be of no consequence to him if anyone fell from grace, the singer asked: "How can court life be boring? The Prince is so talented and intelligent." — "If these skills were supplementary to something else, that would be very nice," answered the chamberlain, "but if these flowering trees bear nothing but blossoms, upon what should the fruit grow for us? Such a gentleman as the Prince is raised on pleasantries and luxuries, if he shows receptiveness and intelligence everyone tries to offer him a selection of the best; he acquires knowledge effortlessly like a rich man inherits gold, and because he does not know how to earn it, he does not know how to use it. He welcomes anything that will do for the moment eagerly because it absolves him from struggling with his own doubt and ability and that gives him an appearance of weakness. Instead of teaching him what character is, they teach him not to deviate from an opinion once it has been put into writing. In this manner he is ruled by everyone and everyone thinks he is a compromiser. Have you something in writing from him?" — "No," said the singer, perplexed, "shouldn't his word, his hand and the very fact that we have exchanged roles be enough?" — "You do not know him," exclaimed the chamberlain critically, "but now it is too late, we are at the gate, the watchman stands on guard." — "But how did they recognize us from such a distance?" asked the singer. — "By the odor of the leather of the carriage," answered the chamberlain, "it is the only new carriage in the whole city, also the thunder-storm conductor, which is attached to it, distinguishes it from other carriages." — "A thunder-storm conductor," exclaimed the singer, "we will ruin the theory of its inventor, the storm moves in with us; everyone is already running about as if a rain cloud were approaching; each person should be notified appropriately and be at his post. Take care of the boating party and the removal of the court parasites when you have time; I want to present a genuine fireworks display with all my tricks for the Princess. I'll be damned, the young girls have already assembled and are shrieking a welcome!"

Amidst such disorderly shouting and running about they went into the castle courtyard where two gargantuan grenadiers with leveled bayonets restrained the pushing of the crowd. The Princess sat with her court at the table and looked at the clock to see if it was time to dismiss the guests; for as the old gods were ruled by fate, so the new ones are ruled by time. Then a messenger reported the arrival of the Prince; following behind him was the singer who with his rare acting ability had quickly learned to imitate every movement of the Prince so well that the Princess herself without a moment's hesitation greeted him as her husband. The head housekeeper could not suppress a subdued reproach over the unexpectedness of this arrival; she looked upon a favorite dish hoping it would not become too cold to eat. But Halbgott, after he had kissed the hand of the Princess, handed a piece of music paper to the stiffly corseted housekeeper and sang a friendly Italian greeting song so that everyone became enthused over the happy mood of the Prince and the good effect his visit to the spa of Carlsbad had had upon him. Now he told them of the festivities which the Kings and the Kaiser had organized at the spa, of the Saxonian Hall, the post-court, how colorful lanterns had lit up everything and ordered gondolas decorated with similar colorful lanterns for the Princess and the court in order that the night be enraptured for them by song and wine. Everyone was alarmed; the Princess apologized for a slight illness and asked to be excused, although the idea pleased her very much; but suddenly many glasses which Halbgott had secretly hidden near the candles exploded with crackling noises. The Princess fled holding on to the singer's arm, the others followed, thus they all went into the fragrant garden of the castle which was encircled by a stream. And what warmth was in the air! In addition there was distant summer lightning and the sound of a forest horn was heard upon the barges which were gradually illuminated! Who would have been able to refuse the pleasant invitation to the boating party? Everyone felt that a strange frenzy had overcome them, so unprepared were they to emerge from their customary circle; the continuous beat of the strokes of the oar was the only thing which eased the restless agitation of the whole court. Other boats accidentally came towards them from the city; our Halbgott ordered that they have a little pirate's war, the boats were steadied and the crew transferred into the main ship, and to the astonishment of the court at this moment the most polite women from the city suddenly found themselves amongst nobility and no one had the courage to point out that this was not proper. Only the Princess wished to exclude herself from them because her mother insulted by the offense to her daughter could start a war; for that reason Halbgott led her across into one of the captured ships and sang at her feet, "La Biondina,"[7] to the accompaniment of his guitar while the Princess sat upon her tall seat and rustled her fan very properly. Then everyone let themselves go in the great pleasure boat, old memories stirred in the hearts of the oldest people; they spoke of the beautiful times when the adjutants of General Tilly and Wallenstein livened up the court, of Max Piccolomini and Seni,[8] who had told them their fortunes; even the head housekeeper joined the lord high chamberlain in a conversation. If only the Prince were here, thought the singer, who sat at the feet of the Princess, he could harvest what I have sowed, he would be satisfied with me; already the Princess has tapped my head with her fan as if she wanted to say something casual to me; she appears quite moved, she moans. — He feared all further comments and yet he did not know how to avoid them although she had requested that they sail back to land. She hung on to his arm tightly, she assured him that if he had always been so amusing, so full of life and so affectionate, the whole quarrel, the separation between them, would not have happened; but she feared to have children who would be born out of boredom and disgust, such a state of affairs would have affected their whole future. Halbgott assured her that the future could straighten out everything between them, they both would probably have many

years to live together, and on this day he had decided to rid the
castle of all the scandalmongers and court parasites who had refused
the warm approaches of the Princess. The bothersome people
would all be removed through the actions of the chamberlain to the
old hunting castle, which lies a quarter of an hour's distance away,
their possessions had already been taken there and they themselves
would be taken there in the large gondolas, thinking to find there a
festival they would find there instead their sleeping quarters, their
whole future household goods, a church in which they will hold
their daily prayer meetings, gardens in which they can enjoy peace
and quiet, in short, this castle would be transformed by the magic
wand of the chamberlain into a prison for useless court parasites
and ambassadors. — "Splendid," cried the Princess, "how your
spirit awakens, your determination ripens, this day must give us
back what our petty differences took away from us!" — The singer
interrupted this speech while he drew the attention of the Princess
to the nightingales which had sounded with unending power their
last call of the year from their leafy abode in the pruned linden trees
by the main entrance. — "The nightingales are our hearts," said
the Princess and when the singer did not reply to her statement,
she withdrew her arm from him and moved towards the castle with
some agitation. But she tried to ameliorate her rash action; she
turned around at the door and said: "I want to look at you in the
moonlight from the distance; you have a splendid noble appearance, I also love you from afar!"

They finally parted and the singer told the chamberlain of the
distress which the unexpected tenderness of the Princess caused
him. "I thought I never would be able to confront the clever,
learned manner of the woman, I feared that I would have to insult
her and I would have to run away from her in order not to endanger
my friendship with the Prince; the charms of the Princess, unlike
those of the Prince, are too much to resist." The chamberlain,
embarrassed, paced up and down the floor and swore that moods
were unpredictable; he would have expected arguments and quar-
rels rather than tenderness, he would rather have believed that

someone could have broken through the ice of the North Pole than the heart of the Princess. — Amidst this conversation a noise was heard upon the secret staircase which led from the bedroom of the Princess to that of the Prince in which they both now found themselves. With a leap the singer planted himself under the bed and ordered the chamberlain to say to the Princess that he had gone for a walk because the weather was so beautiful. Instead of the Princess an old lady-in-waiting appeared with a request from the Princess to let her know the time since her clock had stopped during the nightly excursion. The chamberlain gave her the clock of the Prince, but the old woman still lingered, turned to the bed of the Prince and fastened a splendid bouquet of flowers to it; then she winked at the chamberlain to be quiet and withdrew again through the secret passage. The imprisoned Halbgott now slipped out from under the bed; the chamberlain pointed to the bouquet, Halbgott could not restrain himself from smelling the flowers with a feeling of happiness as if they were the first flowers he had found on earth. But still more: he found a note attached to the flowers; his heart beat so fast that he could scarcely read it. What did it say? A spiritual song: "Now all the forests rest!" — "What does that mean?" — The chamberlain laughed. "One of her old peculiarities with which she so often alienated the Prince; her tenderness has turned into a religious fervour like one who has become excited while turning the pages of a magazine and whose transformation is difficult to see!" — "Oh, I can understand this," exclaimed the singer, "I will sing from out of my window my part from Pergolesi's *Stabat Mater* which I find here upon the piano of the Prince; that should please her and touch her heart. Damn it! I cannot totally repress the courtesies due a beautiful woman."

The windows were opened, Halbgott sang the *Stabat Mater* to the accompaniment of the piano like a complete god; his voice had returned to him with full force, and with the agility of a sleep-walker he knew how to descend from the highest tones of his voice to his lowest and then to climb upwards again. The chamberlain kissed his hand enthusiastically, the nightingales moaned during the pauses in the music, the fountain pushed its huge stream of water higher up to the stars in the sky, the glowworms like the messenger of the stars floated through the open window and flew around the head of the singer like a circle of stars; only a cursed cat began to meow terribly on the terrace so that almost simultaneously the singer, the chamberlain and the Princess on the top floor hissed and scolded out of the windows; but it did not help, the beast wanted to be heard as was customary for a cat and in its own way received applause, for from all sides came its brothers and sisters, dear ones and not-so-dear ones who alive and biting gathered around their howling relative. — And now the servant of the Princess came quietly again and walked up the secret staircase with a little letter for the alleged Prince from her mistress. The singer read it when he was alone with the chamberlain:

> No more time should be lost,
> My clock stands still today.
> And that which my lips do not want to say,
> I hear ringing in my ears.
> Ringing ear, what do you want to say?
> Does he not think of my love?
> Should I be afraid, should I risk it?
>
> What seemed like ringing in my ears,
> Is his divine singing in the night,
> And he sings a *Stabat Mater;*
> But accompanying it is the meowing of a cat!
> Whoever heard of something like that?
> Is it a devil who disturbs us?
> Is it an angel who warns us,
> Because the devil ensnares us?

The singer wanted very much to answer that it was a good angel, but he was supposed to answer in rhyme only which he was not capable of doing; he could not express himself in writing especially well. What was he to do? From the window above the Princess asked him what he thought of her verses, she could not sleep, he

187

should keep her company. The old servant came in with a light in order to show the way; the chamberlain rubbed his forehead. "In a minute, in a minute!" said the singer in embarrassment. "Yes!" he continued, — then something slid toward the window on wheels like those of a spinning wheel which has gone out of control. "Is that the grandmother?" — "No, it is the grandfather!" — "It is the Prince upon his Drasine,[9] he orders us to help him in through the window." — It was the Prince, with the help of the singer he climbed in through the window. — "Greetings, brother," exclaimed the Prince, "let me kiss you, you have worked wonders; but I also did my part, I travelled fifteen miles today in my Drasine; tomorrow in return for your help I have something good to tell you which concerns you; rest here for the night, I will hurry to the Princess!" — With these words he hastened after the servant of the Princess who was waiting with a light and left the singer in a state of happy suspense to ponder over the news which he would hear in the morning. But the day which should explain everything already began to rise in the east like a red apple blossom and his eyes closed from fatigue, while the chamberlain drove the Drasine of the Prince through the main entrance of the garden towards the rising sun. — "I call that healthy snoring, you sound like a pair of bellows blowing upon a fire!" said the Prince who had already been sitting in front of Halbgott's bed for a long time when suddenly the singer opened his eyes. "I call that happy dreaming," answered the singer, "was I dreaming correctly? Was your majesty the cat, and are you my brother?" — "Truly God gave you a sign in your sleep!" answered the Prince and embraced him, "I was the cat, I am your brother; and like a cat I had to disturb you, you don't know what your voice caused; the Princess cried so much from the top floor that her tears made the flowers glisten. As your brother I have put everything in order for you. Your mother knew my father intimately, but only for a short time, her stubbornness separated them; she ran away took another name out of spite in order not to be reminded of their relationship; she tormented you because you look like our father. My father instructed me in his will to take care of her, he knew nothing of your existence. Brother, come to my heart, you are blood of my blood, I have no brother who is more genuine than you; I thank you from the bottom of my heart, I thank you for the love of the Princess; because of you I have found happiness. We will all live joyously from now on, only my wife feels ashamed in your presence because she said such affectionate things to you. However, I have become just like you in only a few days; I eat and drink what tastes good to me; I am healthy like a fish; and just think of the joy I had when I appeared using your name, my playing and singing met with such approval that the hands of the audience almost dropped off from clapping so much. Imagine that everyone thought you were dead; a corpse who looks like you was found in a stream; your tormenters thought you had committed suicide because of the misery they had caused you; then when they finally realized what great talent you had, they glorified you and cried over you at your funeral. And when I suddenly appeared a rapture overpowered these stubborn people, they believed you were being resurrected from the grave on the day of judgement. I want to help you with your art, help me, brother, to rule my kingdom; especially today when all the administrators from the nearby provinces will greet me after my happy homecoming and request my orders. Please take over for me today when I am distracted by so much joy and want to live only for my wife; you know the world, these people are no different from anyone else; thunder down upon them like they have never experienced before. They are all probably worth nothing, for I who knew nothing have never been worth much. Everything will become different under your leadership, and from now on we will concern ourselves with something other than looking at skirts. I am no longer a Hans Boring, the stony shell of my princely habit has burst open; even the spring itself had burst its heavy stone cover as if it was celebrating the sealing of our living, endearing bond as we left Carlsbad; it had to be as fate ordained it. Brother you are also no longer the same, you already walk ceremoniously like a minister of state and that you shall become, put everything in harmonious order through the power of your song, you second Orpheus!" — "Heaven grant it, I thank you for the honor, brother of my heart!" exclaimed the singer, "I will take your administrators down a peg, bring your cooks up to date, bring depth into your theater, make your orchestra sweat and bring laughter to your court! But brother keep my mother away from me with her mice!" — "Upon my return from the spa my provincial councils are coming to present their good wishes," exclaimed the Prince, "I hear them already in the antechamber clearing their throats and blowing their noses. Now wait, I will hide with the Princess!"

The chamberlain announced the delegation and Halbgott nodded graciously. The members of the board of finance were introduced and the director expressed how pleased he was that the Prince looked so well. "You alone gentlemen," said Halbgott, "can cure me; both my people and I are ill, we are sick of your wasteful ways; you cost the human race more time on earth than there is in all eternity. A penny gained is worth little if it is bought with a dollar. I forbid you to write any more decrees, use the wit you waste on paper in another direction. What have you accomplished with your countless edicts? Paper has become expensive, my country is a wasteland, yet those of my neighbors are gardens. Instead of cultivating decrees, cultivate the land; you have many caterpillars in your head, take them out before it is too late. First learn the beat before you ask the people to dance to the tune of your pipe; it is better to do nothing at all than something clever and inopportune, think before you do something if you don't want your actions to backfire. Listen, I am asking you to do one more thing for me, history is not an adding machine, it is not predictable, that which is past cannot be changed much less erased. Thus do not always trust the philosophy you learned in school, it is neither imaginative nor practical; also do not think that you have to compromise your ideas for protocol. Look further than the end of your nose and don't stick it into affairs which do not concern you. When you start something you cannot foresee the end; therefore do not disturb things for which you have no alternative, do not draw any conclusions if you are in doubt. Learn from the doers, not from words, and don't think you can teach them because you can speak more eloquently. Do not control honest people, the rascals don't want to be controlled. Do not try to find fault with rights which are justly earned because you are bored, convince yourself that the past is not unreasonable and that you too must think. Heaven will give its blessing to the least demanding, not the highest bidder, therefore, never ask too much at one time from the people, only ask that which is justifiable. See how you would feel if you had to follow for only a few weeks the many thousands of decrees you issue which only an eternity could fulfill!" — With these words Halbgott's mother came in to the astonishment of the attentive council with the angry expression of a Welsh rooster upon her face, heavily made up and wearing an enormous curly wig covered with old gauze bonnets which resembled a balloon. The Prince had not been able to hold her back and was pulled into the room by her. "Cospetto di Bacco,[10] for the love of God!" she shrieked, "you bad boy!" — "But mother," the singer answered, "are you not impressed with the way I am playing the role of the Prince here, soon I will become a minister of state. The department of justice and the clergy are still waiting for me to graciously admonish them. Look at the painting of the Prince's father upon the wall, whom you almost annoyed to death with your whims, isn't his face frightful. Look he is rolling his eyes at you, telling you to have respect for me." — "Damned Prince!" she exclaimed and looked angrily at the painting. In the meantime the members of the council, realizing that the Prince who had scolded them was an imposter, began to protest. Likewise the exiled court parasites and ambassadors broke in and stormed the Prince with their complaints about the way the double of the Prince had mistreated them. The clergy appealed to the conscience of the Prince. The Prince looked towards the singer for help, but the latter was overcome by the stormy assaults of his mother. The Prince uncertain of what to do asked the members of the council and the courtiers whether the singer had not shown them some sort of a legal document, he himself knew nothing of

191

such a thing. They all cried out unanimously: "No, nothing has been put into writing." — "Well then everything can still be changed," said the Prince, "I had never intended such a thing, my will is unshakable, that you all know!" — At the same time he gave a reprimand to the chamberlain which was really intended for the singer. The latter heard the reprimand even though he was standing in another part of the room and feared that now he would be hissed at even more in the state theater than at the provincial theater where he had last been employed. Fortunately, the Drasine is still standing in front of the window, he thought, and wanted to jump on it and escape. But first, not wanting to leave anything behind, he seized the bouquet of the Princess which she had sent to him during the night; then, as if the flowers had some magic power, the Princess came into the room through the secret entrance. She probably had been eavesdropping, the sun had broken through the clouds with her entrance; smiling graciously she ordered the court parasites and council members to accept the following decree otherwise she would request they be executed by her noble father. Then she kissed the Prince tenderly and said that her husband had ordered her to acknowledge Halbgott as his rightful half-brother before the highest dignitaries of the land through her kiss. The singer knelt down; she kissed his forehead and said: with this kiss he would receive an edict which would allow him to say everything that he thought; no one can be offended by him. — "Oh, blessed moment!" exclaimed the singer, "so I am to be appointed court jester!" — "No, as minister of state," the Princess contradicted him, "here are the legal documents signed by my husband." The singer seized them and exclaimed, "Yes, truly, now I have it in writing, a thousand thanks! But if I should raise this land to the highest peak of happiness then my mother is to be given the post of official state fortune teller with a salary agreeable to her and give the old paper documents to the mice to eat so that there will be room for new decrees. The mice and the cards are her crystal ball and they will tell us something about the future which should be particularly helpful in ruling the country; she also has a billy goat which is sitting now in the garden, employ him as a gardener with an appropriate salary; her blind dog will be satisfied with the honor of receiving a medal to wear on his collar. So in this way the country would come to order." The Prince authorized these requests and Halbgott's Italian mother declared that she was totally satisfied. — Now happy wishes could be heard from all sides, the small cannons in front of the castle were fired, the Japanese bell was rung solemnly in the castle church to summon the city to a celebration. In order to fill out the interval between the announcement and the celebration, the singer sat at the piano and sang with the most splendid variations:

> What has to be, will be,
> Nothing can escape fate,
> Nothing can alter its final decision,
> That is proven by the kiss of the Princess.

From ON FOLK SONGS[11] [1805]
To Johann Friedrich Reichardt

When the people untie the horses from the hero's wagon as he enters the city and pull the wagon themselves, they do so not because they can pull the wagon better, but because this is their way of paying homage to their hero. In the same manner I will discuss folk songs with the best of intentions and gratitude to you, but at the same time I do not wish to suppress or give up the important ideas I have concerning this type of music. I have addressed this essay to you, Reichardt, because of our friendship and our mutual interest in folk songs. You have done more for old German folk songs than any living musician, you have brought these deserving melodies to the attention of the learned class. Noble pursuits can never be boring, thus I hope you will join me as I turn my thoughts toward a subject of great value. I will present to you many observations from various periods and places. These remarks will demonstrate unanimously that the only thing which moves our nation is the folk song, nothing so thoroughly else captures its attention.

What is it that people hear in the folk song? Everything which happens in the world, everything which has been put aside, but yet is not forgotten, and all those things which cannot rest until they are allowed to bring a higher form of pleasure to mankind, these are the things one hears in the folk song. I did not realize this for a long time and I do not expect everyone to believe what I have to say. One cannot arrive at any type of understanding until one studies the history of mankind, until one literally works one's way back to the beginning of the world, a process which is arduous, but necessary if we are to gain any insight into man's place in the universe.

When I pause to think about folk songs[12] then a sense of the present, of the orderliness and clarity of life overcomes me. These songs never leave my mind although I have not heard them for a long time. I heard them as a child from my nurse as she was cleaning the room, her melodies accompanying every sweep of the broom. As I listened to these melodies a feeling of utter stillness came over me. I often wondered why these songs affected me in this manner. Children hear them less often now, I wonder how they occupy their minds. Afterwards when I attended various social gatherings I heard all kinds of melodies in Schulz's songs.[13] My tutor praised them saying that only the poems of Gellert[14] were greater than the songs of Schulz. Now I must admit that the songs of this composer helped me during a time when my mind was in a state of disorder, when I was attracted to sentimentality. The songs were able to help me because I sensed in them a true tone comparable to that kind of laughter which comes from the bottom of one's heart. Later on in my life I saw the power of these songs strangely diminished, many things of greater glitter passing by attracted people more. These glittering things pass by the crowd which stands there gaping and then submerge into the witches' cauldron of the overworked, the hackneyed and the trite.

That which I love in poetry I never hear sung, generally speaking, hence I would rather whistle the beautiful melodies in order to get rid of the false cuckoo eggs[15] which are laid in the nest of the noble song bird. However, if I happened to be so fortunate as to hear some learned person singing, "Kennst du das Land?"[16] accompanied by the piano as you suggested, Reichardt, then I imagined I saw the four walls around me become like the Herculean columns,[17] which for a long time have separated the busy segment of the people from the fiery bed of the sun. If I then saw someone quietly reading Goethe's wonderful poem, "Der Fischer,"[18] it seemed to me as if I could see the magnificent image, half sinking, half submerging into the water, suffocating. This same fate befalls everything splendid, it is smothered.

Mediocre, common words gain new significance when spoken in the theater, this is particularly true of those contrived idiomatic expressions which are commonly used today to create a nationalistic atmosphere, but instead of being nationalistic, these phrases become more and more alien to our culture. The theater in the end even imagined that it actually stood above the nation (but I think only like the gallows made of a few feet of wooden boards, which looks over the city). The noble tones of music, however, pulled these vulgar words down the street where they reverberated like an echo and the serious choirboys in their blue robes standing embarrassed before the audience had to sing them, had to perform these songs which were the result of the disagreement which occurred between the poet and the musician who were no more united than the doctor and the pharmacist.[19] A beautiful poem set to an inferior melody only endures for a while, like a person exhausted from merry-making, it is drained of all strength; the music ensnares us into this confusing maze and frightened by the poetry which appears like an imprisoned dragon to us we try at once to find the thread which will lead us out of this labyrinth of tones and words. Thus empty poetry often draws us away from music, perhaps, even spoils the music for us.

New ideas cause old ideas to become obsolete, not because new ideas are more valuable, but because people demand so much constant change. This quest for novelty has cleared the road for the arrival of frivolous types of songs which are the antithesis of true folk songs. In this whirlwind of novelty, in this kind of confused rush to create an alleged paradise on earth almost all folk songs have been extinguished. This occurred, for example, in France (perhaps, even before the Revolution, which itself might have contributed to the disappearance of the folk song) where few folk songs exist today. Yet it is only the folk song which can bind a people to that which is everlasting. Folk songs are not sung as much as they used to be in Italy and Italian opera is also declining because of the cravings of empty-headed people for novelty. Even in Spain several folk songs have disappeared and nothing of importance is created now in that country. Oh, my God, where are the old trees under which we rested yesterday, where are the ancient signs of our values, what has happened to them, what is happening? They are almost forgotten amongst the people, every once in a while we stumble across them and it is painful. Once the summits of the high mountains are completely eroded and the rain drives the earth downward no trees will grow there again. That Germany does not suffer this fate is our main concern.

Where I first experienced the full energetic power and feeling of the folk song was in the country. Once on a warm summer night lively shouts awakened me. Then I saw out of my windows through the trees the servants and the village people singing to each other:

> Up, up brothers and be strong!
> The departing has come;
> We travel over land and sea
> Into hot Africa.[20]

They stopped their singing and departed for their regiment which was preparing for war. Many sounds pleased my ears at that time, everything which I heard sung came from people who are not trained singers and their music charmed me immensely whether they were miners or chimney sweeps. Later I realized that what singers strive for is actually accomplished by these folk, namely, that one sound echoes in many persons and unites everyone. This unity is the highest prize that a poet and a musician can attain. This prize, however, is seldom obtained and has not been earned for a long time (yet for every flower that is trampled upon a thous-and bloom in its place); thus when a song of the people which is a hundred years old appears either in spirit or in some melody (usual-ly both) it is of value.[21]

Man has become a servant to materialism, this miserable state of affairs is as conspicuous as the yellow dust of worm-eaten wood. Everyone has something to say about his life, however, there was no spiritual life. Life became disdainful, death fearful and in this poverty originality was devoured. Wisdom was vain, empty (as plain as the servant girls of Saint Petersburg who should go and beg for some makeup). Suddenly the whole world became poor, times were hard, there were no morals, the end of the world was at hand, all had occurred during peaceful times, during a time of plenty, in the spring, and no one realized that the world had reached such a point. People were short-changed, like in the market place, their minds cheated, no one wanted or was able to follow the spiritual side of his nature, physical impulses dominated mankind. No class of people felt they were good enough simply because there was a need for their existence, as there is for the fruits of the earth, rather they had to convince themselves of their worth by making up rules. Thus the aristocracy wanted to improve their lineage, the mer-chants imagined that they truly belonged to the moral culture of the world, the intelligentsia thought that there was a divine qual-ity in everything they said, but those who scorned everything be-lieved they knew it all. A lot could be said still about the general aspects of these phenomena, just take a look at the nearest collec-tion of paintings hanging on the walls of an old house and see how true ugliness and picturesque falseness have come into the world. It is more important, however, to observe the consequences of this general trend on the folk song; in many regions folk songs have completely died out, sunk amidst the dirt and the emptiness of the heavily travelled street.

People tried to desecrate these songs when folk festivals took place by removing from them every trace of life, or performing them in awkward ways until the songs broke into pieces and became slanderous music. Music, stage plays and plays whose purpose it is to fool the audience, how the city needs all three of these forms of entertainment to reconcile itself to the fact that its people are imprisoned, how different is the countryside, how it enjoys its three day wedding festivals and its continuous fairs. But soon the purpose of these entertainments was to provide money for a select group of individuals. Joy and spirit remained locked up in isolated circles, a mockery against those left out, but at the same time these select circles became the object of mockery. The existing public entertainments, masked balls, bird hunts and processions became for the most part divertissements in which few participated, they became like the old Christmas trees of poor families which were lit up year after year, each time losing more and more of their leaves. Also the cheerful sounds of the triangle of the Bohemian miners no longer sounded for the children to come and start the procession, the custom of the three Kings no longer exists.[22] But why should I talk about children when the politicians let the world turn itself ten times in a quarter of an hour from enlightenment to darkness simply because they are bombarded with suggestion from all corners to get rid of old customs? But could it be that while all this was going on, something else happened which was not noticed simply because it happened? The journeying of the tradesmen is becoming restricted, at least encroached upon, military service in foreign countries is completely stopped, students are forced to remain in the fatherland. Yet the highest and most important part of a student's life is to experience foreign culture to the fullest in order to compare their own customs with those of other lands, in order to balance out their education.

Who doubts in these times that the participation of the people is really missing? It is missing in war, it is missing in peace, an insurmountable burden is being placed upon the young men of future generations. Since the time when I was able to think I have noticed that human activity is becoming slower and slower like the hours of rest and eating supplant one another and yet diminish one another; thus all passions and enjoyments do not last as long any more, their effect on our lives is diminishing. Most people turn away from their true nature like dry wood jumps away from the fire. Many never reach that point in life when they feel a unity between themselves and the world, when one thing is enough to truly satisfy and fulfill their lives; such persons are forever longing, they are only the embryos of living beings and few of them ever experience youth or old age. Just as the beams of our ceilings are today weakened by an unknown mold, men are suddenly becoming hollow and empty, they carry no burden, support nothing, accomplish nothing, strive for nothing. Where have the songs disappeared to? They lie lost in that which is commonplace, lost in the sea of the world amidst a thousand treasures. I would like to signal the storks to stay away! Don't fetch anyone out of the sea of the world, do not bring a human being into the world for he would only long to return again to the sea of triviality, even if the sea is being washed away and the tide is low. There is only one devil and many angels. Is it still possible to be delivered, or is the choice only one of pain? I wonder if the world will stop long enough to allow something extraordinary to happen. Those that speculate about it earnestly seem to feel it is possible, for this is the dream of activity, only we ourselves are conscious of this morning dream.

When in the evening during a winter storm I walk past the theater where light and life have been extinguished, I think probably that the quiet clock will strike once, its sound hovering above the lingering hours. Then the lid of the coffin will open itself and the larva is broken apart by a colorful choir, the new group of larvae will rise up and fly across the land as all kinds of different musical sounds are dispersed into the air awakening everyone who had already been asleep. Ice stays frozen for a long time before it breaks

under the strain of a great weight. But that person who only once
walked with strength through all the wonderful entwining paths of
his predecessors, his eyes having seen the lustre of the sun spring-
ing up before him, that person can foresee the joyous life in the free
stream, he wishes to swim in it, sail upon it, ride in and through it,
chasing after the rustling stag, then he will rest upon the green turf
of its bank, see the stars in it, stars which submerge into eternal
reflection. He who only once lost and forgot himself in the dance,
he who saw a balloon rising upward quietly like the sun and
through it receives the last greeting of insignificant man, he who
also found himself carried away by the *Janitscharen*,[23] an enemy
against him and looking to see if his courageous comrade is still
with him, he who saw the riders coming towards him upon the
clouds and irresistibly like a trumpet blow stopped the mighty
stream, he who even saw the anchor lights of a war fleet in the
sunshine upon whose decks a few moments ago are filled with activity, to see those golden castles and galleries float quietly away into
the dense ocean, like the fins of a fish, these are all things which
surround us and which we encounter in our daily lives, he must
believe in a Sunday after the six work days which everyone experiences and from which everyone derives pleasure. All the trombone
players in the tower even if they had played a thousand times and
were never heard, on this day and in this morning hour, they would
be allowed to accompany the songs of the people and the bells one
more time. No matter how gently we rest, we would rather be
awakened, and then everything will rise like the anchor of a ship as
the sailors sing their simple song, as long as they sing together.
What I hope for is no empty dream, history has proved how the
pure striving of mankind steps forward victorious and singing.

Listen as the migrating birds beautifully sing of the new spring,
already the valiant craftsmen with their bundles and leather carrying cases walk across the paths in long rows; see how they draw
comfort from the song of the bird, see how the window pane and
the metal sign which hangs outside the house tremble from the
sound of the clavier, where there is singing, there is unity, where

Germans are needed from London to Moscow to Rome there is no
half-hearted song:

> Arise, comrades, travel along,
> Fetch your bundles and skins!
> But before we turn our backs
> To the city with our last steps,
> Give us, girl, a kiss and a glass of wine,
> To travel on with toward the sun.[24]

In the autumn when everything was almost still and all the trees
had lost most of their leaves, it so happened that I came across a
thick leafy tree with branches entwined and full of starlings singing and flying about. In a similar manner the songs of the German
craftsmen elevated my spirits as I stood in the damp night air by
the Dutch canals; their songs caused a small sail to flutter, and it
seemed to me as if the ship was being quickly pulled away by
colorful ribbons. Have not others experienced something like this,
even if it were only in a dream? Thus I heard over the London
Bridge fugitives from Hanover[25] singing: "A free life"[26] and as I
looked into the surface of the water towards my fatherland with
longing, that land with its angry red evening sun appeared to me
like a friend.

Now if such a simple art, like these songs, can be so moving,
how is it possible that grandiose intellectual works so often produce no feeling at all? He who does not want to achieve the highest,
also cannot achieve the smallest. That person to whom the circumstances of life are favorable creates simple art naturally and effortlessly reaps a great harvest and nourishes everyone and everyone can
live as God planned it. To one who comes in touch with the people
and gets to know them intimately, the wisdom of the ages is an
open book and he may proclaim to all, songs, sagas, knowledge,
sayings, stories, prophesies and melodies. He is like a fruit tree
which a gentle gardener has pruned and made a garland from its

white and red roses. The power of simple songs allows everyone to call mightily into the heart of the world which usually only a few can do with only their strength. This person of whom I have been speaking gathers his scattered people together under his banner, no matter how divided they are by language, political prejudices, religious beliefs, and idle novelty through song, and by singing of a new era. And although his banner has no trophies and, perhaps, is only the torn sail of the ship of the Argonauts[27] or the blown coat of a poor singer, whoever carries it may not find distinction in it, but he may find his duty in it. For we all seek something higher, the Golden Fleece, which belongs to everyone, which is the wealth of our entire people, and which has formed its own inner living art, we all search for this fabric which belongs to ages past and mighty powers, for this fabric is the faith and wisdom of the people and all that accompanies them in life and death, the history of mankind is contained in their songs, sagas, knowledge, sayings, stories, prophecies and melodies.

NOTES

1. Although I translated Ganzgott as whole god and Halbgott as half-god or demigod in the Introduction (p. 20), it seemed more appropriate to retain the German names Arnim used for the two brothers in his story in the actual English rendition.
2. This story dates from Arnim's own stay in Carlsbad, a celebrated spa in West Bohemia. Thus this tale, like Körner's *Edward and Veronica,* is partly autobiographical and contains many references to local sites.
3. Titans, race of ancient Greek deities connected with the power of nature who were overthrown and succeeded by Zeus and the Olympian gods. The "humiliated son of the gods" probably refers to Atlas, one of the second generation of Titans who was condemned to support the sky on his shoulders for eternity because of his part in the war against Zeus.
4. The god Apollo and the demigod Orpheus equated with Halbgott are related in Greek mythology; Orpheus is said to be the son of Apollo, who taught him to play the lyre.
5. Hebe, a daughter of Zeus and official cupbearer of the gods.

6. "That Greek," possibly Timagenes, Greek historian and contemporary of Augustus (63 B.C.-14 A.D.). Although a friend of the Emperor for a time, Timagenes later became an outspoken critic of his policies.

7. "La Biondina," a Romance by the composer, Ferdinand Paer, ED.

8. Wallenstein, Tilly, etc., historical personages in the Thirty Years War (1618-1648).

9. Drasine, early type of bicycle with a wooden frame, two wheels and a saddle seat named after its inventor, Baron Karl Drais of Mannheim, ED.

10. Cospetto di Bacco, i.e., Bacchus, Roman god of wine and revelry, ED.

11. In the most recent edition of Brentano's works edited by Heinz Rölleke (Berlin: W. Kohlhammer, 1975-) Arnim's essay, *On Folk Songs,* has been placed where it originally appeared in 1805, i.e., in the appendix to *Des Knaben Wunderhorn.* Unless otherwise indicated "ed" in the following notes refers to the edition of Arnim's works edited by Monty Jacobs.

12. Arnim uses the term "Kirchenlieder" here. I do not think, however, that he means church songs as such, but rather simple devotional songs of the people.

13. We have here another reference to the popular songs of Johann Abraham Schulz.

14. Christian F. Gellert (1714-1769), German poet and moralist.

15. The European cuckoo bird lays its eggs in the nests of other birds and leaves its young to be reared by foster parents. When the cuckoo eggs hatch the young birds because of their size soon push the others out of the nest. In Arnim's metaphor, the false cuckoo eggs are the bad lyrics which are destroying the noble song bird, i.e., the folk song.

16. "Do you know the Land Where the Lemon Trees Bloom?" is one of the ten "songs" in Goethe's *Wilhelm Meister.* This favorite poem of the Romantic composers was set by Reichardt, Schubert, Schumann and Liszt; Arnim is referring to Reichardt's version, in which it would appear he felt the lyrics and the melody were well-matched. In this poem Mignon expresses her yearning for her homeland, Italy.

17. Herculean columns, term used in the writings of the Greeks to refer to the promontory of the Strait of Gibraltar which symbolized the boundary between earth and the world beyond, Heinz Rölleke, ED.

18. A brief summary of Goethe's poem, "Der Fischer," might be helpful here in understanding Arnim's imagery. In this poem, a fisherman glances into the water as he watches his rod. Suddenly from out of the water a woman emerges singing and talking to him. She asks him why he disturbs her with his wit and devious manner. The fish, she tells him, are happy down in the water. The fisherman becomes full of longing and follows her into the water, never to return again.

19. Arnim is referring here to the comic opera, *Doktor und Apotheker (The Doctor and the Pharmacist)* by Karl von Dittersdorf, ed.

20. Arnim is quoting from the first stanza of Christian Daniel Schubart's well-

known poem, "Kaplied" ("Cape Song," 1787) which appears in *Des Knaben Wunderhorn* under the title, "Das heisse Afrika" ("Hot Africa," ed.). Incidentally, Heine quoted the same lines in his Preface to *Salon* I.

21. The following long but important footnote is by Arnim: While speaking of the above I cannot refrain from telling you about the wonderful splendid preface which Georg Forster wrote for his *Frischen Liedlein,* Nürnberg, 1552, a passage which is a favorite of mine. "Dear friendly singer and lover of noble music, in the past few years many song books have been printed and I let the people who have knowledge of songs judge their value. I deliver my little song book to you and with it old German songs which if I may say so are almost the best, as are the composers who wrote them, composers who were brought up with music, dealt with music, and ended their life with music. I present these to you so that they are not completely forgotten and so that many new unrhymed compositions will not be used instead of these, for these new ones are not part of the real tradition of song. I am also publishing this collection so that during the various festivities fresh German songs should be sung or played so that a lot of unnecessary babbling, unflattering toasting, arguments, unfair play can through the singing of these songs be avoided. I often heard the following said by a splendid man: 'among all the ways one could spend his time there is no more honest, beautiful or divine entertainment than music. All other ways to pass the time such as playing games, fencing, wrestling, jumping, are all oriented in such a manner as to make everyone determined to do their best and to outdo the others which then causes many disagreements and anger. Music, however, has no other purpose than to maintain harmony, the unity of mankind, of all voices.' Some of the best songs in our collection come from the marvelous selection of Georg Forster which shows that merit does not disappear." (By "collection" Arnim means *Des Knaben Wunderhorn.*)

22. Arnim is referring here to the old German Christmas custom of children dressing up as the three Kings and going from door to door asking for treats.

23. Janitscharen, a group of soldiers who since 1329 consisted of war prisoners converted to the Islamic faith. Since the fourteenth century this group continued to grow in size and was incorporated into the regular Turkish army in the seventeenth century.

24. At the end of this poem Arnim had written, "Liebesrose, Lied 18." According to Heinz Rölleke this title refers to a collection of old German poems, the manuscript of which (YD5161) is in the Preussischer Kulturbesitz.

25. Arnim is looking back to his London journey of 1803; in July of that year Hanover was besieged by French troops.

26. Quotation from Schiller's *Die Raüber* (*The Robbers,* 1781), Heinz Rölleke, ED.

27. In Greek legend the men who sailed with Jason to search for the Golden Fleece (Argo being Jason's ship).

Heinrich von Kleist

[1771-1811]

HOLY CECILIA OR THE POWER OF MUSIC [1810]

NEAR THE END of the sixteenth century, when the iconoclastic riots raged in the Netherlands, three brothers, young students at the University of Wittenberg, met together in the city of Aachen with a fourth brother, who had been appointed to a clerical post in Antwerp. They came together in Aachen for the purpose of collecting an inheritance which had been bequeathed to them by an unknown uncle and because they knew no one in that city they stopped at an inn. After several days had passed, during which time the three brothers listened to their brother from Antwerp describe the events which occurred in the Netherlands, it so happened that the nuns of the Convent of Holy Cecilia, which then stood before the gates of the city of Aachen, were about to celebrate the Corpus Christi Festival and that consequently the four brothers, incited by their youthful enthusiasm and the example of the Netherlands, agreed to organize an iconoclastic riot in that city.

The fourth brother, the preacher, who had on many occasions led similar riots in Antwerp, assembled beforehand in the evening several young students and sons of merchants from Aachen who sympathized with the new iconoclastic movement and who consequently spent the night in the inn drinking, eating and cursing the Pope and, as the day rose over the pinnacles of the city wall, this group equipped themselves with axes and all kinds of destructive tools in order to begin their wild attack. Happily they agreed upon a signal at which time they would begin to smash the window panes decorated with biblical stories; and, convinced they would find a number of followers among the people, they went to the cathedral determined to destroy everything in sight during the hour when the bells would ring.

The Abbess, who at the beginning of the day had been informed by a friend of the imminent danger which threatened the convent, sent repeatedly in vain for the officer of the Kaiser under whose jurisdiction Aachen lay and begged for a guard to protect her cloister; the officer, who was himself an enemy of the Pope and sympathetic to the iconoclastic movement, knew how to deny her request and, under diplomatic pretense, told her she was imagining the whole thing and that the convent was not in the least in any kind of danger. In the meantime the hour had dawned when the festivities were expected to begin and the nuns prepared for Mass amidst anxiety and prayer and pitiful forebodings of the danger which threatened them. No one protected them but the cloister's seventy-year old warden who, with a few armed helpers, stood guarding the entrance to the convent.

It is generally known that in the convents the nuns were trained to play all types of instruments, often performing their own music with a precision, an understanding and a feeling which one misses in a male orchestra (perhaps, on account of the feminine generic character of this mysterious art). Now adding to the distress of the nuns, it so happened that the music director of the convent, Sister Antonia, who always conducted the orchestra became ill a few days before due to a violent nerve fever. Thus not only were the nuns troubled by the four blasphemous brothers, whom one could already see under the pillars of the church hidden in cloaks, but they were deeply embarrassed because they were unable to perform the music expected of them for the festival. The Abbess, who had in-

206

structed on the previous evening that a stirring, old Italian Mass by an unknown composer be performed, which the choir had executed on several previous occasions with great success due to the very special and magnificent qualities of this Mass, persevering, again sent one of the sisters to inquire about Sister Antonia's health; the nun, however, who undertook the task, came back with the report that Sister Antonia was in a state of total unconsciousness and was in no condition to direct the performance.

In the meantime, serious events had already taken place in the church in which gradually more than a hundred persons of all professions and ages had appeared with axes and crowbars. The unruly mob had teased some of the workers stationed near the entrance and had taken the liberty of insulting the nuns, who now and then were seen in the halls performing acts of piety, so that subsequently the warden of the convent proceeded to the sacristy and implored the Abbess on his knees to stop the festival and go into the city and put herself under the protection of the commandant. But the Abbess insisted unflinchingly that the established festival would have to be given in honor of God; she reminded the cloister warden of his duty to protect with his body and life the Mass and the solemn event which would be held in the church, and since the bell had just rung she ordered the nuns, who gathered around her trembling and quivering, to begin at once, in spite of everything, the performance of an oratorio, no matter which one or how important it is.

Just then the nuns took their place on the platform by the organ; the parts of a music composition, which they had already previously performed, were distributed, the violin, oboe and bass players examined them and tuned their instruments. Then Sister Antonia, her face somewhat pale, appeared on the staircase fresh and well; she carried the parts of the old Italian Mass, upon whose performance the Abbess had so earnestly insisted, under her arm. Concerning the questions of the astonished nuns, from where had she come and how did she suddenly recover, she answered, "No matter friends, it is of no importance," and distributed the parts which she carried with her and sat down glowing with enthusiasm at the organ bench from where she directed the performance of the excellent music composition. Her appearance thus came as a wonderful, heavenly consolation to the hearts of the pious women; in a moment they took their places by their stands with their instruments, even the anguish which they had experienced helped carry their souls as if on wings through all heavenly harmonies. The oratorio was executed in the highest and most magnificent musical splendor; in the halls and among the benches no breath stirred, especially when the *Salve Regina* and the *Gloria in excelsis Deo* were performed,[1] it was as if the whole population of the church were dead, so that not even the dust upon the stone floor was disturbed by the four Godforsaken brothers and their insolent followers, and from that time until the end of the Thirty Years' War when it was converted from religious to civil use, the convent remained free from all danger.

Six years later when this event was long forgotten, the mother of these four young men arrived from the Hague and under the sad pretense that her sons were lost asked the magistrate of Aachen to help her legally investigate the whereabouts of the four brothers. The last news which they had had from them in the Netherlands, where they truly belonged, was a letter written the evening before the Corpus Christi Festival of six years ago. On four crowded pages the preacher gave a preliminary report to his friend, a schoolmaster in Antwerp, in which he wrote with great enthusiasm and even greater exuberance about the plans to attack the Convent of Holy Cecilia, but the mother, however, did not want to discuss this any further. After various futile efforts to find the persons whom the distressed woman sought, the magistrate finally remembered that four young people whose country and origin were unknown were found not long ago in the lunatic asylum of the city, an institution supported by the generosity of the Kaiser, and that they had been there for a period of years which corresponded to those mentioned by the mother. The four young persons lay ill because of their extreme religious fervor and the court in addition vaguely recalled that their behavior at that time of the festival was extremely dis-

208

turbed and melancholy, all this the mother did not understand for she was unfortunately well-acquainted with her sons' attitudes and it seemed that the report to which she paid little attention indicated that the four young men were Catholic, which indeed her sons were not.

Nevertheless, strangely affected by some of the characteristics which the report described, she went one day in the company of a court messenger into the asylum and asked the chief administrator to allow her to examine the four unlucky, confused men whom they kept there. But who could describe the fright of the poor woman when upon first glance she immediately recognized her sons as she walked through the door: they sat in long black robes around a table upon which stood a crucifix, which they appeared to worship with folded hands silently leaning upon the table top. Concerning the questions of the mother, who, having lost her faculties had sunk upon a stool, as to what the men were doing, the directors assured her that they were only occupying themselves with the glorification of Jesus, who according to their allegations they believed to be the Son of the one true God. The directors added that for the past six years the four young men had lived this spiritual life, that they slept little and ate little, that no sound came from their lips and that only at midnight they stood up and intoned the *Gloria in excelsis Deo* with a voice which burst the windows of the house. The directors closed with the assurance that the young men were physically perfectly healthy, that one could not deprive them of a certain serious solemn tranquility, that if one declared them mad they would sympathetically shrug their shoulders, and that they had already many times said that if the good city of Aachen knew what they knew, it would set aside its business and kneel down in front of the crucifix of the Lord singing the *Gloria*.

The woman, who could not bear the frightful appearance of her unfortunate sons, and, who subsequently was taken home again, her knees shaking, went on the following morning to the home of Veit Gotthelf, well-known draper of the city, in order to obtain information about the cause of her sons' alarming condition. Viet

Gotthelf, who had meanwhile married and had several children and had taken over his father's important business, received the disturbed woman kindly. Since he had been informed beforehand of the reason for her visit, he bolted the door and after having offered her a chair, said to her: "My dear woman, if you will not involve me, who was closely associated with your sons six years ago, in an examination, then I will speak frankly to you without reservation. Yes, we were strongly resolved to go ahead with the plans which the letter mentions. How this course of action, whose performance was arranged so precisely with irreligious sagacity, failed is incomprehensible to me. Heaven itself appears to have protected the convent of the pious women. Be aware of the fact that your sons even at the very beginning had allowed several annoying, mischievous jokes, which were to be the introduction to the final events, to be performed while the divine service was going on. More than three hundred villains equipped with axes and wreaths of tar came from within the walls of our misguided city and waited for the signal that their leader, the preacher, was to give to begin the destruction of the convent. But when the music began, your sons suddenly simultaneously took off their hats in a manner which seemed strange to us, folded their hands before their bowed heads and little by little were overcome by a deep inexpressible emotion and after a shuddering pause the preacher turned around and called to us to take off our hats in a loud frightful voice. Meanwhile a few companions whispered to him in vain, nudging him frivolously with their arms to give the signal upon which they had agreed previously for the rioting to begin. Instead of answering the preacher fell down upon his knees with his hands folded crosswise upon his chest and his forehead pressed fervently into the dust and murmured along with his brothers the whole series of prayers which he had ridiculed only a short time ago. During this moment the crowd of pitiful fanatics robbed of their leader, stood deeply confused, inert and indecisive until the oratorio, which thundered joyfully down from the platform, was finished and in this minute by order of the commandant several arrests were made and a few evildoers who had already created disturbances were apprehended and led away by a guard, so that the miserable band had no other choice than to speedily withdraw from the convent under the protection of the crowd which was then dispersing.

"In the evening when I had asked at the inn several times in vain about your sons who had not returned, I went, not without considerable uneasiness, with some friends to the convent in order to ask the doorkeepers, who were left to help the guard of the Kaiser, about them. But how can I describe to you my fright, noble woman, when I saw lying prostrate before the altar of the church these four men just as before, full of fervent ardor with their hands folded and kissing the ground with their chests and tops of their heads as if they had been turned into stone. The warden of the convent, who at this moment had just come by, asked them to leave the cloister, in which it was already growing dark and there was no longer anyone present, while he tugged at their coats and shook their arms, but, half-standing as if in a dream-like trance, they did not listen to him until finally the warden with the help of the servants took them by the arms and led them out through the door, subsequently they followed us into the city while moaning and looking back at the cloister, which sparkled brilliantly behind us in the glow of the sun, with frequent heartfelt glances. On the way back the friends and I asked them repeatedly kindly and lovingly, of all the dreadful things in the entire world, what could have struck them in such a manner as to be capable of transforming their innermost minds. They clasped our hands and rubbed them while glancing at us and then looked down upon the ground deep in thought and from time to time wiped the tears from their eyes with an expression which still even today pierces deep into my heart.

"Upon arriving in their living quarters, they cleverly and neatly fastened a cross together out of birch rods and inserted it into a small mound of wax, then they set the mound between two candles, which the maid had fetched, upon a large table in the middle of the room while the friends, whose number grew larger and larger from hour to hour, stood in scattered groups at the side wringing their hands, speechless from grief over their ghastly actions. The four miserable men sat down around the table and, as if they were totally oblivious to everything around them, prepared quietly with folded hands to pray. They did not want to eat any of the food which was ordered in the morning for the celebration which they earlier had planned to take place after the riots and which now the maid brought in, nor, as, as night approached, did the four young men desire to sleep in the beds which the maid had prepared in the adjoining room because they appeared tired. The friends, however, in order not to provoke the indignation of the innkeeper, to whom the performance seemed strange, had to sit down at the lavishly prepared table and partake of the sumptuous feast seasoned with the salt of their bitter tears. Suddenly the clock struck midnight, your four sons listened attentively for a moment to the dull sound of the bell and then all at once rising simultaneously from their seats, while the rest of us put our table napkins down and looked at them full of anxious expectations of what was to follow, they started to intone the *Gloria in excelsis Deo* with a dreadful ghastly voice. The sounds they made were not unlike those of leopards and wolves howling to the sky during the icy wintertime. The pillars of the house, I assure you, shook, and the windows, hit by the visible breath of their lungs, threatened to shatter as if one had thrown handfuls of sand against their surfaces. With this horrible event we dashed out, senseless, in scattered groups, our hair standing on end, leaving our coats and hats behind, into the surrounding streets, which in a short time were filled with, instead of us, more than a hundred persons roused from their sleep. The mob, forcing open the doors of the house, pressed up the staircase to the hall in order to find the source of this horrible and disgraceful roaring, which came as if from the lips of damned sinners rising out of the flaming bowels of the earth, full of pity in order that God should hear them. Finally when the clock struck one, they became silent, having previously been totally unaware of the anger of the innkeeper or the pitiful exclamations of the surrounding crowd. With a cloth your sons wiped the sweat, which fell down from them in great drops upon their chin and chest, from their foreheads and spreading open their coats they laid down upon the inlaid wooden floor in order to rest an hour from such an agonizing business.

"As soon as he saw them sleeping the innkeeper let them alone and made the sign of the cross over them and, happy to be rid of the misery for the moment, he instructed the group of men who were present and who were muttering secretly with one another to leave the room assuring them that in the morning the four young men would be themselves again. Unfortunately, however, with the first cry of the rooster, the four miserable beings stood up again around the same bare cross which lay opposite them on the table and began the same strange religious ritual, which only exhaustion had forced them to abandon, all over again. They would not accept any admonition or help from the innkeeper whose heart melted from the sight of their pitiful appearance and instead they asked him to gently send away the friends who were in the habit of assembling with them every morning. They asked nothing of the innkeeper but bread and water and, if it was not too much trouble, some straw beds for the night so that consequently the man, who previously had derived a great deal of money from their earlier merry escapades felt distressed that he now had to notify the court about all that had happened and to ask the magistrate to take the four young men, over whom, without doubt, the evil spirit must have control, out of the house. Upon the order of the magistrate they were given a medical examination and, as you know, since they were found insane they were placed in the lunatic asylum which was established by the kindness of the lately deceased Kaiser to provide the best care for persons of this kind within the walls of the city."

All this Veit Gotthelf, the draper, said and still more, which we suppress here, because in our opinion we believe we have said enough about the events, and he asked the mother once again not to involve him in any legal investigations which might ensue. Three days later, the mother, deeply affected by this report, decided, because the weather was beautiful, to walk to the convent, holding on to the arm of a friend, with the melancholy purpose in mind of viewing the horrible place where God had, as if with lightning bolts, destroyed her sons. Upon their arrival at the cloister the two women found that the building was being renovated and the entrance was barricaded by boards so that they raised themselves up painstakingly in order to look inside through the opening in the boards, but all they could see was the magnificently sparkling rose window in the background of the church. Hundreds of workers singing joyful songs upon various intertwined scaffolds were busy lifting the towers a third higher and covering the roofs and pinnacles, which until now had only been covered with slates, with strong bright copper which glistened in the rays of the sun. Meanwhile, a dark, black thunderstorm with golden rims hovered over the building, it had already been blowing up over the vicinity of Aachen and after it hurled several weak lightning bolts against the cloister sank down in the east, dissolving into vapors and muttering discontentedly.

Now it so happened that as the two women stood upon the steps of the spacious monastic quarters lost in thought contemplating this double spectacle, a sister from the convent who passed by accidentally discovered who the woman under the portal was so that the Abbess who had heard about the letter which described the fateful Corpus Christi Festival and which the mother carried with her thereupon immediately sent the sister down to her. The mother, although taken aback by the request which was announced to her, nevertheless, respectfully obeyed and while the friend, upon the invitation of the sister, withdrew into an adjoining room, the nuns opened the folding doors of the beautiful, tasteful balcony to the foreigner from the Netherlands, who in the meantime had to climb up the stairs. There upon the balcony the mother found the Abbess who was a noble woman of quiet queenly bearing sitting upon a footstool which was supported by legs which looked like dragon claws; upon a desk at her side lay the parts of a music score. The Abbess, after she had offered the mother a chair, disclosed to her that she had already been informed of her arrival in Aachen by the mayor and after the Abbess herself had inquired about the condition of her unfortunate sons she urged the mother to accept the fate which had befallen them because it was irrevocable and expressed to her the wish to see the letter which the preacher had written to his friend the schoolmaster in Antwerp. The mother, who was endowed with enough common sense to foresee to what results this step could lead, felt herself momentarily embarrassed, but since, however, the honorable face of the Abbess necessitated unquestioning trust and in no way could it be possible to believe that her intention could be to make the letter public, therefore took the letter from her bosom and handed it to the noble woman while kissing her hand warmly.

While the Abbess read over the letter, the mother happened to glance at the desk upon which the score of the musical composition lay opened, and since suddenly it occurred to her because of the report of the draper that it could probably have been the power of the music which had bewildered and destroyed her sons on that terrible day, she turned around and timidly asked the sister who stood behind her chair if that was the music which had been performed six years ago on the morning of that remarkable Corpus Christi Festival in the cloister. Upon the answer of the young sister that, yes, she remembered hearing of it and that it was customary to place music which they did not need in the room of the revered Abbess, the mother, shaking violently and disturbed by many thoughts, stood up and walked over to the desk. She looked at the unfamiliar, magic signs, which appeared to have been used by a terrible frightful spirit to mark a circle for himself and thought she herself would sink to the ground when suddenly upon the opened page she saw the passage, *Gloria in excelsis Deo*. It seemed to her at that moment as if the whole horror of sound that had ruined her sons moved thunderously over her head and she believed that the mere sight of those words had made her lose her senses, whereupon moved by a deep inner humility and subjection to the Almighty, she quickly pressed the score to her lips and then sat back again in her chair.

Meanwhile, the Abbess had finished reading the letter, and while she folded it together said to the mother, "God himself on that wonderful day protected the convent against the arrogance of your erring and grievous sons. The means he used can be of little concern to you who are a Protestant and you probably will not understand that which I am about to tell you. For learn that no one knows absolutely who quietly directed the score, which you find opened there before you, from the organ bench during the oppression of the frightful hour when the iconoclastic riots were about to overtake us. Through a testimony which was received on the morning of the following day in the presence of the convent warden it was proved that Sister Antonia, the only one who could have directed the music during the interval of time, lay ill and unconscious in the corner of her cloister cell, her limbs robbed of all strength; a nun in the convent, who because she was a relative, was ordered to care for her during the morning as the Corpus Christi Festival was celebrated, did not leave her bedside. Yes, Sister Antonia would herself have unquestionably verified and established as true that it was not she who appeared in such a strange manner upon the altar by the organ if her mentally confused mind would have allowed it and if in addition she had not died that night of the nerve fever which had earlier confined her to her bed and which had not appeared dangerous. Also the Archbishop of Trier, to whom this incident was reported, had already expressed the opinion which alone explains it, namely, that the holy Cecilia herself had performed this frightful and at the same time glorious miracle and from the Pope I have at this very moment received a papal brief in which he confirms this."

Following these words the Abbess then gave the letter, which she only requested from the mother to learn more information about the event with which she was already quite familiar, back to the woman from the Netherlands with the promise that she would make no use of it; thereupon the Abbess asked the mother whether there was any hope for the recovery of her sons and whether she could help her with some money or other form of aid that could serve this purpose, to which the mother, crying, replied, no, while kissing the habit of the Abbess, who greeted the woman warmly and ended the meeting. Leaving behind a small fund which she deposited with the court for the care of her sons the woman, whose presence in Aachen was totally in vain, went back to the Hague, where one year later, greatly affected by this event, she converted to Catholicism. The sons, however, lived to a ripe old age and died happily and joyfully after they once more, as was their custom, intoned the *Gloria in excelsis Deo*.

HAYDN'S DEATH [1809]

Since 1806 Haydn no longer went out of the small dwelling which he occupied in a suburb of Vienna[2] because of his extreme old age. His frailty was so great that a special piano was built for him whose keys by means of a special apparatus were especially easy to depress. Since 1803 he no longer used this instrument to compose, but played it in the solitude of his old age when he felt the inclination to amuse himself. Friends who came to inquire after his health found instead of an answer a card fastened to the door upon which the following sentence from one of his last songs[3] was engraved in copper: "My strength is exhausted, old age and weakness weigh me down."

In the meantime during the winter of 1808 leading families of Vienna formed a society which on Sundays performed the works of the great composer before a large gathering. One of the most ornate and most magnificent salons of the city which at the very least could accommodate five hundred people was the scene of this musical festivity;[4] women and men from the upper class arrived here partly to enjoy the concertos and oratorios which were performed and partly to participate in the performances accompanied by the most capable musicians of the city. At the close of the winter season, on March 27, 1808, the society decided to perform Haydn's *Creation*. They received from Haydn in one of his cheerful moments the promise that he would come himself: and everyone who had respect for music, for merit and old age accordingly made a great effort to be present on this day. Two hours before the beginning of the concert the hall was already full; in the middle, three rows of chairs were occupied by the foremost virtuosos of the city, men like Salieri, Gyrowetz, Hummel,[5] etc.; in the front a chair of still greater distinction was reserved for Haydn, who did not suspect what a triumph awaited him.

Scarcely had the signal been given for his arrival than everyone stood up in spontaneous agreement as though hit by an electric bolt; people pressed forward and raised themselves up from their seats in order to see him and all glances were directed toward the doors through which he was supposed to enter. Princess Esterházy at the head of a gathering of persons of noble birth or of unusual superior talent stood up and walked towards the foot of the stair-case in order to welcome him. The famous old man, carried upon a sedan chair, appeared under the doorway; he arrived at the chair which was intended for him amidst cheers and applause and fan-fares from all the instruments. Princess Esterházy took her place to his right, the author of *Danaiden*[6] to his left; the Princess Traut-mannsdorf and Lobkowitz,[7] as well as several foreign ambassadors, etc., followed; and two women[8] appeared who presented to him two poems in the name of the society, one, an Italian sonnet by Carpani,[9] the other, a German ode by Collin.[10]

Haydn, who had not anticipated this reception, decided in his simple and modest manner to express in words the emotion he felt. The audience heard only single broken utterances from him: "Never—never did I feel—! That I would like to die this moment—! I would slumber happily in the other world!" At just this moment the signal to begin was given by Salieri who directed the concert; Kreutzer,[11] at the piano, Clementi[12] (with the first violins), Radichi,[13] Weinmüller[14] and a selection of amateurs began the performance of Haydn's *Creation* with wonderful unity

218

and sincerity. This work, perhaps, has never been performed with such perfection; the talented performers outdid themselves and the listeners experienced what they will never experience again. Haydn, whose heart was old and weak, was overcome by his feelings and melted into tears, he was capable of nothing more than raising his hands to heaven, speechless, as a sign of his gratitude.

In the meantime the organizers of this festival had anticipated what the performance could do to the health of this venerable old man because of the emotional upheavals connected with it and already at the end of the first part the sedan chair appeared again to take him home. Haydn, not wanting to cause a disturbance in the hall, signaled to the carriers of the chair to go away; but they urged him to leave and thus he was taken away with the same triumph with which he had appeared earlier although now no longer with the same amount of happiness.

Every heart believed when he left the hall, that they had said good-by to him for the last time.

In the antechamber he extended his hands once more over the gathering as if to bless them; and a presentiment of grief overcame the earlier enthusiasm with which they had welcomed him.

This presentiment was only too correct. Haydn having arrived in his home, lost consciousness and two and a half months later (May 31) he was dead.

CENDRILLON [1810]

The opera, *Cendrillon*,[15] which Madame Bethmann[16] has chosen for a benefit performance and which Herr Herklots has already translated into German for this purpose is said to be called "Ascherlich," "Ascherling" or "Ascherlein" and not "Aschenbrödel,"[17] because the music, written originally to a French text, requires a word with three syllables. *Brödel* from *Brot*[18] or from the old German, *Brühe* (*brode,* in French), is the name of a woman covered with grease and dirt; this meaning has lived on among the people because of its use in the fairytale, where this word with the wantonness of friendly irony is given to a delicate sweet child who is extremely poor, but pure of body and soul. Instead of changing the title and name of the heroine of this fairytale into something else, which although well-chosen, is, nevertheless, arbitrary and meaningless, why not consider the music and combine the "del" into "dl" or eliminate the "d" altogether. An Austrian poet would, without doubt, not hesitate to say "Aschenbrödl" or "Aschenbröl."

"Ascherlich" or "Aschenbrödl" will be performed by Mademoiselle Maas, Madame Bethmann, I am told will be one of the jealous sisters. It is more than mere youth which qualifies Mlle. Maas for this role, but, regarding Madame Bethmann, it would be sad if she believed that she was not given the part of the heroine on account of her age. It is much too early for her to resign (regarding this opinion we believe that we have the support of, if not the largest part of the public, than at least the most intelligent). The performance of this artist can well be compared to many an old musician as he sings accompanied by the piano.[19] In many respects his voice lacks many of the qualities which a young, vigorous singer possesses. Yet, at the same time, by applying his knowledge and immense delicate feelings to his performance and avoiding the defects in his voice, the older singer leads our imagination at certain times along the right paths so that everyone can easily supplement that which he lacks and, in addition, experience a higher form of pleasure, the same kind which a better voice, but one of lesser genius, would be able to provide. Madame Bethmann's greatest glory will begin in only a few years (at an age when others lose their glory) when she learns how to deal with her abilities in a different manner.

THEATER NEWS [1810]

The Singspiel, *The Swiss Family,* by the Kapellmeister, Weigl, which has been met with lively, almost extravagant applause in Vienna, Munich, Stuttgart, Frankfurt, etc., is also being rehearsed here in the local Royal National Theater of Berlin.[20] The direction deserves our most enthusiastic gratitude, we doubt that the charm and enjoyable character of this work will ever be equaled or rivaled. Whether the role of Emmeline (who as the leading figure determines the success of this work) will be given to Mademoiselle Schmalz because of the range and solidity of her voice or to Madame Müller because of her dexterity and considerable theatrical experience or to Madame Eunicke[21] who happily unites both elements (which probably would be the most suitable) is a question. In Vienna the role has been given to Madame Milder, one of the most able singers as well as one of the most excellent actresses which Germany possesses at this time.

THEATER [1810]

Yesterday, *The Swiss Family* was supposed to have been repeated under the direction of the Kapellmeister, Weigl. However, the audience applauded loudly and vigorously when Mlle. Herbst appeared, this ovation was puzzling because it was followed by the audience shouting "da capo"[22] before she even uttered one sound, this outburst necessitated that the curtain be closed. Herr Berger then appeared and explained that another opera would be performed. Whether the public, if a part of it can be called that, did not like the selection or whether the public was dissatisfied with the choice of Mlle. Herbst for the role of Emmeline or whatever

221

other reason caused this reaction, concerning this we do not wish to speculate. Regarding the first performance of the opera it was generally felt that everyone enjoyed the pleasant music and even Mlle. Herbst performed her part better than one expected considering her rather limited musical and dramatic talents. By the way, the public was more than compensated by the performance of the other two selections: *Die Geschwister* by Goethe and the Singspiel, *Der Schatzgräber*.[23] In the first Mlle. Schönfeld performed her part quite valiantly and Herr Gern in the other was, as usual, a master performer.[24]

NOTES

1. Kleist has made two errors here. First, the nuns now under the direction of Sister Antonia performed the old Italian Mass, not the earlier substituted oratorio. Second, the *Salve Regina* ("Hail O Queen") and the *Gloria in excelsis Deo* ("Glory to God in the Highest") belong to two different classes or services of the Roman Catholic liturgy: the former belongs to the Offices or Canonical Hours, the latter is the second item of the Ordinary of the Mass.

2. Haydn's address at this time was 73 Kleine Steingasse, Wundmühle, Vienna; today this street is known as Haydngasse.

3. Kleist is referring to "Der Greis" ("The Old Man"), a quartet for soprano, alto, tenor and bass with piano accompaniment composed by Haydn in 1799 (poem by Gellert).

4. The concert described here probably took place at the University of Vienna (see Karl Geiringer, *Haydn, A Creative Life in Music*. New York: W. W. Norton, p. 170).

5. Antonio Salieri (1750-1825), Italian composer, conductor and teacher; Adalbert Gyrowetz (1763-1850), Czech composer and long time friend of Haydn; Johann Nepomuk Hummel (1778-1837), composer, pianist and pupil of Mozart and Salieri. In 1804 upon Haydn's recommendation Hummel took over the aged composer's duties at the court of Prince Nicholas Esterházy II.

6. Danaiden, probably *Les Danaides,* an opera composed by Salieri in 1784.

7. Prince Franz Joseph von Lobkowitz (1772-1816), member of an Austro-Bohemian noble family of musical patrons; the Prince was a patron of Haydn and Beethoven.

8. The "two women," i.e., the Baroness Spielmann and Magdalene von Kurz-

böck; the latter was a talented pianist to whom Haydn dedicated his last piano sonata and last piano trio.

9. Giuseppe Carpani (1772-1852), Italian poet, dramatist, translator, librettist and close friend of Haydn. Carpani translated the text of *The Creation* into Italian and in 1812 published an important study of Haydn, i.e., *Le Haydine*.

10. Joseph Heinrich von Collin (d. June, 1811), German poet and dramatist, friend of Beethoven.

11. Rodolphe Kreutzer (1766-1831), French violinist, composer and acquaintance of Haydn and Beethoven. Beethoven's Sonata in A Major for violin and piano (op. 47, so-called "Kreutzer Sonata") was dedicated to him.

12. Muzio Clementi (1752-1832), composer, virtuoso pianist and personal acquaintance of Haydn, Mozart and Beethoven. Kleist has confused these two participants, for undoubtedly it was Kreutzer who was in the first violin section and Clementi at the piano.

13. See following note 14.

14. Karl Friedrich Weinmüller (1763-1828), well-known German bass and friend of the young Franz Schubert. Weinmüller was associated with the Kärntnertor Theater in Vienna for many years where he specialized particularly in the operas of Gluck. In 1821 he made his farewell appearance in the first performance of Weber's *Der Freischütz*. Weinmüller and Radicchi performed together in the 1814 production of *Fidelio:* Radicchi sang the role of Florestan, Weinmüller, that of the jailor, Rocco.

15. *Cendrillon (Cinderella),* opera by Niccolo Isouard (1775-1818). Kleist's essay discusses the preparations for the performance of this popular opera in Berlin in German; it was not until eight months later (June 4, 1811), however, that the opera was actually produced.

16. Friederike Bethmann (1760-1815), wife of the actor, H. E. Bethmann. Madame Bethmann is often referred to as one of the greatest actresses of the early Romantic era performing in such works as Schiller's *Maria Stuart, Macbeth* and several of Kotzebue's plays. She was also an equally gifted singer. Her musical abilities are discussed in: *Meyers Grosses Konversations-Lexikon,* Leipzig, 1903, II, 768.

17. Aschenbrödel (*asche,* ashes + *brodeln,* to boil), is the German name for Cinderella. Kleist would have been pleased to know that when the opera was performed in Königsberg in 1812 in German, the title, Aschenbrödel, was used.

18. Brot, i.e., bread.

19. Kleist uses the mid-18th century term for the piano, i.e., Fortepiano, in this passage which does not appear very often in the literature of this period. It would seem that the poet wanted his readers to imagine his old musician sitting at the piano and not at the harpsichord (clavier).

20. *The Swiss Family* (first production, Vienna, March 14, 1809), was performed in Berlin on November 21, 1810. The following is a brief summary of the plot of this popular opera: Count Wallstein, whose life has been saved by a

Swiss shepherd, brings his benefactor and his family to live with him on his estate. Emmeline, the daughter of the shepherd, is overcome by extreme melancholy. The Count, thinking that she is homesick, has an exact replica of her father's chalet built for her. But the true cause of Emmeline's unhappiness is soon revealed when Jacob Freiburg, blowing his Alpine shepherd's horn, appears. Reunited with her lover at last, Emmeline marries Jacob and the Count blesses the happy pair.

21. Therese Eunicke (1776-1849), second wife of the tenor, Friedrich Eunicke (1764-1844). Their daughter, Johanna, was also a well-known singer and sang the title role in the first performance of Hoffmann's *Undine* at the age of eighteen. Amalie Schmalz (1771-1848) was another famous German soprano with a range of three octaves. Müller, see p. 168, no. 61.

22. Da capo, musical term which literally means go back (i.e., to the beginning of the piece).

23. *Die Geschwister, The Brothers; Der Schatzgräber, The Treasure Digger.*

24. The critique of *Cendrillon,* the essays, "Theater," and "Theater News" were published in Kleist's journal, *Die Berliner Abendblättern (The Berlin Evening News).*

Joseph von Eichendorff
[1788-1857]

MAGIC IN AUTUMN[1] *A Fairytale* [1808]

ON A CLEAR autumn evening the knight Ubaldo had wandered far
from his companions and as he rode along the paths of the fir-
covered mountains he saw a man in strange, colorful clothes climbing down from one of them. The stranger did not notice him until
the knight stood close to him. Ubaldo saw now with astonishment
that this same person wore a very elegant and splendidly decorated
jacket which, however, had become old-fashioned and out of place.
His face was handsome, but pale and covered by an unruly beard.

The two men greeted each other with surprise and Ubaldo related to the stranger how he unfortunately had lost his way. The
sun had already gone behind the mountains and this area was far
from any human dwellings. Therefore, the stranger proposed to
Ubaldo that he spend the night with him; tomorrow as early as
possible he would show him the only path which leads out of these
mountains. Ubaldo was quite willing and followed his guide
through the deserted forest ravines.

They soon came to a high cliff at the bottom of which was a large
carved out cave. A large stone stood in the middle of it and upon
the stone was a wooden crucifix. A sleeping area of dried leaves
filled the back of the den. Ubaldo tied his horse to the entrance of

the cave while his host silently brought some bread and wine. They sat down next to one another and the knight, who thought the dress of the stranger looked like that of a hermit, could not restrain himself from inquiring about his past. — "Don't ask who I am," answered the hermit seriously as his face became sinister and unfriendly. — Ubaldo noticed, however, that when he began to mention the many journeys and glorious deeds he had accomplished in his youth the stranger listened attentively and then sank into deep contemplation. Feeling tired Ubaldo finally stretched himself out on the bed of leaves which was offered to him and soon fell asleep while his host sat down by the entrance of the cave.

In the middle of the night Ubaldo was startled by troubled fearful dreams. He partially raised himself up. Outside the bright moon shone upon the quiet circle of the mountain. Ubaldo saw his host pacing restlessly back and forth under the tall quivering trees near the cave. With a hollow voice he sang a song and from the broken utterances Ubaldo could only make out the following:

Fear drives me out of the abyss,
Old melodies reach toward me,
Sweet sin, let me go!
Or cast my whole being down there
Amidst the magic of these songs,
Concealed in the womb of the earth!

God! Fervently I would like to pray,
But memories of the earth continually
Separate You from me,
And the howling through the forest
Fills my soul with horror,
Harsh God, I fear You.

Ah! Then tear apart my chains,
You died a bitter death
To deliver all men,
I wander lost at the gates of Hell.
Ah, how quickly I am lost.
Jesus, help me in my need!

The singer was silent again, sat down upon a stone and seemed to murmur some indistinct prayers, which sounded much more like intricate magic formulas. The murmuring of the brooks from the neighboring mountains and the soft whistling of the fir trees sang strangely along with him and Ubaldo sank back upon his bed of leaves overcome by drowsiness.

No sooner had the first beams of the morning light shone through the treetops when the hermit appeared before the knight ready to show him the way out of the ravines. Joyously Ubaldo mounted his horse and his strange, quiet guide walked silently next to him. Soon they arrived at the summit of the last mountain; before them lay the sparkling world below in the beautiful morning light with its streams, cities and castles. The hermit himself appeared moved. "Ah, how beautiful the world is!" he cried with dismay, covered his face with his hands and hurried back into the forests. — Shaking his head Ubaldo now followed the familiar path to his castle.

Soon curiosity drove him back to that original desolate place and with some difficulty he found the cave again, where this time the hermit seemed to him to be less sinister and very reserved.

Ubaldo had gathered already from his nocturnal song that the hermit wanted to repent for his deep sins, but it appeared to the knight as if his soul were wrestling in vain with the enemy for his behavior showed no evidence of that kind of joyful trust one associates with a truly devout person, and quite often, as they sat talking with one another, a heavy suppressed, worldly longing broke out from the mad flaming eyes of the man with an almost frightful violence and his expression showed a total lack of self-control and seemed to be completely transformed.

This moved the pious knight to repeat his visits often in order to embrace and sustain the disturbed one with the complete strength of his own untroubled, innocent soul. The hermit in the meantime continued to keep his name and earlier occupation a secret, and it appeared that he had a dread of the past. With each visit, however, he became more tranquil and trusting. Indeed, the knight finally succeeded once in persuading him to follow him to his castle.

It had already become evening when they arrived at the castle. Therefore, the knight started a warm fire and brought the best wine he had. For the first time the hermit appeared to feel somewhat at ease. He looked very attentively at a sword and another piece of armor which hung on the wall sparkling in the reflection of the fire and then looked again silently at the knight for a long time. "You are happy," he said, "and I look at your strong, joyful manly form with true respect and timidity, how you move and quietly rule life untroubled by sorrow and joy while you seem at the same time to devote yourself entirely to life like a navigator who knows precisely where he should steer and who would not let himself be lured off his course by the magic songs of the sirens. In your presence I have often felt like a cowardly fool or a madman. There are people who are intoxicated by life—ah, how horrible it is to suddenly become sober again!"

The knight who did not want to lose the opportunity of taking advantage of his guest's emotion, urged him with good-natured eagerness to now finally tell him the story of his life. The hermit became reflective. "If you promise me," he said at last, "never to repeat what I tell you and allow me to omit all names, then I will do it." The knight gave him his hand and promised him joyfully what he asked, and called in his wife, whose silence he vouched for in order to allow her also to hear the story which they both had desired for so long to hear.

She appeared, one child on her arm, another holding on to her hand. She was a divine, beautiful vision of fading youth, quiet and gentle like the sinking sun, whose delicate vanishing beauty was mirrored once again in her lovely children. The stranger was totally bewildered by their appearance. He forcefully opened the windows and stared out for several moments onto the nocturnal forest floor in order to pull himself together. Calmer he then walked back to them; everyone moved closer around the blazing fire and he began to speak in the following manner:

"The autumn sun rose lovely and warmly over the tinted mist which covered the valleys around my castle. The music stopped,

228

the festival was over and the merry guests departed in all directions. It was a farewell party which I gave for my dearest childhood friend who on that day gathered with his small troop of men to go to the Holy Land in order to help the large Christian army recapture the promised land. Since our earliest youth this journey was the singular object of our mutual wishes, hopes and plans and I still now often think with an indescribable melancholy of that quiet, beautiful morning when we sat together under the tall linden trees upon the rocky slope of my castle and in our minds followed the sailing clouds to that blessed wonderland where Gottfried and the other heroes lived and fought amidst the bright lustre of glory. — But how soon everything changed within me.

"I had been seized by an unconquerable love for a girl, the flower of all beauty, whom I had seen only once, and this love held me spellbound in the quiet confines of these mountains. Just when I was strong enough to fight I could not depart and left my friend to go alone. This girl was present at the festival and I became intoxicated by the happiness which her magnificent beauty caused in me. Only in the morning when she wanted to depart and I helped her on to her horse did I dare to disclose to her that I gave up going to the Holy Land for her. She did not reply but looked at me with big eyes and as it appears alarmed and then quickly rode off." —

With these words the knight and his wife looked at one another with apparent astonishment. But the stranger did not notice their glances and continued:

"Everyone had departed. The sun shone through the high arched windows into the empty room in which the only sound was the echo of my lonely footsteps. I leaned for a long time against the balcony; I heard the sound of the woodcutters coming out of the forest. Amidst this loneliness I was seized with an indescribable passionate excitement. I could no longer endure it, I swung myself upon my horse and went hunting in order to ease my oppressed heart.

"I wandered about aimlessly for a long time when suddenly I found myself to my astonishment in a part of the mountains which

229

until now was totally unknown to me. I rode deep in thought, my falcon upon my hand through a beautiful heath over which the slanting beams of the sinking sun passed away; the autumn webs flew like veils through the warm blue air, high over the mountains the farewell songs of the departing birds fluttered away.

"Then suddenly I heard several forest horns which some distance away from the mountains seemed to answer each other. Several voices accompanied them. Never before had music filled me with such wondrous longing as these tones did and still today I remember several verses of the song as the wind carried it across to me between the sounds of the forest horns:

> Beyond streaks of gold and red
> Birds migrate in the sky above,
> Wandering lost, thoughts vanish,
> Ah, they find no secure resting place,
> And the lament of the horns
> Penetrates deep into your heart.
>
> Do you see beyond the forest
> The light of the distant blue mountains,
> And the streams of the still valley
> Rushing onward out of sight?
> The clouds, brooks and birds alive with life
> Strive onward into the distance.
>
> My golden locks flow and flutter,
> Sweetly my young body still blossoms —
> Soon all beauty must wither,
> Time consumes the brightness of summer,
> Youth no longer blooms,
> The horns are silent everywhere.
>
> To impart upon a pair of red lips a kiss,
> To embrace slim arms like dew,
> To press against a pure heart,
> The tones of the horns bring you
> A rich, full greeting of love.
> Come, ah come! Before they fade away.

"It was as if I were bewitched by these tones which penetrated my entire being. As soon as the tones emerged my falcon became afraid and flew up into the sky, circling wildly and disappearing high in the air never coming back. But I could not resist and followed without stopping the enticing song of the forest horn, which, bewildering my mind, seemed at one moment to come from out of the distance and the next as if the wind carried it closer to me.

"At last I came out of the forest and saw a shining castle standing upon a mountain. From the top of the mountain down to the edge of the forest a wondrously beautiful garden with a variety of different colored flowers smiled and enclosed the castle like a magic circle. All the trees and shrubs in this garden were brilliantly colored, some were purple-red, others were golden-yellow and some bedecked in fiery colors; tall asters, these last stars of the fading summer, burned in an array of multi-colored gleaming tints. The sinking sun threw its beams directly upon the lovely knoll and the fountains and the windows of the castle, which sparkled dazzlingly.

"I noticed now that the tones of the forest horn which I heard before came from out of this garden and in the middle of this splendor amidst wild vine leaves I saw to my astonishment—the girl who occupied all my thoughts and who was walking about singing between the tones of the horn. She became silent when she noticed me, but the horns continued their music. Handsome pages in silk dress hurried down and took my horse.

"I flew through the elegant, trellised, gilded gate to the terrace in the garden where my beloved stood and overcome by her great beauty I threw myself down at her feet. She wore a dark red robe, long veils transparent like the spider's web in autumn and held together on her forehead by a magnificent aster made of precious sparkling stones flowed loosely around her golden-yellow locks.

"She lifted me up tenderly and said with a voice which sounded as if it were broken-hearted: 'Handsome, unfortunate youth, how I love you! I have loved you for a long time and each year when autumn begins its mysterious festival my desire grows with new overpowering force. Unfortunate one! Why did you come into this circle of my music? Leave me and flee!'

"I shuddered at these words and entreated her to explain the meaning of them. But she did not answer and we walked silently next to one another through the garden.

"Meanwhile it grew dark. A serious nobility spread over her whole form.

" 'For know then,' she said, 'your childhood friend who left you today is a traitor. I am forced to become his bride. He has hid his love from you because of his wild jealousy. He has not gone to Palestine, but will be here tomorrow in order to claim me and hide me in a remote castle forever where no human eyes can look at me. — I must depart now. We will never see each other again unless he dies!'

"With these words she pressed a kiss upon my lips and disappeared amidst the dark paths. A stone from her aster sparkling coldly bedazzled my eyes; her kiss burned through all my veins with a sensuousness that was almost unbearable.

"With horror I thought about her terrible words which she had thrown like poison into my healthy blood when she bid me farewell and confused I wandered aimlessly down the lonely paths which surrounded the castle and meditated for a long time. Exhausted I finally threw myself down upon the stone steps in front of the castle door; the forest horns still sounded and I fell asleep troubled by strange thoughts.

"It was a brilliant morning when I awoke. All the doors and windows of the castle were firmly locked up, the garden and the whole area was still. Amidst this lonely scene the picture of my beloved and the whole magic of the evening before awoke in my heart with the new beautiful colors of morning and I felt the blessedness of being loved in return. Now and then when her frightful words came to my mind I was seized by an impulse to fly far away from here; but her kiss still burned upon my lips and I could not leave.

"A warm almost sultry air blew over the area as if the summer wanted to return once again. For that reason I drifted dreamily into the nearby forest in order to distract myself by hunting. There at the top of a tree I noticed a bird with wondrously beautiful feathers which I had never seen before. As I arched my bow to shoot him, he quickly flew to another tree. I followed him eagerly; but the beautiful bird fluttered continuously from one treetop to another while his bright golden wing feathers gleamed charmingly in the sun.

"In this I way I came to a narrow valley which was enclosed by high rocks. The air was calm here and everything was still green and blooming as if it were summer. A wondrous song sounded forth from the middle of this valley. Surprised I pulled the branches of the thick bushes apart by which I stood—and my intoxicated eyes were blinded by the magic which was revealed to me here.

"A quiet pond stood amidst the circle of high rocks upon which ivy and strange reeds grew voluptuously upwards. Many beautiful girls were singing and dipping their beautiful legs up and down in the tepid water. Without any covering the girl stood magnificently above all the others and while they were singing she looked silently past the sensuous waves playing about her ankles transfigured and bewitched by the reflection of her own beauty in the intoxicated water. — I stood there for a long time with my body permeated by a flaming shudder and I hurried away quickly in order not to be discovered. I plunged into the deepest part of the woods in order to cool the flames which raged through my innermost being. But the further I fled the more lively those scenes reappeared before my eyes and the more the splendor of those youthful limbs consumed me.

"In this state of mind nightfall descended over the forest. The whole sky had changed and became dark; a wild storm rose over the mountains. 'We will never see each other again unless he dies!' these words echoed in my mind continuously and I ran as if I were chased by ghosts.

"It seemed to me sometimes as if I heard the deafening noise of horses' hooves in the forest. Whenever the din come close to me I fled fearing every human face. I often saw the castle of my beloved standing in the distance whenever I climbed the summit; the forest horns sang again as they did the evening before; the candles glowed throughout the windows like mild moonlight and lit up the circle of the nearest trees and flowers like magic while the whole area outside the castle was full of the sound of wild confusion, of a storm and sinister goings on.

"At last, scarcely knowing what I was doing, I climbed up a rock at the bottom of which a raging storm rushed past. When I arrived at the top I saw a dark form which sat upon a stone quiet and motionless, as if it were itself made of stone. Just at this moment the clouds galloped across the sky and broke into many pieces. The moon came into view for a moment, blood red—and I recognized my friend, the bridegroom of my beloved. As soon as he saw me he quickly raised himself up standing tall, I shuddered with horror as he drew his sword. Enraged I attacked him and we wrestled with one another for some time until at last I threw him over the side of the cliff into the abyss below.

"Suddenly everything became still, no sound could be heard from the gorge below or from the surrounding area, only the stream below roared with more force than before as if my whole previous life had been buried under its swirling waves and everything was over for me.

"Quickly I rushed away from this horrible place. Then it seemed to me as if I heard a loud repugnant laugh coming from out of the top of the trees behind me; at the same time I believed in my confused state that I saw the bird which I had followed earlier above me in the branches. — In this hunted, fearful and half-conscious state of mind I ran through the wilderness and leaped over the garden walls to the girl's castle. With all my strength I tugged at the hinges of the castle door, 'Open the door,' I cried distraught, 'Open the door, I have slain the brother of my heart. Now you are mine on earth and in hell!'

"The wings of the gate quickly opened and the girl more beautiful than I had ever seen her before fell in total surrender with burning kisses upon my chest which was heaving with violent emotion.

"Let me be silent now about the splendor of the castle rooms, the fragrance of the exotic flowers and trees, of the beautiful singing women who peered out between the branches, of the waves of light and the music, of the wild, indescribable lust which I felt in the arms of the girl —"

At this point the stranger suddenly jumped up. Outside could be heard a strange song flying past the castle windows. It consisted only of single phrases which now and then sounded at one moment like a human voice and the next like the high tones of a clarinet which the wind blew over the distant mountains to us, these tones seized the whole heart and then quickly went away. — "Be calm," said the knight, "we have experienced these sounds for a long time. Sorcerers are said to live in the neighboring forests and often in autumn such tones wander in the night to our castle. They disappear as quickly as they come and we trouble ourselves no longer about them." — A great excitement, however, appeared to be fermenting in the heart of the knight which he suppressed, but only with difficulty. — Outside the tones had already died away again. The stranger sat absentmindedly, lost in deep thought. After a long pause he pulled himself together again and continued his story although not as calmly as before.

"In the midst of the splendor I noticed sometimes that the girl would be overcome by an instinctive melancholy if she looked out of the castle and saw how the autumn finally wanted to bid farewell to all the meadows. But a healthy, undisturbed sleep through the night made everything all right again and in the morning her beautiful face, the garden and the whole surrounding area looked revived once more, fresher, as if it had been reborn.

"Only once, when I stood next to her by the window did she look quieter and sadder than ever before. Outside in the garden the winter storm played with the fallen leaves. I noticed that she often shuddered secretly when she gazed out upon the pale wintry area. All her women had left us; the songs of the forest horn sounded today, but only out of the distance, until finally they would be heard no more. The eyes of my beloved had lost all of their glow

235

and appeared to flicker out like a flame. Just at that moment on the other side of the mountain the sun set and enveloped the surrounding gardens and valleys with its pale glow. Then the girl embraced me with both arms and began to sing a strange song which I had never heard before and which penetrated the whole house with endless melancholy tones. I listened enchanted, it was as if these tones pulled me down with the sinking sunset, my eyes closed against my will and I fell asleep lost in dreams.

"When I awoke it was nighttime and everything in the castle was still. The moon appeared very bright. My beloved lay upon a silk bed asleep next to me. I looked at her with astonishment, for she was as pale as a corpse, her hair hung tangled around her face and bosom as if tossed by the wind. Everything around us stood still and lay untouched just as it did before I fell asleep. It seemed to me as if that had been a long time ago. — I walked to the open window. The area outside appeared transformed and completely different to me than I had seen it previously. The trees whistled wondrously. Then I saw below by the wall of the castle two men standing, who, murmuring mysteriously and conversing, bowed and bent towards each other moving back and forth as if they wanted to weave a spider's web. I could not understand anything, I only heard my name being mentioned frequently. — I looked back once again upon the form of the girl, which just at that moment was illuminated by the moon. It seemed to me as if I saw a stone statue, beautiful, but dead, cold and motionless. A stone sparkled upon her rigid breast like the eyes of a basilisk,[2] her mouth was strangely twisted.

"A horror which I never experienced in my life overcame me there suddenly. I let everything remain as it was and hurried through the empty desolate halls where all the splendor had faded away. As I rushed out of the castle I saw in the distance the two strange men suddenly stop their motions and stand still like statues. On the other side, far below the mountain, I noticed by a lonely pond several maidens in snow white garments, who, singing, wondrously, appeared occupied, strangely spreading webs upon a meadow and bleaching them in the moonlight. This sight and this singing increased my horror even more and I jumped faster over the garden wall. The clouds galloped quickly over the sky, the trees whistled behind me, I hurried away breathless.

"Little by little the night became quiet and warmer, nightingales were singing in the bushes. Outside, deep below the mountains I heard voices and old long-forgotten memories returned to me again in a half-conscious state and consumed my heart while before me the most beautiful spring morning rose over the mountain. — 'What is that? Where am I?' I cried astonished and did not know what had happened to me. 'Autumn and winter have gone and spring is here again. My God! Where have I been so long?'

"Finally I reached the summit of the last mountain. Then the sun rose magnificently. A delicious movement flew over the earth, streams and castles sparkled, the people, ah, quietly and happily they went about their daily tasks, as of old, and countless larks jubilantly flew high into the air. I fell upon my knees and cried bitterly over my lost life.

"I did not understand then nor do I understand now how all that happened; but I did not want to fling myself upon the happy guiltless world with my heartfelt sin and unrestrained lust. Amidst the deepest solitude I wanted to ask heaven for forgiveness and I wanted never to see human dwellings again until I had washed away with tears of fervid repentance all my sins, the only thing from the past which has remained clear and evident to me.

"Thus I lived for a year when you met me by the cave. Very often fervent prayers emerged from my tortured heart and sometimes I believed I had overcome my sin and I had found forgiveness, but it was only a blissful deception of rare moments and quickly everything was gone again. And when autumn now stretched its wonderfully colored net over mountain and valley the familiar tones came out of the forest and penetrated my loneliness and dark voices within me resounded and answered them, and in my innermost being the tones of the bells from the distant cathedral still frightened me when they reached across over the mountains on a clear

237

Sunday morning as if they were looking for the divine grace of childhood in my heart, but it was no longer there. — Look, a wonderful dark kingdom of thoughts lives in the hearts of men, crystals and rubies sparkle there and all the petrified flowers of the depth look up with an awe-inspiring look of love and magical tones moan in the midst of them, you do not know from where they come and whence they go, the beauty of earthly life shines in subdued light outside, the invisible springs rustle, beckoning you sadly and constantly and pull you forever downward—downward!"

"Poor Raimund," cried the knight who had observed the stranger with compassion during his tales.

"In the name of heaven, who are you that you know my name?" cried the stranger and jumped up from his seat as if struck by lightning.

"My God," replied the knight and embraced the quivering one in his arms with heartfelt love, "don't you recognize us any more? I am your old faithful comrade in arms, Ubaldo, and here is your Berta whom you loved secretly and whom you lifted upon her horse after the farewell party in your castle. Time and an active life have very much blurred the clear pictures of youth and I only recognized you again after you began to tell me your story. I have never been in an area of the type you describe and never fought with you on the rocks. I went immediately to Palestine after that party where I fought for several years and then after my homecoming the beautiful Berta became my wife. Also Berta had never seen you after the farewell festivities and everything which you relate here is only fantasy. — An evil magic, awakening anew each autumn, and then disappearing again in you, my poor Raimund, has ensnared you with false games for many years. Unnoticed by you you have lived through months as if they were single days. When I came back from the Holy Land no one knew where you went and we believed you lost long ago."

Because of his joy Ubaldo did not notice that his friend trembled more and more violently with each word he said. Raimund looked with wide open eyes at both of them alternately and now suddenly recognized his boyhood comrade and love of his life, Berta, over whose tall, withered figure the flame of the fire threw its quivering light in a playful manner.

"Lost, all is lost," he cried from the depth of his heart and pulled himself out of Ubaldo's arms and fled swift as an arrow out of the castle into the night and the forest.

"Yes, lost, my love and my whole life has been a long illusion!" he said over and over again to himself and ran until all the lights in Ubaldo's castle had vanished behind him. Almost unconsciously he took the path to his own castle and reached it just as the sun came up.

It was again a warm autumn morning just as it had been when he left the castle many years ago and the memory of that time and the pain of the lost splendor and glory of his youth suddenly seized his whole soul. The tall linden trees upon the stone castle courtyard still rustled continuously; but the site and the whole castle was empty and desolate and the wind swept past over everything and through the decaying windows.

He walked into the garden. It lay there also deserted and wasted, only single, late-blooming flowers still shimmered here and there amidst the yellow grass. Upon a tall flower a bird sat and sang a wonderful song which filled his heart with endless longing. They were the same tones which he heard last evening as he told his story and which wandered past Ubaldo's castle. With alarm he now also recognized again the beautiful golden-yellow bird from the forest. — But behind him from out of a high arched window of the castle, a tall man looked out over the area during the song, still, pale and dripping with blood. It was Ubaldo come alive.

Horrified, Raimund turned his face from the frightful form and looked below into the clear morning before him. Then suddenly below the beautiful magic girl rode past upon a slender horse smiling, in the bloom of luxuriant youth. Silver cobwebs flew behind her, the aster on her forehead threw long golden-green beams upon the heath.

With his mind whirling, Raimund hurled himself out of the

garden and after the charming form.

The strange songs of the bird preceded him as he went. Gradually the further he came these tones transfigured themselves into the forest horn song that previously enticed him.

> "My golden locks flow and flutter,
> Sweetly my young body still blossoms —"

he heard separately and broken off again from afar.

> "Rustling within the calm still earth
> The brooks wander to the distance." —

His castle, the mountain and the whole world growing dark sank behind him.

> "The tones of the horn bring you
> A rich, full greeting of love.
> Come, ah, come! Before they fade away."

It echoed and lost in madness, the poor Raimund went into the forest following the tones and was never seen again.

Selections from

EICHENDORFF'S CRITICAL WRITINGS [1854]

I

It was inevitable; the immense boredom which characterized the scholarly tragedy finally led to disaster; yawning and laughter, which as you know are infectious, followed each performance in abundance. For that reason frightened poets in order to maintain their leading position searched like soldiers for troops to support them and at last hit upon the idea of seeking the aid of music which historically is the art closest to poetry. This occurred, for example, in the old mystery plays and allegorical morality plays, the latter of which placed an even greater emphasis on music and extravagant scenery,[3] and as we have seen Klai[4] gave the signal for the rise of the new cantata and the oratorio. As far as secular music is concerned the pastoral plays of the Pegnitz Society were in effect true *Singspiels* and when Opitz[5] translated the libretto of *Dafne* into German, the signal for the complete conversion to opera was given. Thus instinctively the poets were compelled towards opera. Indeed in the beginning opera showed its early association with the Catholic church by the fact that its subjects were still drawn from biblical material: for example, *Der erschaffene gefallene und aufgerichtete Mensch, Michael und David, Esther, Die macchabäische Mutter,*[6] etc., and all types of mysteries, heaven and hell, dragons, devils and choirs of angels once more moved across the stage. But these products were only appreciated as theater, the strict pious spirit which mysteriously once gave them life was gone forever and only the empty form remained. In the same manner in which they had used the tragedy scholars now employed this empty shell to their hearts' content and in order to please and attract the public filled it with the heavy load of their wisdom and their strange curios. Then Iphigenia, Clytemnestra and the whole world of Olympia itself condescended to sing arias, then morality, geography, ethnology, yes, with incomparable universality, even breweries and butcher shops were set to music. But the poets were not satisfied with their new domain. They had carelessly awakened the insatiable curiosity of the crowd, this terrible lion who lay in wait everywhere for the poetry and ravenous with hunger could not get enough to eat. The learned texts were no longer sufficient and in the general bankruptcy which followed, the opera exploded into nothing but decorations, splendid clothes, battles, cannon-thunder, flakes of turpentine resin, processions and ballets in which quite often the courts and nobility themselves took part.[7] In Postel's *Mustapha,*[8] German, Mongolian, Polish and Turkish armies marched on stage, in the opera, *Semiramis,*[9] old women were transformed into fire-spitting spears, in *Jason*[10] the ship, Argo, climbed singing into the sky where it turned into a star and this operatic rage brought forth the first theaters, something the drama had never been able to accomplish, in Hamburg, Braunschweig,[11] and Vienna, where every opera cost 60,000 gulden and around the year 1700 there were approximately ten opera texts written to every drama. But these texts had violated not only the three unities,[12] but on the whole every dramatic custom and discipline. Hanswurst[13] knocked down the most respected persons, horses, bears and camels performed, incredible monsters rumbled and roared in between, and the women, whom the opera now introduced to the public stage, because of the singing, aroused the anger of many through their emancipated manners and their mode of dress and the most holy material was shamefully profaned until at last the wrath of the church was inflamed and the best opera librettists, Postel, Leessand, Hunold and Feind[14] drew back ashamed of the scandal. In a word the music had completely stifled the pitiful poetry and out of the frantic operatic tumult of that time only a few sounds of Hasse,[15] Handel and Graun[16] have survived.

2

The modern poet is like an Aeolian harp, a harp which breaks the living breath of the world into melody and each impartial person will admit that Goethe's harp with its three main chords, feeling, fantasy and intellect, is tuned harmoniously throughout and hence produces a fine sound everywhere, no matter how the wind blows. But the instrument rings peculiarly if by chance it is strung with only one string. In other words, all meaning actually depends upon the performance, which is demonstrated quite well by the almost contemporary *Siegwart,*[17] a cloister tale by Martin Miller which basically has the same fundamental theme as *Werther* and yet with all its seriousness and honorable intent appears only as a caricature of it. Here, love as the only key to happiness is stressed, love which opposes the tyrannical world like a conspiracy of especially selected sacred souls. Cloister life is here described as comfortable, secure, almost idyllic, without any negative attributes, but it is depicted also in the most sentimental manner, the story consisting of nothing but sighs, and Siegwart is like a man of butter, totally melted by the hot sun. But let him introduce himself to you personally. Siegwart and his school friend one evening are playing an "Adagio" of Schwindl[18] on their violins: "And now they played so sweetly, so tremulously as if the instruments themselves were moaning, that their souls became as soft as wax. They laid down their violins, looked at each other with tears in their eyes, said nothing, except: 'excellent' and went to bed." These violins give quite appropriately the keynote of the whole work. Siegwart, although he had already decided with youthful ardor to become a monk, fell in love as a student with Mariane, who looked at him during a concert "with a gaze so full of longing and questioning that tears came to his eyes." When one time they were both sitting together in the forest, they noticed near them the nest of a warbler and went deep into the forest thicket in order not to disturb it. "The warbler twitted to them its naive song. 'Listen, she thanks you,' said Mariane and fell into his arms. A divine melancholy filled their souls. Mariane lay in his arms and cried from tenderness. She reached for her handkerchief to wipe away her tears. 'Don't wipe away your tears,' he said, 'I must kiss them away!' For a half hour neither of them spoke." Amidst such blessed circumstances, Siegwart naturally right away abandoned his religious vow in order to marry his beloved. But Mariane's proud father unfortunately had other plans for his daughter and wished her to marry a rich Privy Councillor, and when she refused to do this, he barbarically had her taken away to a cloister.

Now Siegwart becomes employed as a gardener in the cloister where Mariane is; the nun, Brigitte, who has become fond of the supposed gardener, arranges secret meetings for Siegwart and Mariane and an elopement is planned. However, the jealous, but cautious Brigitte, betrays everything to the Abbess, Mariane is removed to another cloister and on the night of the planned elopement it is announced to Siegwart that she is dead. The disappointed Siegwart so overcome by despair returns to his early religious vow and becomes a Capuchin monk. "Now I belong to God and my angel and soon my tears will end!" But in the meantime he still has many stored up; during his farewell to his sister and brother-in-law and friends, he cannot speak from sobbing. "He took a glass of wine and said: 'See my tears flow into the wine. They are tears of friendship, separation and gratitude, everyone drink and cry into the glass and then let me empty the goblets. And now give them to me so that my life from now on will be holy! O, God bless you, my beloved for the many tears!' " And in his cloister his eyes gaze for hours upon the still melancholy moon and he writes essays to God and Mariane and from memory certain lines from Klopstock, Haller, Kleist, etc. Finally he is called one evening into the neighboring cloister of nuns in order to hear the confessions of a dying sister. The nun is Mariane, they recognize each other, Mariane dies immediately. Siegwart the whole night is seized by one fainting spell after another. But on the following night he secretly creeps into the churchyard with a bouquet of flowers and dies thereupon on Mariane's fresh grave entering into the land of peace "where offended tenderness and humanity shed no more tears."

3

Who asks in springtime, what is spring? We do not see the air which refreshes us, we do not see the light which tints the foliage around us. One reproaches the Catholic church so often for using the power which is inherent in art to affect the senses without considering here that all art is only the symbol of the mysterious essence of the divine. Instead of slandering the church without understanding, one should learn from it. Why have the portraits of the saints survived all modern classical art? Because those works like those musical tones are sustained by indestructible traditional religious feelings and in spite of it, or, perhaps, because of it they remain independent works of art, works whose most profound inner core has never been touched by the changing mood and coquettishness of time. It is very common, but completely useless, and deceives our pride to dispense with this eternal foundation in art as well as in the drama and to replace this foundation only with morals and intelligence. Whenever one turns away from faith, from the mystery of God and religion, superstition will inevitably result.

4

The writers of comedy, whose works are a reflection of everyday life, have, it is true, an advantage, but it would be more profitable if, until the present situation improves, our poets would return to the humanitarian aspects of mankind which are present in all ages and which in themselves contain sufficient material for comedy and foolishness; in other words, let us dare to write in a more individualistic manner, let us adopt that form of comedy known as high comedy. However, only a small group of poets will make this their goal. It is no wonder, therefore, that our repertoire consists of so many translations of superficial French works which impart to poetry a certain Parisian elegance and crudeness which is acceptable in our salons as it was in the time of Gottsched,[19] but nothing is changed, only the casual costume. A further consequence of the impotence and poverty of our theater is the childish opera and ballet rage.[20] We recognize despite every sculptor the symbolic beauty and poetry of the human body. But no one should try to convince us that the body with its affected distortions is still beautiful or that the obscene jokes of that horrible figure, Hanswurst, are any less immoral or improper than the transparent, perfumed scene of the ballet which transfers the Walpurgis Night scene from the Brocken[21] to the stage for all to watch.[22] On the other hand we really have to admire the sentimental, self-sacrifice of the modern opera which is seriously concerned with copying the truly convulsive sounds of its slovenly half-sister, the ballet, i.e., the sounds of tip-toes, foot trills and emancipated leg movements which delight everyone and are quite a success.[23]

NOTES

1. Eichendorff's *Magic in Autumn* as mentioned in the introduction was influenced by the Singspiel, *Das Donauweibchen, Ein romantisches komisches Volksmärchen mit Gesang nach einer Sage der Vorzeit (The Woman of the Danube, A Romantic-Comical Fairytale with Singing Based upon an Old Legend)*, music by the Austrian composer, Ferdinand Kauer (1751-1831), libretto by F. J. Hensler, first production, Vienna, January 11, 1797. Eichendorff heard *The Woman of the Danube* in Breslau and again in Berlin in 1804. Wagner's niece, Johanna Wagner (1826-1894), appeared in Kauer's popular work at the age of six. The relation of *The Woman of the Danube* to Eichendorff's tale is discussed by Ursula Wendler in: *Eichendorff und das Musikalische Theater*, Band 75 of *Abhandlungen zur Kunst-Musik-und-Literaturwissenschaft* (Bonn: H. Bouvier, 1969), pp. 162-173.

2. Basilisk, a Greek mythical lizard-like monster with supposedly fatal breath and glance.

3. The liturgical drama with music which Eichendorff is discussing here dates back to the tenth century or earlier and encompasses a variety of subjects: mystery plays representing scriptural stories, morality or allegorical plays in which the actors-singers represented such characters as charity, faith, other virtues and vices, death, the soul, etc. The liturgical drama which was popular in the late Gothic and Renaissance periods is especially important to the development of both the drama and the opera, as Eichendorff mentions in this selection.

4. Johann Klaj (or Klai, 1616-1656), German poet who helped establish Nürnberg as one of the important centers of German literature in the seventeenth century. After studying theology in Wittenberg, Klaj settled in Nürnberg where he founded in 1644 along with Georg Philip Harsdörfer the literary society known as the Pegnitz order, a group which specialized in the performance of pastoral musical-plays, liturgical dramas, cantatas and oratorios. Klaj wrote many of the librettos of the Pegnitz productions.

5. Martin Opitz (1597-1639), German poet who introduced Italian Renaissance literary theories into Germany. *Dafne* (1597), a product of the Renaissance humanist circle, the Florentine Camerata, is considered the first opera in the history of music (libretto by Rinuccini, music by Peri and Corsi). In 1627 Opitz translated Rinuccini's libretto into German for the composer, Heinrich Schütz.

6. Eichendorff is referring here to the operatic ventures of the earliest center of German opera, Hamburg. *Der erschaffene gefallene und aufgerichtete Mensch (The Created, Fallen and Resurrected Man* or as it was sometimes called, *Adam and Eve)* was composed by Johann Theile (1646-1724) for the inauguration of the first public German opera house, the Hamburg *Theater am Gänsemarkt* (January 12, 1678); the text of this opera is still preserved, but the music is lost. *Michael and David* might refer to the operatic-passion by Theile (1679)

246

or the opera of the same name by Johann Wolfgang Franck (1641-?). *Esther* was composed by Nikolaus Adam Strungk (1640-1700) for the new opera house in Hamburg as was *Die macchabäische Mutter* (*The Maccabean Mother*, 1679) by Franck.

7. Theile's *Adam and Eve*, for example, contained a lavish full-fledged ballet. An example of a Baroque opera which was lavishly decorated with extravagant sets and effects was Antonio Draghi's *La Lanterna di Diogene* (1674), in which twenty-six members of European high society took part; Emperor Leopold I not only participated in the performance of this work, but wrote one of the arias.

8. *Mustapha* (name of the Sultan of Turkey, 1591-1639), opera by Franck composed in 1686 (Hamburg) with libretto by Christian Heinrich Postel (1658-1705). Postel, a lawyer by profession, was also closely associated with the development of opera at Hamburg. He was frequently engaged as librettist by Gerhard Schott, founder of the new opera house in Hamburg.

9. *Semiramis*, either the opera by Franck (1684) or Strungk (1683), both of which were produced at Hamburg; see also Ludwig Börne's selections, n 50.

10. *Jason*, opera by Johann Siegmund Kusser (1660-1727), composed in 1692 and performed in Hamburg in 1695.

11. This first opera house in Braunschweig opened in April, 1690, with a performance of *Cleopatra* by Kusser (libretto by F. C. Bressand), see also selections from Jean Paul's *Hesperus*, n 6.

12. The three unities, i.e., time, action and place (Sophocles).

13. Hanswurst, see Börne's essays, n 39.

14. Along with Postel, the other names mentioned here belong to that group of early seventeenth century German librettists all of whom specialized in dramatized biblical stories.

15. Hasse, see *Musical Sorrows and Joys*, p. 133 and n 12.

16. Carl Heinrich Graun (1704-1759), tenor and composer of several operas, associated with the operatic activities at Berlin and Braunschweig, see also Introduction, part 2, n 21.

17. Johann Martin Miller (1750-1814) wrote *Siegwart* in 1776; *Werther* was written in 1774. Martin's novella was quite popular in the late eighteenth century; there is, for example, a reference to *Siegwart* in Jean Paul's *Flegeljahre* (no. 59).

18. Friedrich Schwindl (1737-1786), Dutch violinist and composer of Singspiels, active in Germany.

19. Gottsched, see Introduction, part 4, pp. 64-65, and selections from Eichendorff's Critical Writings, p. 240, and n 19.

20. See Introduction, part 4, pp. 67-68 and n 36.

21. Goethe's *Faust*, Part II, Act 2, see also *Musical Sorrows and Joys*, n 10.

22. It is difficult to know exactly which stage work Eichendorff is referring to in this sentence. The nineteenth century operas based on the legend of Faust such as that by Spohr (1816) or Ignaz Walter (1799) do not contain the

Walpurgis Night scene and Gounod's *Faust* (1859) which does set this part of Goethe's drama as a ballet was written after Eichendorff's essay. It also seems unlikely that the poet has in mind the puppet plays *(Doktor Faust)* by Wilhelm Hamm (1850) and Christoph Winter (1847). Since Eichendorff mentions the figure of Hanswurst here it is entirely possible that he has in mind Josef Anton Stranitzky's *Leben und Todt Doktor Faust* (1700), a type of opera characterized by a great deal of spectacle and action (see Otto Rummel's *Die Alt-Wiener Volkskomodie,* Vienna: Anton Schroll, 1952). According to Rommel, Stranitzky played an important role in the use of the Hanswurst figure in the Baroque theater.

23. It should be remembered that when Eichendorff expressed these views the ballet as we know it today was a very new art form; the earliest use of toe shoes is attributed to the famous nineteenth century dancer, Marie Taglioni, who made her debut in Paris in 1822.

Theodor Körner

[1791-1813]

THE HARP

In Defense of the Belief in Ghosts [c. 1810]

THE SECRETARY lived with his young, petite wife during the happy, early months of their marriage. Neither practical considerations nor a passing fancy had unified them, rather, a glowing love which had withstood the test of time was the seal of their union. They had been acquainted with each other when quite young, but Sellner's delayed appointment forced him to postpone the goal of his heart again and again. Finally he received his commission and on the following Sunday he led his faithful sweetheart as his wife into their new home. After the long legal proceedings associated with marriage, receptions and family festivities, they could at last enjoy the beautiful evenings in intimate solitude, disturbed by no other person. The hours which were filled with plans for the future and the music of Josephine's harp[1] and Sellner's flute passed by only too quickly for the lovers, and the deep harmony of their tones seemed to them to be a friendly foreboding of what the future held for them. One evening when they had enjoyed playing their instruments for many hours, Josephine suddenly complained of a headache. She had not told her anxious husband about the attack she had had in the morning, and a fever which was initially slight had now risen quite high because the great enthusiasm she felt while playing her harp had put a strain upon her nerves which from early childhood had never been at all strong. She now, however, no longer concealed her illness from her husband and anxiously sent Sellner for a doctor. He came, but felt that her symptoms were insignificant and promised that by tomorrow they would see a great improvement. But after an extremely restless night, during which time she raved incessantly, the doctor returned to find poor Josephine's condition much worse and her symptoms now quite serious suggesting a grave nerve disease. Sellner was beside himself. On the ninth day Josephine herself felt that her weak nervous system could no longer endure the disease; the doctor had informed Sellner earlier of her grave condition. She knew that her last hour had come and with peaceful submission she waited for her fate. "Dear Sellner," she said to her husband while she drew him to her breast, "I depart from this beautiful earth where I found you and heavenly bliss in your heart, but even though I may no longer be happy in your arms, Josephine's love like a faithful spirit will hover over you until we see each other again in heaven." And with these words, she sank back and gently died. It was nine o'clock in the evening. What Sellner suffered was unspeakable; he struggled a long time with life; the pain had destroyed his health and when he stood up for the first time after many weeks of illness all the youthful energy of his body was dissipated, he lapsed into gloomy daydreams and withered visibly. Deep melancholy took the place of despair and a quiet pain sanctified the memories of his beloved. He had left Josephine's room in the same condition as it was before her death. Her working tools still lay upon her sewing table and the harp stood peacefully, untouched, in the corner. Every evening Sellner made a pilgrimage to this sanctuary of his love, took his flute along as in the time of his happiness, leaned against the window and breathed his longing for his beloved shadow into the sad tones. One night he thus stood in Josephine's room lost in his fantasies. The breezes of a bright moonlit night blew at him

The Harpist, drawing by Caspar David Friedrich, c. 1823. Courtesy, Stadtische Kunstsammlung, Karl-Marx-Stadt.

through the open window and from the near castle tower the watchman signaled the ninth hour; then suddenly the harp as if touched by a magic spirit began to sound along with his flute. Wonder-struck he let his flute be silent and when he stopped playing the ringing of the harp also ceased. With deep trembling he began now to play Josephine's favorite song and as he did so the strings of the harp echoed his melodies louder and louder with more and more power and when the music of the two instruments reached the highest unison the tones entwined themselves around each other. Then with a joyous shudder he sank to the ground and stretched out his arms to embrace the lovely shadow and suddenly he felt himself breathed upon as if by warm spring air and a pale shimmering light glided past him. Glowing with rapture he cried out, "I recognize you, divine shadow of my radiant Josephine! You promised to hover over me with your love; you have kept your word: I feel your breath, your kiss upon my lips, I feel myself embraced by your radiance." In profound bliss he seized the flute anew and the harp sounded again, but softer and softer until its whispering dissolved into long chords. Sellner's entire life's energy was roused by the supernatural experience of this evening; restlessly he threw himself upon his bed and in all of his heated dreams the whispering of the harp called to him. He awoke late and exhausted from the fantasies of the night, he felt his entire being wondrously transformed and a voice was now living within him which foreshadowed the end of his torment and the victory of the soul over the body. With endless longing he waited for the evening to come and full of hope he passed the time in Josephine's room. The music of his flute had already lulled him to sleep when the ninth hour struck and scarcely had the last clang of the bell rung when the harp softly began to sound until at last full chords could be heard issuing forth from its trembling strings. When his flute was silent, the spirit tones became silent, and, as before, the soft shimmering light glided over him and amidst such bliss all he could utter were the words, "Josephine, Josephine, take me to your faithful breast." Like the evening before the harp bid farewell with soft tones until its whispering dissolved into long quivering chords. Sellner, intensely exhausted as he was the first time by the evening's events staggered back to his room. His faithful servant was frightened by the appearance of his old master and hurried to the doctor, who was Sellner's long time friend, although he had been told not to fetch him. The doctor found him with a violent fever and the same symptoms which Josephine had, but this time they were even worse. The fever rose quite high during the night while Sellner had incessant visions of Josephine and the harp. In the morning he became calmer, for the battle was over and he felt his end very near, although the doctor would not hear of it. Sellner told his friend about the events of the last two evenings and no matter how much the coldly intelligent physician objected, nothing could dissuade him from his belief. When the evening came he became more and more exhausted and finally asked with a quivering voice to be taken to Josephine's room. His wish was granted. With endless serenity he looked around the room, greeting again the beautiful memory with silent tears, he spoke calmly, but was firmly convinced that the ninth hour was the time of his death. As the decisive hour drew near he asked everyone to leave the room except the doctor who wanted to remain. Then finally the ninth hour announced itself gloomily from the castle tower and Sellner's face was transfigured, a profound emotion shone once more upon his pale face. "Josephine," he cried, as if touched by God, "Josephine, greet me once more with your spirit so that I know you are near me and will conquer death with your love." Then the strings of the harp rang with wondrous loud happy chords like battle songs and a shimmering light glided around the dying Sellner. "I am coming," he cried and sank back struggling with life for the last time. Softer and softer rang the tones of the harp, then with great intensity the last bit of energy departed from Sellner's body and as he died the strings of the harp suddenly broke as if torn by the hand of a spirit. The doctor shook violently all over, clasped the transformed Sellner, who now in spite of his great struggle lay there as in a deep slumber, closed his eyes and left the house deeply moved. For a long

253

time he could not erase the memory of this hour from his mind and he would not allow himself to speak of the last moments of his friend with anyone, until finally in an uncontrolled voice he shared the experience of that evening with some friends and at the same time displayed the harp which was bequeathed to him by the deceased.

Concerning the Performance of
HANDEL'S ALEXANDER'S FEAST:
Extracts from Körner's letters to his family from Vienna

OCTOBER 31, 1812

Now the rehearsals for the performance of Handel's *Alexander's Feast*[2] have begun by the great academy. The production is being executed by five hundred amateurs. There are seventy basses alone of which I am one. The whole performance is for the benefit of the society of women of noble birth. Until now the rehearsals consisted only of practicing each of the separate voice parts. We basses have rehearsed twice by ourselves. I cannot describe how well we sound together considering that this is the first time we have sung together. But there is a passion here, an enthusiasm which one would hardly find anywhere else. Streicher[3] directs the entire production; he is enthusiasm personified. Tomorrow all the voice parts will rehearse together for the first time. The sustained low E flat of the bass choir makes a great effect, the voices of the numerous singers swell into a powerful magnetic force. The professional musicians are very annoyed by our zeal.

NOVEMBER 21, 1812

Yesterday the dress rehearsal of Handel's *Alexander's Feast* took place. This time I detached myself from the singing and sat in the orchestra pit. Never have I felt such a wave of enthusiasm. Nothing is more superb than the chorus, "Break the bonds of sleep asunder."[4]

DECEMBER 5, 1812

Our great concert has been received both times with great enthusiasm. Allow me to be silent about the unending effect which this
great music made upon me. I have written nine stanzas in honor of
the music and they have been well received by the public. Streicher
was so enchanted that he thanked me with tears in his eyes. I will
send these verses to you one of these days.

SELECTED POETRY

Following the Performance of Handel's Alexander's Feast
in Vienna [November, 1812]

A festival of songs draws the happy crowd
Of thousands into the ornate hall;
The proud structure of the house is almost too narrow,
Enthusiasm guided the selection of the bravely chosen site.
Yet it is still quiet, the music has not begun,
The song still slumbers, the beam of tones still sleeps,
Then the master signals, the trombones resound,
And the beam of tones awakens and blazes through the large
    halls.

And alternating in the magic circle of musical tones
Power and grace flow into the devouring passage of music;
Now the song revels in the bright full beauty,
Then it gently blows away into a sweet bridal song,
And it soars upward and crowns the unison,
The exalted sound of the choir proudly raises itself,
And with the awakened harmonies
Wants to draw the longing of the heart heavenward.

Then suddenly the power of the tones flows down,
A sea of harmonies gushes forth.
What is it that roars and rages amidst the flight of the songs?
What is it that strikes melodious and thunderous against the ear?
Wake up! Wake up! thus it reverberates quiveringly.
The swelling voices of the choir unleashes its furious rage with
  joy,
The power of the tones cuts through the last barrier,
And the thoughts freely revel in space.

The high walls of the hall become too narrow for every heart,
An enthusiasm moves the entire audience,
And without stopping the vast crowd
Now breaks forth in uncontrolled bacchanalian enthusiasm.
Look! Look! The magic of the songs
Exerts its ancient power upon every heart!
A nation which is so roused by these beautiful sparks
Has not yet been destroyed by time.

It is the highest of the poet's rights
That he speak when the crowd is silent.
Thus let me boldly weave the wreath of gratitude,
Which today rises out of a thousand hearts.
The world is full of shallowness and wickedness,
The divine is only rarely visible;
Yet today the divine was heard amidst the music
And its great power was unmistakable.

I must give the first gratitude to the singers,
Who lit the flame of this altar.
What can strength and courage accomplish
If they are intimidated by continuous hard labor?
It was inevitable that you succeeded in this beautiful victory,
And a world of song was awakened,
And from the never fading springs of music
Your own hand plucked the garlands of enthusiasm.

Above all you elevated the blossoms of talent,
To the stars in the world of music;
To you noble ones who endured every pain,
Before your enthusiasm every fear was destroyed,
To you no gratitude is great enough,
No praise is sufficient;
But in our hearts is engraven
That which no words can utter.

And I see a beautiful temple being built,
High above near the glowing altar of joy,
Where tears of enthusiasm fall down,
There love dries up many eyes.
A star-wreath of noble German women
Makes the holy significance of life a reality,
Human endeavor and human happiness
Bloom amidst a bouquet of flowers plucked by your hands.

Yet a great deal remained in this unexamined hour,
Which stood in harsh contrast to their wishes,
The news came to the throne of the Kaiser,
Uncalled for he held out his hand,
And participated enthusiastically in this beautiful German union!
Hail to you my people! Long live my countryland!
As long as such a Kaiser sits upon the throne,
And art and love live in our hearts.

The Human Voice

More courageous because of the call of the trombone
Rushes the warrior into battle and death,
Happier the hunter welcomes the glowing red dawn
With the tones of the forest horn.
The more melodious exalted song of the organ

Inclines toward devotion;
But that which glows powerfully
Trembling deeply through all hearts,
That which calls the soul with words of longing
And whirls it heavenward into holy delight,
That is the everlasting realm of tones,
The harmony of the voice which issues from the human heart.

To My Zither

Sing amidst the holy night, you, the confidant of my heart,
Friendly zither, sing a song here where the loved one lives.
May your tones whisper amongst the sweet dream of the beloved,
And may slumber magically bring forth the image of the singer.
Ah! how you are like my heart: your strings are my feelings;
And—is it not love which tuned my heart harmoniously?

To the Romance of the Troubadour
From the Opera, Johann von Paris[5]

Do you hear the sound,
Which celebrates your name?
The son of songs
Has renewed his oath.
Are you already slumbering?
Enveloped in sweet dream?
Star of my life,
Am I longing in vain
For your light?
You do not show yourself!

How my heart beats,
If I only could confess it out loud!
That which moves me,
I would like to express in songs.
Once inspired,
Will I be able to subdue it?
The longing of love
Wakes sweet tears,
And sympathy never slumbers.

Night remains.
Star, don't you want to reveal yourself?
The north wind blows cold
From the branches of these trees.
Continue slumbering
Through the dance of colorful dreams!
Love is clear,
Therefore good night!
Love watches.

Minstrel and Zither

The minstrel sat on a rock
And looked downwards into the sea,
And saw the waves dancing,
And flowing back and forth.

The zither lay at his side,
The air was pure and mild;
And as if out of the distance
Many a lovely portrait came to him.

Slumber also came faithfully,
Played around his silver hair,
And closed so quietly and divinely
His tired eyes.

And with the circle of dreams
The delights of youth came back to him,
And many crushed buds
Blossomed anew.

And the beautiful hours of long ago
Were reborn,
As if he had found his love,
And as if his love were faithful to him.

Then suddenly a shudder,
Like a gusty storm seized him,
And he heard the waves,
And saw his loved one drown.

And now, from out of his dreams,
The minstrel quickly awakes,
And sees the waves foaming,
And the dark foreboding ripples.

And he hears the winds whistling
And raging about him,
He gropes for the zither,
He cannot find it any longer.

The zither swims in the waves,
The storm pulled it down,
And tears well up in his eyes,
And flow upon the waves engulfing the beloved
    instrument.

Then it seems to him as if the zither were calling,
As if the strings sounded;
And he throws himself into the depth,
And makes a path through the waves.

And from the distance he already sees the zither
        gleaming,
And struggles to reach it.
And holds it up; then the
Minstrel like the zither sinks into the sea.

To Paisiello's Music from Nel cor piu mi sento[6]

How still the longing glows through me
And causes my spirit to quiver
And draws me restlessly through life
And storm and night!
Soon the heart sighs,
Soon the heart beats
In extreme happiness
In deep sorrow.
The morning dream flees.
Ah! Longing, longing, longing!
How the total striving of the soul
Glows in one picture.

The Realm of Song

What sweetly rules in holy power,
What shimmers in the splendor of the stars,
What is related to the divine?
Who enlightens the earth for us,
Whenever the sound of the song is heard from the singer,
Whispering through the strings?
    Carried away
    The heart swells
    And the Muses come closer,
Happily they hover around the one who perceives.

And the tones of the song become clear,
And the song appears boldly before our eyes
Like an image of God.
The harmony seizes the heart
And swings it heavenward
And the tones want to embrace the word.
    Mighty, powerful,
    Never sinking
    The spark glows;
    Moving along
    The tones fly through vaporous waves.

And higher than the day's light
The tones flee, never tiring;
There the realm of songs blooms,
There the poetry of ancient Greece sparkles,
And rejoicing the harmony plunges
Down to the feet of Hellas.
    Sounding, singing,
    The stars shimmer
    In the distance
    Beyond the sun
The goal of the singer is won.

NOTES

1. In this tale, Körner uses the name Josepha, the older form of Josephine, for his heroine.

2. *Alexander's Feast* is a large cantata written by Handel in 1763. The cantata is a setting of a text by Dryden describing Alexander's celebration of the conquest of Persepolis. The composition is also connected to Saint Cecilia in a somewhat incongruous manner. The patron Saint of music appears miraculously at the end and enters into a musical competition with Timotheus, Paul's disciple. For more information regarding this work see Paul Henry Lang, *Handel* (New York: W. W. Norton, 1977, pp. 292-293).

3. Johann Andreas Streicher (1761-1833), acquaintance of Schiller, composer and conductor, active in Vienna.

4. "Break the bonds of sleep asunder," famous chorus of warriors accompanied by trumpets and drums in Handel's cantata.

5. *Johann von Paris* (*Jean de Paris,* 1812), a French comic opera in two acts by Boïeldieu (1775-1834). This opera which dealt with the adventures of a troubadour was one of Körner's favorite works. For a summary of the plot see: *Litteratur Francaise,* 2 vols. (Paris: Larousse, 1967), I, 53. The Romance is from the second act (no. 11).

6. Giovanni Paisiello (see *Musical Sorrows and Joys,* n.18). *Nel cor piu mi sento* is an aria from Paisiello's popular opera, *La Molinara* (*The Maid of the Mill,* 1788). This melody was quite well-known in the late eighteenth and early nineteenth centuries; Beethoven and Dussek each wrote a set of variations on it for piano.

Robert Schumann

[1810-1856]

ON THE INNER RELATIONSHIP
OF POETRY AND MUSIC, *A Speech* [1827]

THE MOST BEAUTIFUL of all the arts, poetry and music, stand there
before us glorious and resplendent in their most beautiful blossom:
they stand alone untainted and refined before our eyes while archi-
tecture crying in back of chaotic irregular walls gazes upon her
great downfall, while sculpture moaning hides her proud face at
the sight of unsavory vulgar statues, while the art of dancing must
abandon every graceful movement which once turned the body into
the loveliest of forms, while painting lifeless and defoliated must
relinquish the divine rights which man had given to her. And truly
poetry and music are not the poorest of children, no, they are the
most beautiful creatures which the earth has plucked from the sky.
How? Could there be anything more beautiful than to enclose the
cold, cautious word with the fetters of the Muse, to sail freely
through space upon the free wings of poetic power, to unveil and
unseal with the boundless regions of fantasy everything which nature creates in her secret realm, or as a great poet speaks of it:

No bond stops me, no barrier chains me,
Uninhibited I swing myself through all space,
My immense kingdom is the thought,
And my winged tool is the word, free like a bird.

Or is there anything more splendid than to unlock the most beautiful feelings of the heart with the melting stream of harmony, with the power of sound which flows beautifully forth from the strings? Or is there any power greater than that which can move the heart in so many ways, which can tune it like an instrument and as the first tones of the chorale are transformed into innocence and purity so the heart can be tuned from cheerfulness and happiness to melancholy and deep contemplation, from kindness and rest to anger and disgust, and its tones which at one time can express love and devotion, the true speech of God, can at another express death and lamentation and blackest despair and can change to sounds of happy triumph? All this music can truly accomplish, but she cannot do this alone, she cannot raise mankind upward to the highest level of beauty, nor can she surround human feelings with glorious magic by herself. Know also that poetry can accomplish such great deeds. Poetry can herself ensnare lovingly the soul of man. She did this in order that the entire world would look astonished at her.

Oh you most beautiful gifts, oh you most splendid gifts, of all the arts you are the most beautiful, you who rob heaven of its divinity and lift the earth up to the sky also quarrel now in our German fatherland about which one should receive the laurel wreath: I do not want to say which of these two arts is the most superior, I do not want to offend any of the heavenly Muses: instead I wish to repeat those words of our great Schiller:[2] "Their quarrel produces greatness, their unity produces even greater things." Yes, their union produces greater things: Whenever the single tone is enhanced by the melodious wave of sound, whenever the free rhythm of verse alternates with proportions of musical time, whenever poetry and music walk hand-in-hand down their heavenly path—their union produces even greater and more beautiful things. But the pleasing sound which results from the union of

265

these two arts is not the only thing which binds music and poetry together, these two arts are bound together by other more delicate ties, namely that both arts have the same origin and the same effect on mankind.

The poet has nothing in common with writers of occasional verses, rhyme patchers, writers of intricate sonnets, madrigal carvers and trio builders, that is people who measure verse by their fingers and then after much effort and pondering finally manage to write something and rejoice heartily that they too have talent.[3] Similarly the musician does not belong to those rows of elegant figure artists, trill beaters, note counters, waltz enthusiasts, I mean those people who assume that the rhythm freely flows without thought into a poem, who do not realize that the metrical design does not govern the thought, but that the thought governs the meter, these persons assume that every tone fits effortlessly together with the others, that musical tones are derived from rhythmical patterns rather than vice versa, I mean by this that those whose inspiration is derived from the highest beauty and not mere rules create works which are truly divine. For it is inspiration which elevates the songs of the singer to the clouds, it is only inspiration which teaches the masterful hand of the harpist how to produce magic harmonies. And it is the feeling for the beautiful, the good and the divine, which nourishes inspiration and allows it to grow. Homer, inspired by the nobility of the mighty warriors, sang about their divine deeds, Pindar, delighted by the greatness of his own world, extolled the singers and the champions in his elevating hymns. And always the lute was not far from the singer.[4] No matter how the poet expresses himself whether in the gentle jesting tones of Anacreon or in the heart-felt speeches of Sophocles' heroes, whether in the critical tones of Aristophanes or in the lovely Idylles of Theokrit: the flute, lute and oboe were his true companions.[5] And if we consider first the heights to which the poets of our time have elevated music, it must be all the more clearly evident that poetry and music spring from one source. Or do you think that a Schiller, a Goethe, a Klopstock and the whole group of splendid

266

singers of the German people did not derive their inspiration for their songs from the same holy fountain which brought forth the harmonies of a Mozart, a Haydn or a Himmel[6] —

> Yes, truly it is beautiful to chain the insensitive word
> With the bonds of the Muses:
> The poet carries mankind to the highest beauty,
> Bravely he swings himself away through all space;
> Only heaven can crown the heavenly,
> There is no place on earth for the gods.
> The world has nothing with which to reward the poet,
> Heaven gives him his most beautiful crown.
>
> Yet it is more beautiful, if the ringing of the strings
> Gloriously raises the song of the poet:
> If, gently the rhythmic structure of the verse
> Hovers above the zephyr wave of the beat,
> If tone battles with tone, word quarrels with word,
> The tone feels and the syllable quivers,
> Until finally both warriors embrace each other with love,
> Amidst the harmonies of the delicate substances.

A MONUMENT FOR BEETHOVEN[7]

The Opinions of Four Voices[8] [1836]

I

The monument for future remembrance stands in reality before me, a tolerable stone, a lyre upon it with the date of birth and death, above it the sky and next to it a few trees.

A Greek sculptor when once asked to suggest a plan for a monument for Alexander, proposed to carve out of Mount Athos a statue which would in one hand hold out a model of a city in mid-air; the man was pronounced insane. Truly, he is less mad than these German penny subscriptions. Emperor Napoleon sleeping far out there in the ocean, you are fortunate that we Germans do not pursue you with a monument for the battles which you won from us and with us; you would rise out of the grave with the shining scroll, "Marengo, Paris, over the Alps, Simplon,"[9] and the tomb would break into tiny pieces. But your D Minor Symphony and all your splendid songs of pain (and of joy) do not seem great enough to avoid having a monument erected for them, you will certainly not escape our recognition!

I see, Eusebius, how my words annoy you, for you would out of the kindness of your heart allow yourself to be turned into one of the statues in the hot spring at Carlsbad if by so doing it would help the committee. Never to see Beethoven, never to press my burning forehead into his hand, do these thoughts not also cause pain in my heart, I would gladly sacrifice a great part of my life to experience these things — I am slowly walking up the stairs to Schwarzspanierhaus No. 200,[10] everything is still around me. I walk into the room, he raises himself up like a lion, crown upon his head, a splinter in his paw. He speaks of his sorrow. At this exact moment a thousand admirers wander beneath the temple columns of his C Minor Symphony. — But the walls would like to fall apart, he wants to get out: he complains how people ignore him, how few grieve for him. — At this instant the basses pause on that deepest note in the Scherzo of his Fifth Symphony;[11] no one breathes. The thousand hearts are suspended as if by a single hair over a fathomless abyss, and now it splits and the splendor of the highest creations produces rainbow after rainbow. — But we run through the streets. No one knew him, no one greeted him. — The last chords of the Symphony sound: the public rubs its hands, the Philistine exclaims enthusiastically, "that is true music."

Thus you honor him in life; no friends held out a helping hand to him: he died in a painful manner, like Napoleon, without a child to press to his heart, amidst the solitude of a great city. Erect then a monument for him—perhaps he deserves it; but one day written upon your fallen gravestones might well be found these verses of Goethe:

Find a person who uses mind and limb,
Who in life is both cheerful and kind,
At once his neighbors will torment him,
And to stone him as well one would find.
But after his life has been spent,
Contributions are raised in haste
To build him a great monument,
To assuage life's bitter taste.
The masses should be made aware
Of the advantage they hold,
It would be smarter not to care,
Let the man's deeds not be told.[12]

FLORESTAN

2

But if anyone should be uprooted from oblivion, so let it be that certain critic of Beethoven who predicts in the *Allgemeine Musikalische Zeitung* 1799, p. 151: "If Beethoven wishes no longer to deny himself and would follow the course of nature, he could with his talent and diligence certainly provide us with instrumental music of immense value" etc.[13] Certainly it lies in the course of nature and in the nature of things. Thirty-seven years meanwhile have passed: the name Beethoven has unfolded like a heavenly flower, during this time, however, the reviewer has shriveled up in his dark little attic into a blunt nettle. Nevertheless, I would like to know the rogue and start a subscription for him to keep him from starving to death.

Börne says: "We would in the end erect even a monument to God;" I say a monument is already a ruin with a deformed front (or conversely, a ruin is like a monument with a misshapen back) and in all fairness we really should consider two, yes, even three monuments. If the citizens of Bonn erect one, then the Viennese would be jealous and would insist upon one of their own, what a joke, for one would then have to ask himself: which monument is the genuine one? Both cities have a right to build a monument for him because he is listed in both of their church registers, the Rhine calls itself his cradle, the Danube (fame is certainly sad), his coffin.[14] People who are particularly poetically inclined, perhaps, might prefer the latter because the Danube alone flows outward toward the east and into the great Black Sea; but others would probably insist upon the holy banks of the Rhine because it is associated with the majesty of the North Sea. But in the end we would have to add Leipzig which as the central point of German culture has the special distinction of having been the first city to show an interest in Beethoven's music, which has brought an abundance of heavenly things to this city. I hope therefore for three —

One evening I went to the Leipzig churchyard to look for the grave of a great person: I searched everywhere for many hours — I found no J. S. Bach — and when I asked the gravedigger about it, he shook his head over the obscurity of the man and said: "there are many Bachs." Upon my way home I now said to myself: "What has occurred just now has a subtle meaning as in a poem! Bach has scattered his ashes to the four winds in order that we do not associate him with ordinary death or think of him as mortal, ephemeral dust and so I wish myself to think of him always sitting upright at his organ in the most distinguished apparel, his music roaring under him and the congregation looking piously upwards and perhaps the angels gazing down." — There you are Felix Meritis,[15] a man whose heart and mind equal his, playing one of his chorale variations: the text is "Adorn Yourself, O Lovely Soul," around the cantus firmus golden leaves entwined themselves and a blissfulness flowed continuously into the hymn, which you yourself admitted to me: "If life has taken hope and faith away from you, this one chorale would restore everything to you again." At this moment I became silent and mechanically walked back to the graveyard, and I felt a sharp pain because I could lay no flowers upon his grave, and those people who lived in Leipzig in 1750 fell in my esteem. Their indifference absolved me from having to speak of my wishes concerning a monument for Beethoven.

JONATHAN

3

One should walk into the church on tiptoe, but you, Florestan, insult me with your violent steps. At this moment hundreds of people are listening to me; the question is a German one: the most esteemed artist of Germany, the highest representative of German culture, not even with the exception of Jean Paul, is supposed to be honored; he belongs to our art; we have been working on a monument for Schiller for many years and are still in the planning stages of one for Gutenberg. If you allow the matter of Beethoven's monument to be taken lightly or allow the project to be abandoned, you deserve all the ridicule of the French Janins,[16] all of Börne's insolence and all the sharp biting anger of a poem by Lord Byron.

I wish to cite an analogy for you. Find your mirror image in it! — Four poor sisters came a long time ago from Bohemia to our city, they played the harp and sang.[17] They had a great deal of talent, but lacked a musical education. A skillful musician took an interest in them and taught them, and through his training they became elegant, happy women. This man had been dead for many years and only his closest acquaintances remembered him. But twenty years after his death the four sisters, who were then living in a distant land, perchance happened to send a sum of money to be used for the building of a monument for their teacher. The monument now stands under J. S. Bach's windows and if the descendants of Bach inquire after their ancestor they will also notice the simple monument, this touching remembrance which the benefactors erected as a symbol of their gratitude will achieve its purpose for all time. And thus shouldn't a monument a thousand times bigger than this one be erected for Beethoven whose every page of music has brought culture and pride to our fatherland and to a whole nation? If I were a Prince I would build a temple for him in the style of Palladio[18] in which would stand ten statues, Thorwaldsen and Dannecker[19] could not of course create all of them for us, but they could supervise their construction; nine of the statues would represent the nine Muses as well as his nine symphonies, thus, for example, Clio would be the *Eroica,* Thalia, his Fourth Symphony, Euterpe, the *Pastoral* and so on and Beethoven himself the tenth statue, the godly male head of the Muses. Or we might do something else: write his name for me in gigantic letters over a whole area of countryside, say upon a hundred hundred-year-old oaks. Or build a gigantic statue of him similar to that erected for Saint Borromeo at Lake Maggiore so that he could command a view of every mountain as he already did when he was alive. And if the ships of the Rhine fly past him and strangers ask: "Who does this giant statue represent?" every child can answer: "That is Beethoven" — and they would think he was a German Kaiser. Or if you want to be practical build an academy for him in his honor and call it, "The Academy of German Music," the main purpose of this academy will be to carry on his ideas, music is not everyone's business, it is not a common trade, it should be revealed to only a chosen few by Priests as if it were something from a magic Kingdom—a school of poets, or, even more, perhaps, a school of music in the Greek manner. In a word, rise up, get rid of your apathy and bear in mind that the monument will be your own.

EUSEBIUS

4

You are both missing the point. Florestan negates the whole concept of honoring a great person, Eusebius lowers it. The highest honor as well as true gratitude is certain to be given great, deceased artists if we continue to absorb their ideas and their goals. Florestan even you also admit that we must show our respect outwardly in some other manner and if we do not make a beginning the next generation will point to our apathy. If we form an opinion about monuments too carelessly here and there common taste and avarice as well as the fear of living up to one's word could find refuge under your impudent cloak, Florestan, which you throw over the matter. Therefore, you should both unite!

In all the provinces of Germany money should be collected, academies, concerts, opera productions and performances of music in churches should be organized. Also it does not seem improper that people should be asked to give a donation at these events. Reis in Frankfurt, Chélard in Augsburg, L. Schuberth in Königsberg have already made splendid beginnings in this direction. Spontini in Berlin, Spohr in Cassel, Hummel in Weimar, Mendelssohn in Leipzig, Reissiger in Dresden, Schneider in Dessau, Marschner in Hannover, Lindpaintner in Stuttgart, Seyfried in Vienna, Lachner in Munich, D. Weber in Prague, Elsner in Warsaw, Loewe in Stettin, Kalliwoda in Donaueschingen, Weyse in Copenhagen, Mosewius in Breslau, Riem in Bremen, Guhr in Frankfurt, Strauss in Carlsruhe, Dorn in Riga—look what a list of distinguished artists I have unfolded for you and there are even more cities and musicians I have not mentioned. Thus may a high obelisk or a pyramid tell the descendants of a great man that his contemporaries took great pains to demonstrate through an extraordinary token how they honor above all else the spirit of his works.

RARO

NOTES

1. This essay was written by Schumann at the age of seventeen, one year before he entered the University of Leipzig as a law student. During the year 1826 Schumann became a voracious reader of Jean Paul and several of his musical images, if not the overall flowery prose style of this "Speech," reflects the influence of this author. Also noticeable are the references to Ludwig Börne in the second selection by Schumann.
2. There is a double meaning implied here by the word "quarrel:" Schumann is referring to the strife between music and poetry; Schiller, however, is referring to the quarrel between himself and Goethe. In a letter to the Weimar poet, Schiller once spoke of two talents: the first which was governed by intellect; he felt he possessed; the second, which characterized Goethe's method, was totally dependent upon inspiration.
3. Schumann, like Wagner's Hans Sachs (Die Meistersinger von Nürnberg), is making fun of writers who think the essence of a poem is form alone and who create entirely according to the rules.
4. The singer, i.e., the poet.
5. Pindar, Anacreon, see Börne's essays, ns. 12 and 20; Homer, Greek poet,

ROBERT SCHUMANN

8th c. B.C.; Sophocles, Greek dramatist, 5th c. B.C.; Theokrit, i.e., Theocritus, Greek poet, 3rd c. B.C.; Aristophanes, Greek dramatist, 4th c. B.C.

6. Freidrich Heinrich Himmel (1765-1814), German composer, court Kapellmeister in Berlin from 1795-1806. See Ludwig Börne's review of his popular opera, *Fanchon*, p. 155.

7. This dialogue as well as Schumann's piano composition, the so-called *Phantasie in C*, op. 17, was prompted by the Bonn Society's efforts to raise funds for a monument for Beethoven. The Bonn project, although begun in 1835, was not completed until 1845; Schumann saw the statue of Beethoven for the first time in 1852.

8. The four voices of this essay are members of Schumann's literary club, *Die Davidsbündler (The League of David)*, which, similar to the "friends" in Hoffman's *Serapionsbrüder*, provided Schumann with a framework for carrying on various discussions regarding music in his journal, *Neue Zeitschrift für Musik (New Journal for Music)*. Florestan and Eusebius gradually became the two sides of Schumann's personality (see this author's "The Piano Cycles of Schumann and the Novels of Jean Paul," *The Piano Quarterly*, Fall, 1969). The name Florestan might have come from Tieck's novel, *Franz Sternbald*, or from one of Schumann's favorite operas, Beethoven's *Fidelio*. Eusebius is the name of several early Christian bishops as well as a Greek philosopher (4th c. A.D.) whose rational and sober mentality seems to fit Schumann's Eusebius. Schumann once hinted that the choice of the name Eusebius had an astrological basis (see Wasielwski's *Life of Schumann*, Detroit Reprints, 1974, p. 85). Jonathan, Saul's oldest son and close friend of David, was aptly applied by Schumann to represent his own close friend, Ludwig Schunke; after Schunke's death in 1834, Jonathan came to represent Chopin. The name Raro was originally associated with Clara Weick's father; later Raro symbolized a combination of the names, *Ro*bert and Cla*ra*.

9. Marengo, a village in northwestern Italy where Napoleon's troops defeated the Austrians in 1800; Simplon, a road built by Napoleon to cross a path in the Alps.

10. Schwarzspanierhaus (The House of the Black Spaniard), the actual name of Beethoven's last residence in Vienna where he died on March 26, 1827.

11. Third movement, possibly measure 51.

12. This verse is taken from Goethe's *Der westöstliche Divan (The West-Eastern Divan*, 1819, Book VI, "Buch des Unmuths"—"Book of Sadness," poem no. 3); Schumann omitted two lines. The bitter tone of Goethe's poem reflects his old age and is quite appropriate here. The poet sees himself forgotten like so many of his friends who have died.

13. *Universal Musical News*, well-known periodical published in Leipzig from 1798-1882; in 1799 its editorial staff consisted of Rochlitz, Finck, Hauptmann and Lobe.

14. Bonn, Beethoven's birthplace, is near the Rhine; the Danube is near Vienna, where Beethoven died.

274

15. Felix Meritis, i.e., Felix Mendelssohn.
16. Janins, possibly an error in spelling; Schumann probably meant the French literary critic, Jules Gabriel Janin (1804-1874).
17. Schumann is referring here to the four Podlesky sisters and the monument they built for their teacher, Johann Hiller.
18. Andrea Palladio (1508-1580), Italian architect whose style was influenced by a profound love and knowledge of Roman art.
19. Bertel Thorwaldsen (or Thorvaldsen, 1768-1844), Danish sculptor, leader of the Neo-classical movement; Johann von Dannecker (1758-1841), German sculptor.

Bibliography

Aristotle on Poetry and Music. New York: The Liberal Arts Press, 1956.

Blankenagel, John C., "The Dominant Characteristics of German Romanticism," Part I of *German Romanticism: A Symposium, PMLA,* March 1940.

Blom, Eric, ed., *Grove's Dictionary of Music and Musicians,* 10 vols. New York: Saint Martin's Press, 1970.

Blume, Friedrich, ed., *Die Musik in Geschichte und Gegenwart,* 15 vols. Kassel: Bärenreiter, 1958.

Börne, Ludwig, *Sämtliche Schriften,* 5 vols. Düsseldorf: Joseph Melzer, 1964.

Brandenburg, Hans, *Joseph von Eichendorff, Sein Leben und Sein Werk.* Munich: Oskar Beck, 1922.

Brandes, George, *Main Currents in Nineteenth Century Literature,* 6 vols. London: William Heinemann, 1923.

Burney, Charles, *The Present State of Music in London.* Oxford University Press (reprint of 1775 edition), 1959.

Claudius, Matthias, *Sämtliche Werke.* Berlin: Tempel-Verlag, 1964.

Coeuroy, André, "The Musical Theory of the German Romantic Writers," *The Musical Quarterly,* January, 1927.

Dent, Edward, J., *The Rise of Romantic Opera,* Cambridge University Press, 1976.

Edman, Irwin, ed., *The Works of Plato,* trans. by Benjamin Jowett. New York: The Modern Library, 1965.

Ehinger, Hans, *E. T. A. Hoffmann als Musiker und Musikschriftsteller.* Cologne: Otto Walter, 1954.

Eichendorff, Joseph Freiherr von, *Werke und Schriften,* 4 vols. Stuttgart: J. G. Cotta'sche Nuchhandlung, 1957.

277

Fetzer, John F., *Romantic Orpheus: Profiles of Clemens Brentano*. University of California Press, 1974.

_____, "Clemens Brentano on Music and Musicians," *Studies in Romanticism,* 1968.

Friedrich, Carl J., ed., *The Philosophy of Hegel*. New York: The Modern Library, 1954.

Forbes, Elliot, ed., *Thayer's Life of Beethoven*. Princeton University Press, 1973.

Geiringer, Karl, *Haydn, A Creative Life in Music*. New York: W. W. Norton, 1946.

Gutzkow, Karl, *Börne's Leben*, vol. 6 of *Karl Gutzkow's Gesammelte Werke*. Frankfurt: J. Rütten, Literarische Anstalt, 1845.

Heine, Heinrich, *Werke,* 4 vols. Frankfurt: Insel Verlag, 1968.

Hewett-Thayer, Harvey W., *Hoffmann: Author of the Tales*. Princeton University Press, 1948.

Herder, Johann Gottfried von, *Schriften*. Munich: William Goldmann, 1966.

_____, *Sämtliche Werke zur Religion und Theologie,* 10 vols. Vienna: G. Haas'schen, 1818-1820.

Herz, Henriette, *Briefwechsel des jungen Börne und der Henriette Herz*. Leipzig: Schulzesche Hof-Buchhandlung, 1805.

Hoffmann, E. T. A., *Poetische Werke,* 12 vols. Berlin: Walter de Gruyter, 1957-1962.

Jacobs, Monty, ed., *Arnim's Werke,* 4 vols. Berlin: Deutsche Verlagshaus Bong & Co., 1908.

Kaiser, Georg, ed., *Sämtliche Schriften von Carl Maria von Weber*. Leipzig: Schuster und Loeffler, 1908.

Kent, L. J., and Knight, E. C., *Selected Writings of E. T. A. Hoffmann,* 2 vols. University of Chicago Press, 1969.

Kindler's Literatur Lexikon, 7 vols. Zürich: Kindler Verlag, 1964.

Kleist, Heinrich von, *Sämtliche Werke*. Berlin: Tempel-Verlag 1964.

Kneisel, Jessie Hoskam, "Mörike and Music," Doctoral Dissertation. Columbia University, 1949.

Kobald, Karl, *Franz Schubert*. Leipzig: Amalthea Verlag, 1948.

Koch, Friedrich, *Heinrich von Kleist*. Stuttgart: J. B. Metzlersche, 1958.

Köpke, Rudolf, *Ludwig Tieck, Erinnerungen aus dem Leben des Dichters,* 2 vols. Leipzig: Brockhaus, 1855.

Körner, Gottfried Christian, *The Life of Carl Theodor Körner,* trans. by G. F. Richardson, 2 vols. London: Thomas Hurst, 1827.

Körner, Theodor, *Sämtliche Werke,* 2 vols. Berlin: G. Grote'sche, 1885.

Kornmüller, Otto, *Lexikon der kirchlichen Tonkunst.* Regensburg: Alfred Coppenrath, 1891.

Kreisig, Martin, ed., *Robert Schumann, Gesammelte Schriften über Musik und Musiker,* 2 vols. Leipzig: Breitkopf und Härtel, 1914.

Leibowitz, René, *Schoenberg and His School,* trans. by Dika Newlin. New York: Da Capo Press, 1975.

Marek, George, *Gentle Genius, The Story of Felix Mendelssohn,* New York: Thomas Y. Crowell, 1972.

Morgan, B. Q., *A Critical Bibliography of German Literature in English Translation, 1481-1927, with Supplement Embracing the Years 1928-1935,* 2nd ed. Stanford, 1938. *Supplement Embracing the Years 1928-1955,* Scarecrow Press, 1965.

Moser, Hans Joachim, *Die Evangelische Kirchenmusik in Deutschland.* Berlin: Carl Merseburger, 1954.

Novalis (Friedrich von Hardenberg), *Dichtungen.* Hamburg: Rowohlt Taschenbuch Verlag, 1963.

Peschel, Emil W., and Wildenow, Eugen, *Theodor Körner und die Seinen.* Leipzig: E. A. Seemann, 1898.

Ramann, L., ed., *Gesammelte Schriften von Franz Liszt,* 6 vols. Leipzig: Breitkopf und Härtel, 1881.

Reinheit, Hedwig Wahl, "Johann Friedrich Reichardt, His Importance to the Romantic Movement in German Literature," Doctoral Dissertation. New York University, 1947.

Richter, Jean Paul, *Sämtliche Werke,* 30 vols. in 17. Berlin: G. A. Reimer, 1860-1862.

————, *Jean Paul's Briefwechsel mit seiner Frau und Christian Otto.* Berlin: Weidmannsche Buchhandlung, 1902.

Rölleke, Heinz, ed., Clemens Brentano, *Sämtliche Werke und Briefe,* 3 vols. in print. Berlin: W. Kohlhammer, 1975-

Royse, N. Y., *Some Ancient Melodies.* Cincinnati: Robert Clark, 1882.

Rummel, Otto, *Die Alt-Wiener Volkskomodie.* Vienna: Anton Schroll, 1952.

Salmen, Walter, *Johann Friedrich Reichardt: Komponist, Schriftsteller, Kapellmeister und Verwaltungsbeamter der Goethezeit.* Zürich: Atlantis Verlag, 1963.

————, *Das Erbe des Ostdeutschen Volksgesanges, Geschichte seiner Quellen und Sammlungen.* Wurzburg: Holzner, 1956.

————, "J. F. Reichardt und die europäische Volksmusik," in *Festgabe für Joseph Müller-Battau zum 65. Geburtstag.* Saarbrücken: Universitäts und Schulbuchverein, 1962.

Schaefer, Albert, *Historisches und Systematisches Verzeichnis Sämtliche Tonmwerke zu den Dramen Schiller's, Goethe's, Shakespeare's, Kleist's und Körner's.* Leipzig: Karl Merseburger, 1886.

Schafer, Murray R., *Hoffmann and Music.* University of Toronto Press, 1975.

Schering, Otto, *Geschichte des Oratoriums.* Leipzig: Breitkopf und Härtel, 1911.

Schlegel, Friedrich, *Aesthetic and Miscellaneous Works,* trans. by E. J. Millington. London: George Bell, 1900.

Schneider, Gerhard, ed., *Hoffmann's Werke,* 3 vols. Berlin: Aufbau Verlag, 1966.

Scholes, Percy, ed., *Oxford Companion to Music,* 10th ed. London: Oxford University Press, 1965.

Schoolfield, George C., *The Figure of the Musician in German Literature.* Chapel Hill: The University of North Carolina Press, 1965.

Schumann, Clara, ed., *Early Letters of Robert Schumann,* trans. by M. Herbert. London: George Bell, 1888.

Seidel, Ina, *Achim von Arnim.* Stuttgart: J. G. Cotta'sche, 1944.

Sembdner, Helmut, ed., *Heinrich von Kleist's Lebensspuren, Dokumente und Berichte der Zeitgenossen.* Bremen: Carl Schünemann, 1957.

Siara, Norbert, "Scenische Bauweise des Erzählers Eichendorff nach dem Opernvorbild Gluck's und Mozart's," Doctoral Dissertation. Frankfurt: Goethe Universität, 1973.

Siegel, Linda, "The Interrelationship Between German Romantic Literature and German Romantic Music in the First Half of the Nineteenth

Century," Doctoral Dissertation. Boston University, 1964.

————, "The Piano Cycles of Robert Schumann and the Novels of Jean Paul," *The Piano Quarterly,* Fall, 1969.

————, "Wagner and the Romanticism of E. T. A. Hoffmann," *The Musical Quarterly,* October, 1965.

————, "Wackenroder's Musical Essays in *Phantasien über die Kunst,*" *The Journal of Aesthetics and Art Criticism,* Spring, 1972.

Smith, Murray F., *A Second Supplement to Bayard Quincy Morgan's A Critical Bibliography of German Literature in English Translations, Embracing the Years 1956-1960.* The Scarecrow Press, 1972.

Stahl, William Harris, *Macrobius' Commentary on the Dream of Scipio.* New York: Columbia University Press, 1952.

Stocklein, Paul, *Joseph von Eichendorff.* Hamburg: Rowohlt Taschenbuch, 1963.

Storck, Karl, ed., *Letters of Robert Schumann,* trans. by H. Bryant. New York: E. P. Dutton, 1907.

Tieck, Ludwig, ed., *Phantasien über die Kunst für Freunde der Kunst.* Hamburg, 1799.

————, *Heinrich von Kleist's Gesammelte Schriften,* 3 vols. Berlin: G. A. Reimer, 1826.

————, *Werke,* 12 vols. Leipzig: Bibliographisches Institut, 1892.

Vetter, Walter, *Gluck.* Leipzig: Veb Deutscher Verlag für Musik, 1964.

Vortriede, Werner, ed., *Achim und Bettina in ihren Briefen,* 2 vols. Frankfurt: Suhrkamp Verlag, 1961.

Wagner, Richard, *Mein Leben,* authorized translation. New York: Tudor Publishing Co., 1936.

Walter, Anton, *Franz Witt, Gründer und erster Generalpräses des Cäcilienvereins.* Regensburg: Puset, 1889.

Warrack, John, *Carl Maria von Weber,* 2nd ed. Cambridge University Press, 1976.

Weisse, Benno von, ed., *Schiller's Werke,* 42 vols. Weimar: Hermann Bohlaus, 1963.

Wendler, Ursula, *Eichendorff und das Musikalische Theater,* Band 75 of *Abhandlungen zur Kunst-Musik und Literaturwissenschaft.* Bonn: H. Bouvier, 1969.

Wernaer, Robert M., *Romanticism and the Romantic School in Germany*. London: A. Appleton, 1901.

Wiora, Walter, "Die Musik im Weltbild der deutschen Romantik," in *Beitrage zur Geschichte der Musikanschauung im 19. Jahrhundert*. Regensburg: Gustav Bosse, 1965.

Worbs, Erich, "Waldhornruf und Lautenklang-Musikinstrumente in der Dichtung Eichendorff's," in *Aurora: Eichendorff Almanach,* ed. by Karl Schodrok. Würzburg: Verlagkulturwerk, vol. 22, 1962.

Zeydel, Matenko and Fife, eds., *Letters of Ludwig Tieck*. New York: Modern Language Association of America, 1937.

Editions

LUDWIG TIECK, *Werke,* Gotthold Klee, ed., 3 vols. Leipzig: Bibliographisches Institut, 1892. *Musikalische Leiden und Freuden,* II, 321-386.

LUDWIG BÖRNE, *Sämtliche Schriften,* Inge and Peter Rippmann, eds., 5 vols. Düsseldorf: Joseph Melzer, 1964. *Henriette Sontag,* I, 432-444; *Die Entführung aus dem Serail,* I, 329; *Die Vestalin,* I, 241; *Der Bergsturz,* I, 245; *Die Schweizerfamilie,* I, 289; *Die Zauberflöte,* I, 558-560; *Tancred,* I, 421, 525; *Fanchon,* I, 540; *Camilla,* I, 516; *Sargin,* I, 541; *Lilla,* I, 381; *Vertrauliche Briefe (Der Freischütz),* I, 117-122; *Briefe aus Frankfurt,* I, 1068-1069.

ACHIM VON ARNIM, *Werke,* Monty Jacobs, ed., 4 vols. Berlin: Deutsches Verlagshaus Bong & Co., 1908. *Fürst Ganzgott und Sänger Halbgott,* IV, 155-164; *Von Volksliedern,* I, 63-66, 72-78, 87-89.

HEINRICH VON KLEIST, *Sämtliche Werke,* Paul Stapf, ed. Berlin: Der Tempel-Verlag, 1964. *Die Heilige Cäcilie oder der Gewalt der Musik,* 974-985; *Haydn's Tod,* 1157-1159; *Cendrillon,* 1104; *Theaterneuigkeit,* 1105; *Theater,* 1106.

JOSEPH VON EICHENDORFF, *Werke und Schriften,* Gerhart Baumann and Siegfried Grosse, eds., 4 vols. Stuttgart: J. G. Cotta'sche Buchhandlung, 1957. *Die Zauberei im Herbst,* II, 971-986; *Zur Geschichte des Dramas* (Critical Writings), IV, 642, 640, 569-570, 716-718.

THEODOR KÖRNER, *Sämtliche Werke,* Ernst Hermann, ed., 2 vols. Berlin: G. Grote'sche, 1885. *Die Harfe,* II, 315-317; *Briefe,* II, 339, 340, 341; *Alexander-Fest,* I, 323; *Die menschliche Stimme,* I, 88; *An meine Zither,* I, 63; *Zu der Romanze des Troubadour,* I, 126; *Spielmann und Zither,* I, 156; *Zu Paisiello's "Nel cor piu mi sento,"* I, 124; *Das Reich des Gesanges,* I, 87.

ROBERT SCHUMANN, *Gesammelte Schriften über Musik und Musiker,* Martin Kreisig, ed., 2 vols. Leipzig: Breitkopf und Härtel, 1914. *Über die innige Verwandtschaft über Poesie und Tonkunst,* II, 173-175; *Monument für Beethoven,* II, 132-136.

Index